My Tenant "Bobo"

My Tenant "Bobo"

Harvey W. Black

VANTAGE PRESS
New York

Although this story is based on the author's real-life experiences, names of people have been changed in order to protect their identity.

FIRST EDITION

Published by Vantage Press, Inc.
516 West 34th Street, New York, New York 10001

Manufactured in the United States of America
ISBN: 0-533-13234-7

Library of Congress Catalog Card No.: 99-94958

0 9 8 7 6 5 4 3 2 1

Contents

Introduction

As I introduce this story about my tenant Bobo, I can truthfully say that this story is about 80 percent true . . . from information that I received from Bobo himself, from his knowledge of his past, as he described to me during his visits to my living room.

Real names are not used in this story.

Someone who has a good outlook for his or her future will prepare himself or herself by making plans to meet this challenge, including providing for such items as:

1. Living quarters.
2. Health plans, retirement plans, and financial plans.
3. Conveniences such as a car to go from here to there.
4. Proper clothing and a good budget plan.

In my case, my plan was based on my retirement from the workplace. First and foremost, I wanted a decent, comfortable, and desirable place to live. I selected a two-family house, because it would provide a place for me to live and I would get an income by renting out the second apartment. This extra income would supplement my pension plan, and it would offset the maintenance expense for the entire house.

I was unfortunate in selecting a good tenant. This tenant only wanted to rent one room, with use of kitchen and a bathroom. I interviewed this tenant, who described himself as a faithful and loyal member of the neighborhood church. He described his friend as a deacon at this church with a good record.

This tenant, called Bobo, to whom I rented the one room, with use of kitchen and bath, turned out to be a nightmare, and that's putting it mildly. My tenant Bobo turned out to have two personalities, which I found out shortly after he moved into the one room upstairs. I can only compare him with the character Dr. Jekyll and Mr. Hyde.

My tenant Bobo often came downstairs to talk to me while I sat in my living room, listening to music. His conversation was, usually, based on his past, as he grew up under his mother's supervision. Bobo told me that his mother died when he was nine years old and continued telling me that when he reached the age of eleven he found himself on the streets of Brooklyn with members of a newly formed Gang. His life, as he described it to me, involved getting into trouble with the law.

Bobo had a lot of friends, female friends; he did not have a lot of male friends visiting him. These female visitors created a lot of traffic, going up and down the stairway, day and night. My bedroom was about eight feet from the staircase, and this traffic noise was unbearable. I, eventually, had to move my bedroom to downstairs in the front basement room.

My tenant Bobo eventually stopped paying rent on the space that he was renting from me. I thought that due to the manner in which the rent was paid, by two-party checks from the Department of Social Services, I was safe and would always get my rent money. I, however, found out that this was not true. Bobo found out how to cash the two-party checks, and he did not pay any more rent.

I contacted his supervisor, who promised me that I would get my rent money from Bobo, but I did not get my rent money. I wrote to the commissioner, but I did not get any results from that contact, either. When my tenant Bobo moved, he owed me something like $4,267.00. No investigation was made by the Department of Social Services. I was just an unfortunate retired senior citizen, living on my fixed income and having to support someone like my tenant Bobo.

Bobo's father was seldom home. Therefore, it was Bobo's mother's responsibility to raise him properly.

After Bobo's mother's death, he became a nightmare for his grandmother, who was trying to raise him as his mother had been raising him.

I am inserting Bobo's stepmother. . . . Bobo never mentioned his stepmother to me at all. It seems that he never accepted her as his stepmother. It was after Bobo had moved that his stepmother came by my house looking for her stepson; that was when I learned that Bobo had a stepmother.

Ironic as it may seem, the Black lawyer I selected to represent me in court turned out to be Bobo's lawyer when he was a member of the street gang.

Since Bobo was creating so many problems for his father while a member of the street gang, his father trained him for a job as a long-distance truck driver. Bobo's career as a truck driver ended when he was involved in an accident when a lady driving a car ran into the right side of his truck.

My court case, landlord versus tenant, amounted to about fifteen appearances. An arbitrator was assigned to my case: landlord against tenant, by a judge filling in for Mr. Swan or Judge Swan when he was absent from court that day. The arbitrator was able to draw up an agreement between the landlord and the tenant, but her findings were never used in this case.

Bobo finally moved . . . not due to court hearings or court proceedings. He was forced to move from my house by a blessing in disguise. A fire that occurred next door left his living quarters with two broken skylights and a hole cut through his kitchen ceiling.

Bobo's timely death was not a natural death. . . . See details in story.

The summary postscript shows that Bobo's mother was a high school graduate, and she raised her son based on the theories of three great educators: Friedrich Froebel, Johann Pestalozzi, and John Dewey.

My Tenant "Bobo"

1

Plans for Your Future

Are you a Planner? We know that a plan, according to the definition, is a scheme of action or procedure. Any theory that you plan for the future, has to be worked out to your satisfaction if it is to be successful.

It is advantageous to make plans for what project that you are about to embark on, what you hope to accomplish and what you hope to develop into a successful venture for your own advantage.

You may approach this plan step-by-step, so you won't leave anything out of what you have to or want to accomplish.

In my case, I recalled the difficulties that I was confronted with in the past, so I planned a different approach, one that I anticipated would be best for me. It is easy to make future plans if you've had problems in the past.

Now, what were my plans? Well, I felt that I had a future and planned to reach that future successfully. So I started at the beginning and went step-by-step, considering such aspects as my retirement, for instance:

1. Financial security.
2. Health benefits.
3. A place to live, like a house of my own in a good neighborhood.
4. Transportation: how I was going from here to there.

In planning my future, I selected a date of retirement several years before reaching my retirement age.

1. Financial security: You could use a plan like the IRA, just to mention one of the plans that are available. You can contribute an amount that you can afford and yet will give you good benefits. These plans are to supplement your pension or your Social Security income benefits.

2. Health benefits: Usually these health benefits are selected through your job and your union, if you have one.

3. A place to live: In selecting a house, certainly you will try to select a nice neighborhood, often in a neighborhood where the houses are one- and two-family houses. In such an area as this, there will be fewer people roaming the streets at any given period of time. . . . That's important.

4. Transportation: How are you going from here to there? This is also important. A car saves time but is a little more expensive. It is very convenient. . . . You can go from here to there at any time of day or night. . . . You pay more for convenience.

Everybody, should think of, first, a place you can call home: a place to rest, socialize, accommodate your friends when they visit you, and feel free to just relax yourself.

It's a good feeling when you visit someone or go to church or anywhere else, and you can say, "It's home, my domain. . . . To a place that I have control over . . . eminent domain . . . the power over private property."

In preparation for "this power of ownership," I purchased a two-family house. This house was old, but I could see a great potential in its future. I felt that with my expertise and experience in doing repairs on houses I could make the necessary repairs to make it livable.

When this house was built, they used bricks between the walls to ensure the proper insulation for the house. When this house was built, it was classified as "cold-water flats." Each tenant was responsible for his or her own heat and hot water.

At the time of my purchase, the house was occupied. But I knew in time these tenants would move. The top floor was occupied by an elderly couple: Mr. and Mrs. Roper. The basement and parlor floors were rented to a Mr. and Mrs. Verner. They had two sons and Mrs. Verner was still having children. The Verners were white.

Mr. and Mrs. Roper were black. Mrs. Roper was a very nice lady. She reminded me of my maternal grandmother. Each time that I visited the house, Mrs. Roper would talk to me. Mr. Roper was at work. Mrs. Roper would also go to work at times. She was doing day work, and she had a lot of time off.

Several years after the purchase date, Mr. Roper reached his retirement age. I was visiting the house the day of Mr. Roper's retirement date, and I recall that he came home with a small bottle of "booze" to enhance his celebration after retiring from his job. He offered me a drink. At first, I refused, but on second thought I agreed to have a drink with him. We held our glasses up, and I said, "To a happy retirement, Mr. Roper, for many years of retirement bliss."

Several years passed and I continued to go by the house to check out the property and to collect the rent. After I had returned from my vacation, I went by the house to check the property and to collect the rent and I found that the top floor was vacant. Mr. and Mrs. Roper had moved. My good neighbor told me that the Ropers had moved. He said that they tried to contact me but failed. I told my neighbor that I had just returned from my vacation.

I did not start making repairs on the top floor, because for the type of repairs needed the whole house would have to be vacant. Fortunately, I only had to wait two more years before the Verners moved. While I was waiting for the Verners to move, my good neighbor told me that Mr. Roper had died and only a few months later Mrs. Roper died.

At this point, I invited a plumbing contractor by to give me an estimate of how much it would cost to install a central heating system to furnish heat and hot water. After the estimate was given, I was able to get the whole job financed. Smaller repairs I could do myself, like cabinetmaking, minor wall and ceiling repairs, and painting. This was in the year 1963, the latter part of the year. I was working full-time at that time and would go by the house after work and work until about midnight.

I would go home after the midnight chimes went off. I went home to relax for the next day at work. I had a portable radio at my "retirement house" that I played constantly while I was working.

On the night of November 22, 1963, that the news reporter announced that "the president of the United States, President Kennedy, had been assassinated. The reporter continued to report the news over and over, and saying, "for more news, stay tuned to this station."

I could not do any more work that night; this tragedy was hard to believe. I went home and my radio was virtually on for the rest of the night. The next day, I, like many people I saw, went out looking for a newspaper with good coverage of the story of President Kennedy's assassination.

In the *Daily News* dated November 23, 1963, I read the following: "Dallas, Texas, November 22, 1963, President Kennedy was mortally wounded by a Rifle Bullet at 12:31 P.M. (1:31 A.M. New York time), as he rode in an open convertible limousine leading a motorcade through the streets of Dallas. He died in Parkland Hospital twenty-nine minutes later." Another headline was: "Suspect Collared in Assassination."

This tragedy of President Kennedy's assassination brought back memories of the death of Franklin D. Roosevelt, April 1945. I was a soldier in the United States Army at the time, during the Second World War. I was sitting in the dayroom, listening to the news over the radio. When the news reporter announced that Franklin D. Roosevelt had died. I felt dismayed, that with the death of our president during the time of war we would lose the war to the enemy. I felt rather insecure. I might have shed a few tears. Fortunately, we won the war.

I completed the repairs on the house, and since it was at least two decades before I would become eligible to retire, I rented both apartments out to new tenants. Now I had to wait several years for these tenants to move. That was no problem, because I had a lot of time to wait.

Several years passed, and these tenants moved. At this point, I had the opportunity to do more repairs on the house. I had the whole house, front and back, remodeled. I had the house covered with siding, and I had new replacement windows installed.

I was now formulating plans for my retirement. I retired rather secretly. I did not make plans for a party like most of the retirees before me did. I simply took care of all of the paperwork required before retiring.

One of my friends in the office told me, "Why don't you tell the supervisor that you are retiring?"

I said, "OK."

I went to the supervisor, who happened to be a female, and said, "I am retiring."

She asked me, "When?"

I said, "Today."

This was on a Friday.

She looked rather perplexed. I will not reveal the secret of why I retired in a secret manner until my autobiography.

I moved into my "retirement house." I occupied the basement and parlor floors. My bedroom was located on the parlor floor, the back room, while my living room was the front room of the parlor floor. I was now fulfilling my dream of living in a house after retirement.

After I settled down, all I needed was a good tenant to rent the top-floor apartment for additional income to supplement my fixed income.

One day, I sat on my stoop, enjoying the sunshine, since my house was located on the sunny side of the street. The sun helps in many ways. . . . It shines on the stoop and furnishes heat in the winter of the year. When it snows on the sidewalk, the sun helps to melt the snow: When the snow is deep, it is easier to shovel when you can get help from the sun.

While I was sitting on the stoop, I was approached by a soft-spoken man, who identified himself as a friend of Jack. I knew Jack. . . . Jack was never a tenant here in my house. Jack was the boyfriend of my tenant Geneva. I recalled when Geneva applied for an apartment, I was hesitant about renting to a young lady. She was single, and she was working at that time. When you have a new person applying for an apartment, you have to "Size him or her up" and try to read his or her personality by looking him or her over and over. You also try to determine what his or her behavior, as a tenant will be. By this time, I had gained a lot of experience as a landlord living in the same house as a tenant. In some ways, you share some of the same things. Therefore, you try to choose a good tenant. When you rent to a new tenant, usually he or she stays for several years before he or she moves. Some tenants are like roving "cowboys" always on the move; going from one place to another. Some tenants, after living in one location for a few years, want to move to a new location. Geneva was a good tenant. She informed me from the beginning that I would not have any trouble with how she lived and how she chose her friends. She continued by saying that she was active in church. I found out, later, that this statement was true.

Geneva *was* a good tenant. She even performed some minor improvements herself in her bathroom, like decorations, etc.

After a few years, Geneva lost her job. I never found out precisely why she lost her job. Liz, Geneva's best friend told me that Geneva had problems with her boss. When Liz implicated Geneva's boss, I asked Liz, "Was it a case of sexual harassment?"

Liz answered saying, "Kinda like that."

Anyway, Geneva got behind in her rent payments. I sorta felt sorry for Geneva, because she was a nice tenant, but you have to collect your rent. Rent payments help to pay your real estate taxes, heating bills, water bills, and, by all means, your maintenance expenses.

Geneva, appearently had some ideas in her mind of how she was going to pay her rent. She virtually flirted with me, a little, but I did not respond. I guess that I sorta gave her the "cold shoulder." She, however, did not give up on her advancements toward me, that is, in a flirtatious manner. One day I stopped by to check on the rent payments. Geneva appearently, saw me parking my car, from her window, and prepared herself for her surprise attack. I knocked on the door, and she opened the door while simultaneously, falling back as if she was surprised to see me coming at this time. She was only in her negligee, revealing the contours of her body, revealing the beautiful profile . . . of her body, that is. What did I do or how did I respond? Well, I guess you can call me chicken. I simply said, "I am sorry," and walked away. I remembered the advice that Jimmy, the truck driver for the wholesale dry-cleaning company, gave me when I purchased a dry-cleaning store. Jimmy said, "If you want to be successful in business, don't go with your customers." I followed his advice with my female tenants.

I could not pay my real estate taxes, heating bills, water bills, and general maintenance expenses with sexual favors. Maybe I was "profiting from the mistake of others." I recall that a man purchased a rooming house and rented to a lot of female tenants. He simply started going with some of his tenants, secretly, he thought, but when the tenants started talking to one another the hidden secret was revealed. The girls stopped paying their rent. . . . The man eventually lost his rooming house.

Geneva, without hesitation, applied for public assistance to pay her rent. Geneva was receiving public assistance for about two years when I stopped by to collect the rent. I knocked on the door. As usual, she opened the door, and I saw a man, who, later, was found out to be Jack, Geneva's boyfriend.

After a few more years passed, Geneva moved. She left owing me something like six hundred dollars rent arrears. Somehow I believe that Geneva did this on purpose. She, apparently, remembered when I ignored her advances toward me. Nevertheless, Geneva had moved.

Several days passed after Geneva moved, and the next month was approaching. About a second or third of the month, a welfare check came to my address, addressed to Jack. Jack apparently knew that the check was coming, and he came by to pick it up. I gave him the check and asked him to change his address, because he was not a tenant at this address. Jack promised me that he was going to change the address on his welfare checks. This, supposedly, was the last check to come to my address.

Anyway, the soft-spoken man said, "Jack asked me to come and pick up his check."

I simply told the soft-spoken man that there was no check for Jack. He referred to Jack as "Deacon Jack." I told the soft-spoken man to change the address on his checks or to tell Jack or Deacon Jack to change the address on his mail. The soft-spoken man promised me that he would deliver the message to Deacon Jack, then left to return to Deacon Jack's place.

Several days passed, and the soft-spoken man returned for the same purpose . . . to pick up Deacon's check. I did have a check, this time, for Deacon Jack. I gave it to the soft-spoken man and asked him, again, to tell Deacon Jack to change his mailing address. The soft-spoken man reached into his pocket and took out a few dollar bills. He said, "Deacon Jack gave this money to me to give to you for taking care of his mail."

I said, "No. I will not accept a bribe for that type of service. I cannot understand why he doesn't change his mailing address. He doesn't live here. . . . He was never a tenant here. He was Geneva's boyfriend, and he lived with her, at her expense and with her consent."

"OK." The soft-spoken man left and returned to . . . wherever Deacon Jack lived, I guess.

My telephone rang. The female voice said, "I heard that you have an apartment for rent. How many rooms are there in the apartment?"

I said, "Well, there are four rooms in the apartment, but I am only renting out three rooms in the apartment, because the hall bedroom is full of my daughter's furniture and I don't know when she is going to take it out."

The caller asked, "How much would the three-room apartment be per month?"

"I said, "It's only five hundred dollars per month."

She asked, "Will you rent it to me?"

"How many people in your family?" I asked.

She said, "I have two children, ages four and two, and I am on Public Assistance."

I said, "First of all, I do not have window guards at the windows on the outside. This is required if there are children ages two and four, to protect them. Therefore, I cannot rent the apartment to you, sorry."

Since one of my relaxing pastimes is sitting on the stoop when the weather is nice or favorable, I returned to the stoop after the phone call. As I sat there watching the girls go by, whom did I see coming? Nobody but the soft-spoken man himself, coming up the street. When he reached the stoop, he spoke to me. Now, I was wondering, what message is he bringing to me from Deacon Jack?

Instead of giving me a message from Deacon Jack, the soft-spoken man said, "Do you have a room that you can rent to me?"

My reply was, "No. I have a three-room apartment for rent."

He said, "I only need one room, with use of kitchen and bathroom." Then he asked, "May I see the apartment?"

I said, "OK, come with me," and we went upstairs, starting from the kitchen, then we went to the back room, the bathroom, and finally the front room."

"Oh," the soft-spoken man said, "this is perfect."

I answered, "The apartment?"

He said, "No, just this front room."

I looked at him for a moment; finally, I said, "If I rent the front room to you, then I would have to rent the back room to somebody else. . . . It would be a sharing proposition with two different tenants." I continued, saying, "This type of sharing an apartment was very common when I got married in 1950."

The soft-spoken man said, "I was sharing an apartment with a family member of a friend of mine. They said that they needed the room for their son, who was scheduled to get his United States Army discharge from military service in, about a month. I agreed and moved in with Deacon Jack. Deacon Jack's place is too small; this room here is just perfect for me. How much rent would it be per month?"

I said, "If I rent one room to you, then I will have to rent the back room to somebody else. This type of arrangement means that you would have to share the kitchen and bathroom with another person in the apartment."

"OK."

"The rent, of course, would be divided between the two of you. For example, if the apartment rents for five hundred dollars per month, then each tenant would pay two-fifty per month, understand?"

The soft-spoken man simply nodded his head, and we returned back downstairs. While we were standing on the stoop, he asked,

"Should I come back to find out if you are willing to let me have the room?"

I said, "I will decide by next month."

He left.

I thought after two weeks had passed the soft-spoken man had found another place to move and I would not see him again. Not so, because two weeks later I saw the soft-spoken man coming up the street again. It was easy to identify him, because I had observed, before that when he walked he had a sorta switching motion about the middle of his body.

As he approached the stoop, he nodded as if he was speaking, but before I could speak, he reached into his pocket and pulled out some bills, saying, "I have security money for you." I was sorta bewildered about this man. As if counting his money, he said, "I have two hundred and fifty dollars."

As I was retired and living on a fixed income, the money did look good to me . . . and all cash money. I had to think quickly whether to accept this money or not. I said, "Well, for one thing, I do not know anything about you . . . like your name, where you are from, the type of work you do, single or married, nothing about you."

He said, "Well, you know Deacon Jack, right?"

I said, "Yes."

"We go to church together on Sunday mornings," he said. He continued, saying, "I am not working because I am a diabetic; my bills are paid by the Department of Social Services." He assured me that I would not have to worry about getting my rent money, because they would send him a check for the rent and he would have to give it to me. My name would be on the check, and he would have no choice but to give it to me.

He continued, saying, "I was married and have a daughter. My wife and I are separated now, and I live alone."

I said, "I do know Jack, or rather Deacon Jack. I did not know that he was a deacon; however, I did know that his girlfriend, Geneva, was active in church. Since I know Deacon Jack, and you said that you are his friend, I will give you a one-year lease." I wrote down his name as "Bobo Ryan."

I issued a one-year lease to "Bobo Ryan," from November 14, 1989, to November 13, 1990. Rental space: one room (front), with use of kitchen and bathroom. I received one month's rent in the amount of $250.00 as security. I put the security money in the bank. He was scheduled to pay one month's rent in advance when he moved into his room.

While I was preparing to type up the agreement on a one-year lease, I was considering how this rental income would help me to meet my obligations of maintaining the house as it should be maintained.

2

The First Phase of Bobo's Tenancy

In previous years, the practice of sharing an apartment was somewhat common. Many times, several relatives would move to New York from the South or from Puerto Rico and end up sharing an apartment together. Not only relatives, sometimes they would be unrelated. Yet they would get along together beautifully. They would share the rent and some of the other facilities.

I was a landlord for a long time. When I purchased the house that I called my family house, it was a four-family house with a lot of space, extending into the backyard. I was accustomed to renting to several relatives who shared the space, the rent, and the facilities. Many of these tenants could be treated like family members. This is why I decided to rent the one room to Bobo, with the option of his sharing the apartment, rent, and facilities.

I remember on one occasion one of our tenants, a young lady, was engaged to get married. The young lady and her sister and other relatives did not know how to go about arranging for this marriage or wedding. My wife and I made the arrangements for this wedding ceremony.

I stood in as the tenant's father, while my wife played a recording of Mendelssohn's Wedding March for them to march into the back room. Ironically, this house was once owned by a rabbi and the back rooms were built to serve as a synagogue. It was long, extending back into the backyard for a distance, and it served as—may I say—a church. It was certainly perfect for this occasion.

We all celebrated their wedding festivities and sent them off on their honeymoon as Mr. and Mrs. Fortunate.

What happened to all of those good tenants? We are living in a new era now, and people have changed their way of life. It seems that new tenants want more than a place to live. What is it that they want . . . to own the house?

The soft-spoken man called Bobo, finally moved into his room in November 1989. He had convinced me that he was a religious man and would be a good tenant. It seems that Bobo had a good answer for all of my questions. He appeared to have an answer for the question before the question was asked. It was me who failed in my perception of the man I accepted as a tenant.

After Bobo had lived in the room upstairs for about three months, it seems that he changed his image. He started harboring young girls. They would come and ring his doorbell constantly, day and night. It was up and down the steps in the hallway all during the night and during the daytime as well. This reaction of my tenant Bobo happened so quickly, it appeared that all he had to do was open a door to a roomful of different girls and they rushed out like a spontaneous reaction. I soon had to start complaining to Bobo about this type of activity. He finally jammed his bell to prevent it from ringing. The constant ringing of Bobo's bell annoyed him. Did the girls stop coming? No, they simply started calling him, Bobo, from the street. Bobo would throw the keys to the girls from the window, and they would simply open the door and go upstairs, where Bobo would be waiting for them.

My tenant Bobo had taken on what you might call a Dr. Jekyll and Mr. Hyde type of image or personality. This type of behavior made me say, "What type of man did I rent the room to?"

It started out as one girl coming to see Bobo, then another girl, and then still another girl. Soon it became a chain reaction of girls coming and going without stopping. It was at this point that I was forced to ask my tenant Bobo to move.

Bobo was paying his rent at this time, and on time. But I could not put up with this type of behavior; it annoyed me.

Next door to my house, a mother and five children were occupying the whole house. That is, they were living on the parlor and basement floors. One of the owners, male, was living on the top floor. This family consisted of the mother's three small girls, and two small boys. One day, I observed the mother of these children talking to Bobo as he sat on the stoop. I could not hear what she was saying to Bobo. . . . I could only assume that she was complaining to Bobo about all of these young girls coming and going all day and at night to see him in his one room, with use of kitchen and bathroom. Certainly, it was impossible for her girls, as well, as her boys, not to see all of this type of behavior going on just next door to them. This was, however, after the second time that I saw this mother complaining to Bobo about his type of next-door neighbor, that she and her five children moved to a different location of the city.

When the mother and her five children moved, the male tenant was left living upstairs. It was at this point that I learned that he was one of the owners of the building. There were three brothers who owned the house next door. This male tenant (one of the owners) told me, one day, that the girls calling Bobo from the street all during the night prevented him from getting the sleep that he needed to relax him for the next day's work. . . . Finally, he moved to another location.

I think that it was at this time that I moved downstairs from my bedroom, which was located on the parlor floor, about eight feet from the stairway, where these girls would go up and down the stairs. This move downstairs put me in the front room of the basement floor, moving me away from the noise of the footsteps of the girls, about eight more feet from the stairway, on the parlor floor.

This move did not shut out the noise that these girls were creating going up and down the stairway.

The next precaution that I took was putting locks on all of the doors: One was on the door of my bedroom on the parlor floor, one on the door of the front room of the parlor floor (my living room door), one on the door of the kitchen floor, one on my new bedroom door, and one on the door leading from the basement to the parlor floor. I was virtually a prisoner in my own house. . . . I was locked in. I had already lost ownership of my stoop to my tenant Bobo.

When I was going out, I would leave by way of the basement door leading to the yard in front of the building. When I returned, I would enter the house by way of the basement door.

My tenant Bobo was not always in a bad mood; he would have good moments, but sometimes he would appear to be vicious. I often sat in my living room, where I prepared income tax returns for a few of my friends and cousins during the income tax season. And I would go upstairs to the living room just to listen to my favorite classical music on my new stereo system. I spent a lot of my time just listening to classical music or a favorite opera.

Sometimes, when my tenant Bobo heard me in my living room, he would come down and knock on the door of my living room. I always kept the doors locked. He would ask if he could come in to talk to me. I could tell from Bobo's action that he missed his father's image in the household while he was growing up. I would let him in and talk to him as I would talk to a child, even though he has bad manners at times. His conversation was mostly about his mother. I could understand that, because his mother had died when he was only nine years old. His father was a long-distance truck driver. He was not around when Bobo was growing up, to help raise him, and he missed his father's image. A child needs both a mother and a father when growing up. A child imitates both images of his or her father and of his or her mother while he or she is growing up.

During this visit of my tenant, Bobo did not mention his mother at all, because he had a proposition for me to consider. He said, "Mr. B., with your permission, I could make some money for you and for me. I could use that back room for some of my girls to patronize some of their friends. All you would have to do is furnish that back room with some furniture, and I would control the whole operation. I would give you fifteen dollars, and I would get ten dollars, out of twenty-five dollars, that the girls would give to me, after deducting their fee for their services for these men." He continued, saying that since he would be responsible for the whole operation, "I think that this would be a fair exchange for all of us, since all you have to do is furnish the room with the proper furniture."

I thought about my tenant Bobo's proposition, and I thought about all of the problems that I was currently having with Bobo. I would have to be out of my mind to accept this proposition coming from my tenant Bobo. I knew that my problems would triple in a short space of time. No doubt, I would have to move out myself. Therefore, my answer was, "No way."

After my tenant Bobo failed to accomplish his aim of getting me to agree on his request or proposition, he apparently formulated his one way to accomplish his aim.

One day, I went upstairs to check on a problem bathroom and observed that the waste line was clogged. I had to take up the whole stool to unclog the waste line. It was clogged up by the basin stopper. The basin stopper was supposed to be used with a strainer. I asked Bobo to tell his girls to use the stopper only with the strainer. Otherwise, the stopper would go down the drainer pipe and stop up the line, again.

Meanwhile, while I was checking on the clogged waste line, I observed that Bobo had a double bed, a single bed, and a chair bed in the room that he occupied.

Bobo told me that the girls did not know that the stopper was supposed to be used only with the strainer. Bobo, however, did not give me a reason for having all of these beds in his one-room occupancy. It appeared that Bobo was going to manipulate his scheme, anyway, without my permission to accommodate the girls and their friends.

It was obvious that Bobo was conducting some type of convenience for the girls to accommodate their friends. In the previous request from Bobo, when he asked me to furnish the back room with the proper furniture, I would get fifteen dollars and he would get ten dollars for the girls to accommodate their male friends. It appeared now that Bobo was getting the total of twenty-five dollars for himself for offering this type of convenience for his girls to service their male friends.

I did not have any concrete evidence that he, Bobo, was conducting this type of operation. Since I had been going to court with Bobo, I learned that you cannot accuse a person of a crime unless you are absolutely sure that he is, without a doubt, a criminal and committing a crime by what he is doing.

One night, one of the shows on television was "The Life of Prostitution on the Street." One girl was asked, "Why do you engage in street prostitution? Why do you do this?" The answer from one of the girls was: "I have four children, ages eleven, nine, seven, and five." She continued, saying that she did not have a job to earn the money to support five children, plus herself, and that's why she engaged in the act of prostitution." This girl continued, saying that she made enough as a prostitute on the street for these men to support her family and herself. One of the girls was asked: "What do you do for these men?" The girl laughed and said, "I don't want to answer that question." Most of the girls admitted to being on drugs. Street prostitution: how does it work?

My tenant Bobo should know what prostitution on the street was, because my tenant was now classified as a pimp. Then the other question is, "What is a pimp?" It seems to work this way: The pimp or the agent gets paid by the customer, and the pimp or agent gets the girls for the customer to perform his act with them. Then the customer has to pay *X* amount of dollars to the pimp or agent and the customer has to pay *X* amount of dollars to the prostitute as her fee for letting the customer perform his act.

These prostitutes are dedicated to one another. That is, for instance, they look out for one another, for their safety or financial help.

For an example, on one occasion one of the girls was sick and did not have any money and did not feel up to going out to "hussle" for herself. She simply relayed the message to one of her friends. This friend went out and hussled for her sick friend. This favor was performed for the sick friend so she could pay some of her bills, get something to eat, and get what they call a fix.

Now the question arises: "What is a fix?" As far as I can understand from the drug users, that is when they can get the amount of drugs that they need to get that extraordinary feeling. I was told that this is what they call a fix.

I did not agree to accept Bobo's request to let him use the back room so he could operate a "prostitutes' den" or "private sanctum" for his girls to, as Bobo stated, "accommodate their male friends." But it seemed that Bobo was trying to carry out his plans, or schemes, anyway.

I continued to sit in my basement room, helplessly listening to footsteps going up and coming down the stairway, wondering what was going on upstairs. For one thing, I did not want to come in contact with all of those different girls. I wondered that since there were so many different girls, were any of them carrying the AIDS virus?

One day, I smelled smoke coming from the area of Bobo's room upstairs. I did not like the odor, and I went upstairs to investigate the origin of the smoke that I was smelling. When I approached Bobo, I asked him, "What was that smoke that I was smelling?"

Bobo's answer was: "It's Ben Gay that I was using for my aches and pains."

I continued to say that the smoke smelled like something burning. Bobo said, "No."

At this point, I could not take Bobo's type of behavior anymore. He moved into the room on or about November 22, 1989. On March 6, 1990, with all of Bobo's activities going on upstairs, I was forced to ask him to move.

It was April 1, 1990, when one of his visitors (one of the girls) broke the windowpane into his room. Reason: I heard that Bobo did not want her to come up to his room at this time of day or hour. She simply got herself a rock and threw it up to the right window, breaking the windowpane on that side, where Bobo usually sat when he threw the keys down to the girls when they came to see him. This was the girl's reaction against Bobo since he would not let her go upstairs. I reported this incident to the Eighty-first Precinct, and a complaint, number 3045, was issued to me against the tenant. Bobo paid to have the windowpane replaced.

When Bobo moved upstairs, he took possession of his room, the upstairs area, and also took possession of the stoop on or at the entrance area downstairs, where I used to sit for relaxation. Bobo had a special pillow that he used to sit on the stoop. I was now going and coming by way of the basement door and the yard. I did not come in contact with him or his girls. Did Bobo have control of the house at this time? It seems that Bobo did have control of the entire house and control of me, the landlord, at this time as well.

On September 7, 1990, one of the girls, Sally, broke the plate-glass window on the right side door, the entrance door from the stoop. Here again I had to file a complaint against my tenant Bobo.

Here again the Eighty-first Precinct issued a complaint number to my tenant Bobo. The number in this case was 7270. I did not have any problem with Bobo; he paid to have the plate-glass window replaced.

It became an ordeal dealing with Bobo's type of behavior. I had reached the point where I did not want to come in contact with him or his girls. If they were his "lady friends," he certainly had a lot of them visiting him.

One day, while I was on the outside washing my car, Bobo called me, saying, "Mr. B., this is my daughter, Sally!" While I was standing on the sidewalk, looking up to the right of the building and the window on the right, Sally was looking down at me. Bobo continued, saying that Sally was only twenty-three years old and that it seemed she had a "crush" on me. "She likes you!" Bobo was looking down from the left window, while Sally was looking down from the right window. Both of them were leaning out of the windows.

My answer was, "She is too young for me."

Sally responded by answering quickly that she was not too young for me. Sally continued, saying that she had a lot of experience with men of my age. "I have no problem with your age," she said.

If you did not know these girls that were visiting Bobo, you would if you were around this area for some time. On my way home one night, about one block away, as I was driving, I saw a girl on the sidewalk to my right. As I looked closer, I observed that it was indeed Sally. She recognized my car, and it seemed that she tried to hide herself from me. I did not say anything to her. I simply drove home and parked the car on the street in front of my house.

I have observed girls on the street, like Sally was, this night. These girls would approach me, saying, "Are you going out?" I soon learned that this was how the prostitutes were able to let the males know that they were looking for business in their profession as prostitutes. However, there are some males who go out looking for these prostitutes. Especially old men go out to look for young girls.

Diagonally across the street from my house was a five-story building. The caretaker of this building lived in the back of the building, which was on the same street as my house. His apartment was on the second floor. He said to me that one night, while he was looking out of his window, he saw one of Bobo's girls outside, adjacent to his window, about four o'clock in the morning. He said that she was talking to someone in a car. It seemed that she was trying to lure him to take her someplace.

After Harv, the caretaker, told me that, I recalled that one night I heard Sally talking to a man while he was sitting in his car. It appeared that her male companion was arguing with Sally. The car was parked in front of my house, and Bobo heard them arguing. Bobo came downstairs to check on Sally and the man in the car. Bobo wanted to know why they were arguing with each other. The male companion told Bobo that he had given Sally thirty-five dollars and she did not keep her promise to him. Bobo told the male companion in the car to wait a minute. Bobo took Sally by the arm and led her upstairs, assuring the male companion that she, Sally, would return to his car soon.

Sally did not return to the man's car. The man in the car started blowing his horn after a few minutes. But Sally did not return to his car. After the man in the car blew his horn several more times, Bobo realized that this noise of horn blowing would annoy the neighbors. He came downstairs to appease the man by telling him that Sally was not feeling well and that she would accompany him on a later date. . . . Bobo assured the man that Sally would take care of her responsibilities in the near future. The male companion drove away.

Bobo returned back upstairs, and I overheard Bobo and Sally arguing with each other. The argument went on for a few hours.

I began to wonder about Bobo and Sally. Bobo has introduced Sally to me as his daughter. I accepted Sally as Bobo's daughter and that was the end of my thinking that she was one of Bobo's girls that were coming to see him.

When Bobo first introduced me to his daughter as being twenty-three years old, maybe he thought that I would accept her because of her youth. There are other factors in a female companion. She should be more mature, not too young, although Sally did not think that she was too young, because of her experience with older men. I observed her as not being able to communicate properly. When she talked, most of her words were muffled. She did not finish high school; therefore, her vocabulary was limited. Maybe she was doing the only thing she was capable of doing, dating different men for a fee. However, I do not look down on any people because they are uneducated or less intellectual. I usually treat people as human beings, regardless of their educational background or intellectual capabilities.

The next and most important reason for not going with her was the risks one takes when he goes out with someone like Sally. Why like Sally? Well, Sally was seen a great percentage of the time on the streets, usually with different men. Personal hygiene should be one of the factors that anyone should be mindful of when dating anybody from the streets. What about a disease like AIDS, for instance? With someone like Sally, you are subjected to someone who is likely to become a victim of the AIDS virus. I, however, would have liked to talk to Sally, to advise her of the risks that she was taking going out with different men from the streets. You cannot deny the possibility of catching the AIDS virus when you take chances like Sally was doing. If you went out with her, you could get what she had. Would you take that chance?

Today you have to be very careful whom you socialize with, especially concerning who is constantly out on the streets. Should I say the girls who are "hustling for a living"? You have to choose your companions very carefully today.

One thing that I could not come to grips with was that Sally was introduced to me as Bobo's daughter. Bobo was my tenant. It seemed that Bobo wanted me to date his twenty-three-year-old daughter. From my experience renting to Bobo, it all seemed that Bobo had other reasons on his mind.

I said to myself, *Here Sally and Bobo are sharing one room together, upstairs. However, there are one double bed, one single bed, and one chair bed in the room. Why are there so many beds in one room? Sally could be sleeping in the single bed, while Bobo is sleeping in the double bed. Nevertheless, they are sharing the same room, for a father and daughter. There is no privacy for either of them. Sharing one space becomes commonplace.*

Different people have different ideals. I suppose that this was only one example of how people lived together like Sally and Bobo. In this case, I began to think that Sally was not Bobo's daughter. Yet Sally called Bobo Daddy several times, different times. The manner in which she called him Daddy seemed to be for real, to me. She did not try to hide any of her emotions. She simply said, "Daddy." I accepted that this couple was for real, father and daughter. However, it could be an incest case.

Bobo and Sally used to argue a lot with each other. One of their arguments seemed to have gotten out of control. I heard Bobo yelling and telling Sally to "get out." He followed by saying, "And don't come back." Sally left. I did not see Sally for several days.

In my opinion, this did not worry Bobo at all. Bobo was never alone. With all of these young girls coming and going out of Bobo's room, Bobo did not have a problem of being lonesome. Bobo had a lot of female companions. I noticed another girl, whom Bobo referred to as "Annie." However, Annie's relationship with Bobo did not last very long. This did not bother Bobo, because he still had a lot of different girls coming and going out of his room. He had a lot of girls from whom to choose one of them. I had a problem trying to figure out why all of these different girls were so loyal to him. He appeared to be a powerful man. Was there any jealousy in these different combinations? The different girls appeared to be very happy to be around Bobo.

With all of this commotion going on upstairs, I could not take it anymore. I issued a termination of tenancy to Bobo, dated October 28, 1990. With my tenant Bobo, it seemed that he decided what he was going to do and what he was not going to do. Bobo simply ignored that termination of tenancy order and continued to do what he was doing as if he did not receive that order to move.

Bobo's lease to rent the room expired November 13, 1990. By November 30, 1990, I issued the second termination of tenancy order to Bobo. As I was waiting for Bobo to move, I noticed that Bobo also ignored the second termination of tenancy to move. I had no choice but to get a lawyer to take my case against my tenant Bobo to court.

Before I rented the room to Bobo, it was my plan to rent the top-floor apartment for $500 per month. This rental income, as I had planned it, was to supplement my retirement fixed income, so I would be able to use that extra money for maintenance of the house and unforeseen expenses as they occurred. I could see the laxity in meeting these expenses, as they were surely to occur, turned out to be only a dream.

When Bobo asked me to rent to him only one room, it sorta changed my plans. However, from my experience renting space in an apartment I said, "Maybe it is possible to rent upstairs in two different units, on what you might call a sharing plan." It worked like this: for instance, Bobo would be renting the front room, while I would be able to rent the back room to another man. This seemed like it would be a simple solution to my rentable unit. It would then be divided into two parts, with the use of kitchen and bathroom. The rental charge would be divided into two parts, as well. Instead of $500 for one tenant, it would be $250 for each tenant.

It did not take me long to find out that this plan would not work with a tenant like Bobo.

As I have mentioned before, Bobo had jammed his bell because so many girls were ringing his bell. . . . It annoyed him. Now these girls, from their point of view, had as their objective reaching Bobo, so they could relay their messages to him, whatever these messages might have been. How could they reach Bobo? Or, how could they let Bobo know that they were outside and wanted to see him? Well, simply by calling him from the street. That's what they did, and constantly. It was "Bobo, Bobo, Bobo!" in the voices of many different girls.

After I had observed this type of behavior by the girls and their constant trek, going up and down the stairway, I knew that it would not be wise to rent the back room to another man, or anybody. Bobo's control of the entire area of the top-floor apartment simply abolished my plans for extra income.

Out of curiosity, I decided to monitor the number of times that these girls would come by to see Bobo. Since his doorbell was jammed, they would call him from the street. This, however, was before Bobo's lease expired.

On March 13, 1990, I started monitoring these calls from the street: A call from the street came at 6:00 P.M. March 14, at 7:00 A.M. a call from the street, a visitor at 2:30 A.M. March 15, a call from the street and a visitor Sunday night, March 18, busy with visitors. On March 19 at 1:23 A.M. a visitor, March 30 at 3:30 A.M., two visitors. I stopped monitoring until on May 10, about 10:00 P.M., a visitor, on May

11, 12:50 A.M. a visitor, 2:45 A.M. a visitor, 5:15 A.M. a visitor. At 10:10 A.M., three visitors, one male and two females. At this point, I stopped monitoring Bobo's visitors and calls from the street. They were not stopping, coming and going. How could anybody in this area get a peaceful night's sleep? What about Bobo himself? Could he get enough sleep?

With all the torture that Bobo was putting me through, he was still behind in his rent payments. Now I had something else to complain about; Bob was not only abusing his room privileges, but he was cluttering up the public hall just outside of the door to his room. There appeared to be plastic bags full of dirty clothing. Dirty clothes that he said he had to have washed.

It seemed with all of these complaints that I had against Bobo, no one was helping me to get them corrected. One of the owners of the house next door, a police sergeant at one of the precincts, told me that there was a place downtown Brooklyn where I, as a senior citizen, could get some help. This place I was going to check out in the near future. But for now I would depend on my lawyer and the New York City court system to help me collect my back rent from Bobo.

In the past, I was lucky to rent to good tenants, considerate tenants. It seems that all of my former tenants could be treated like members of my family. If you have good tenants, it makes you, the owner of the house a good landlord. With my tenant Bobo, it was a different story. It seemed that at this point of Bobo's tenancy he was now revealing his true identity. It seemed that Bobo's character was changing. Therefore, my character as a good landlord also would have to change, so I could deal with Bobo's change of character. I could not have any more sympathy for Bobo. He did not have any feeling for me. He did not care if I had money to pay my bills on the house or would be able to maintain the house as it should be maintained.

Having all of those girls visiting Bobo created more problems with the upkeep of the house. They were using the bathroom, the kitchen, Bobo's bedroom, causing my maintenance of the house to go up and up. Who cared?

As a landlord, a considerate landlord, I tried to deal with my tenant Bobo on agreeable terms. He was behind in his rent. I asked him to pay his back rent or move. Bobo ignored my request to move or pay his rent, and he continued to allow his friends to come and go as he pleased. I informed Bobo that his lease had, in fact, expired and if he did not pay his rent he would not be considered a tenant anymore.

It appeared at this point that Bobo's visitors had increased to an unbearable number of visitors, coming and going all day and all night. Most of his visitors were young girls. I was hesitating in my effort to get a lawyer, hoping that Bobo would come around and pay up his rent. No such thing with my tenant Bobo.

I finally asked my lawyer, Mr. Jasper, to take my case against my tenant Bobo. I had known Mr. Jasper for a long time. However, I had never used Mr. Jasper to represent me on a case before. I asked for an appointment to see Mr. Jasper as soon as possible. When I arrived at his office, I mentioned several complaints that I had against my tenant Bobo. Then I gave my lawyer a breakdown of Bobo's rentable payments.

The total rent Bobo owed me as of this date was $892.50. Mr. Jasper issued a court order to collect the overdue rent in February 1991. The court order read, and I quote: "The petition and precept in the above matter was served upon your tenant in or on the 16th day of February, 1991.

There was another quote in the court order issued by Mr. Jasper: "Please be advised that the trial of the entitled matter has been set down to be heard on the date, March 5, 1991, time and place; 9:30 A.M., Housing Court, part 18, first floor, and you should arrange to be present."

After this court order was issued to my tenant Bobo, I thought that my problem with Bobo was over. No way.

Bobo did not accept Mr. Jasper's court order without a fight. It seems that Bobo knew exactly what to do in this case or cases of this magnitude. Bobo knew what to do in order to get more time to stay in his rented room upstairs. Bobo started putting pressure on me right from the beginning of Mr. Jasper's court order for him to pay for the back rent that he owed me.

Mr. Jasper, apparently not knowing that Bobo was fighting these court orders, notified me when a court hearing was scheduled to be heard, starting from February 1991. But since Bobo was fighting each scheduled court hearing date, the court hearings dates were: March 5, 1991; March 20, 1991; May 28, 1991; June 6, 1991; June 28, 1991; August 19, 1991; September 30, 1991; November 12, 1991; January 22, 1992; and February 10, 1992.

I visited Mr. Jasper's office several times on these court hearing dates. One or two of these times that I visited Mr. Jasper's office, he informed me that I had a lot of problems or would have a lot of problems with my tenant Bobo. Mr. Jasper did not elaborate on what types of problems I would have with my tenant Bobo.

On one of my visits to Mr. Jasper's office, he told me that Bobo had been by his office. Mr. Jasper did not explain why Bobo stopped by his office or what he said concerning his tenancy at my house or what he was going to do about the rent that he owed me.

I finally found out what Mr. Jasper was referring to from Bobo himself. On one of Bobo's visits to my living room, he revealed to me that Mr. Jasper had been his lawyer a few years ago. Bobo continued, saying that Mr. Jasper had represented him in court on many occasions and that he, Bobo, was familiar with how Mr. Jasper handles his cases. At first, I thought that Bobo had decided to pay up his rent or decided to move out . . . without a court hearing.

3

The Second Phase of Bobo's Tenancy

I appeared in court as scheduled March 5, 1991. At the hearing, Bobo only paid $752.50. The total due was $892.50. When I returned home, I called Mr. Jasper and informed him that Bobo did not pay all of his rent. Mr. Jasper issued another court order: "Please be advised that a notice has been served terminating tenancy of the above named tenant, Bobo, effective as of May 13th, 1991. You may accept rent from this tenant for any period through and including May 13th, 1991, but no rent for the period commencing May 14th, 1991, and thereafter."

On March 8, 1991, Bobo started fighting back. He went downtown to the Civil Court Building and filed a complaint against the landlord:

Whole Apartment	No heat throughout apartment
Bathroom	No cold water, bad plumbing
	Mice-infested
Kitchen	Bad Plumbing
Whole Apartment	Bad electrical wiring
	Signed by ____Bobo____

As a result of Bobo's complaints, an inspector was sent out to check the apartment for those complaints. According to the inspection sheet, the inspector was from the Department of Housing Preservation and Development, Office of Rent and Housing Maintenance.

Bobo was a recipient of the Department of Social Services, and that added emphasis to the violations, even if Bobo was the cause of some of those violations. Anyway, the inspector came. I was not at home at the time. I found out about the violations when I received the violations sheet sent out by the inspector.

As a result of Bobo's complaints, he was given more time to stay in his room, in my house.

Our next appearance in court was March 8, 1991. Usually, when we stood before the judge the respondent stood on the left and the petitioner stood on the right of the judge. The judge virtually leaned over from his seat, which was up above my head, and pointing his finger at me said, "I will charge you with contempt of court and will put you in jail if you fail to correct those violations."

As a rule, I was a quiet person; I think that I am a good and considerate landlord as well, but when the judge made that statement I felt senseless for a while. After I was able to recompose myself, I stood there, motionless, until the judge finished questioning Bobo. I then returned to my seat. I noticed that the judge would only ask the tenant questions, not the landlord. Many times I was in court without a lawyer, because Mr. Jasper did not attend all of the hearings. I had to represent myself, although I was not given a chance to say anything. Maybe, Mr. Jasper stayed out on purpose, because the judge sorta ignored Mr. Jasper on several occasions.

Returning home, I made sure that I did not get on the same subway train as Bobo. I purposely pretended to do some shopping in order to use up some time. Usually, when I arrived home I would find that Bobo arrived earlier.

Now as for the violations, I will take them one at a time:

1. No heat throughout the apartment. Maybe the apartment felt cold to Bobo because he spent a lot of time leaning out of his window, answering the calls of all of his girls. As one looked up from the sidewalk, it was the window on the left side of the building. This window was directly over the radiator. Certainly if the window was opened for several hours during the day it would cool the room down to a lower temperature. Would you think that Bobo would be able to realize why it got cold in the room? Maybe he was not capable of realizing this phenomenon . . . this change in temperature.

In the past, I had heard some of Bobo's friends saying, "It's too hot in here." I am sure that Bobo did hear some of his friends saying "It's too hot in here." At the next court hearing, if I told the judge that some of Bobo's friends complained that it was too hot in his room, the judge would not believe me and would ignore what I was saying.

2. No cold water in the bathroom: Pause a minute and recheck that statement. Cold water was flowing in all of the pipes in the entire house at all hours, day and night.

The main water line was piped in from the street. There was always cold water flowing through the pipes. If he had said, "No hot water in the bathroom," then you could believe his statement. The judge would still believe Bobo's complaints.

3. Bad plumbing: When I renovated the entire house, I had the contractor install all new brass plumbing throughout the whole house. Do you know what brass plumbing means or is? It's the best type of plumbing: it doesn't rust; it doesn't corrode, either. Yet Bobo said that I had "bad plumbing." If the judge would see that I did, in fact, have all brass plumbing, he would still agree with my tenant Bobo.

4. Mice-infested: You might find it hard to believe my statement about mice infestation in my tenant Bobo's room. I have a habit of overbuying when something that I can use is on sale. The merchants in one of the nearby stores that I patronize put a new brand of mice-rat poison on sale. . . . I stocked up on this new brand of mice-rat poison. When Bobo complained about mice infestation, I went upstairs and asked Bobo where he wanted me to put this poison. He pointed out several areas; I put several containers of this poison in small containers in those areas where he saw these rodents visiting more often. This included the bathroom, the kitchen, and his room.

One day, while I was upstairs, Sally asked me, "How much did you pay for that brand of mice-rat poison?" I wondered why would she ask me how much I paid for that brand of mice-rat poison. Anyway, I told her how much I paid for the poison and left the area. Would you believe that after a few days passed I went upstairs to check on something and I noticed that those containers were empty?

What did I do about the empty containers of poison? I simply put some more of this new brand of mice-rat poison in those empty containers again, but not as much as I did the first time. I do not recall Bobo complaining about mice-rat infestation anymore. At each court hearing, Bobo had to have a complaint against the landlord in order for the judge to continue being in favor of the tenant and not the landlord. It seemed that the judge wanted to enforce his threat against me, charging me with contempt of court, so he could put me in jail, as he had so eloquently stated in the past. It seemed that he got a great deal of pleasure out of making that statement.

I hardly said anything while I was in court. The judge did not listen to me anyway, so why should I say anything? Maybe my silence in court made him think that I was ignoring what he was saying. Therefore, he continued to let me know that he could charge me with contempt of court and would put me in jail, as if to say, "I have the power to charge you with contempt and will, in fact, put you in jail." OK, what could I say about it? I simply remained helpless.

I did, however, continue trying to "rid" the house of all of those violations; that's all I could do. Bobo was the "jury" at all of my court hearings. I simply sat and waited for the judge to say, "Court is adjourned."

5. Bad electrical wiring: In this case of bad electrical wiring, the inspector was referring to the exposed wiring in the public hall, first floor, and leading up to the top floor. The only exposed wiring in the public hall was the doorbell wires and the wiring for the timer. Usually, this type of wiring is insulated wires.

Bobo did not mention his bell not working on his report of violations, but the inspector put the bell down as one of the violations on his inspection report: "Properly repair the broken or defective doorbell, second story." By now, the "doorbell violation" stood out in "bold print." Because it was Bobo himself that jammed the bell. Could I tell the Judge that? I recall telling the judge that Bobo jammed his bell because of the numerous girls coming to see him, ringing his bell, and that he himself purposely jammed his own bell because the constant ringing of the bell annoyed him.

Since the inspector put Bobo's doorbell down as a violation. I had to figure out a way to fix his bell, so he could not jam it. How could I do that? I ran a complete new circuit for the bell from the first floor. The hall bedroom was used for storage and kept locked at all times. The door to enter the hall bedroom was just outside of the door leading to Bobo's room. I ran the new bell circuit wires from the bell button, outside, just above the stoop, up through the walls, up into the hall bedroom. I put Bobo's bell just inside the door of the hall bedroom. It was about three feet from Bobo's entrance door.

When I made all of the connections for Bobo's bell, I pressed the bell button for Bobo's bell and I heard it ring. Bobo could also hear it ring, but he could not reach the bell to jam it. Unless, however, he broke the lock on the hall bedroom door, to gain entrance to the bell.

Did that stop Bobo from jamming the bell? When I was away on vacation or just away for a few days, I had to leave the door leading to the basement hall, or public hall, if you will, open or unlocked. Remember, I used to have my bedroom in the back room on the parlor floor.

When I moved downstairs into the basement room I always kept all doors locked, just in case some of Bobo's girls might want to pay me a visit without being invited. I did not want any uninvited guests coming to visit me. Another reason was that today you have to be careful whom you date. Otherwise, an uninvited guest might turn out to be an infected guest. I certainly didn't want an unwanted "bug" to invade my terminals. Because it might be a "bug" that you cannot kill with a "fly swatter."

Once, when I returned home from a trip, I was unloading the inside of the car; Sally approached me and offered her help in unloading the car. Usually when I am traveling, I always have a few plastic shopping bags with something in them on the front seat and sometimes on the backseat as well. On the front seat were almost always bags with lunch, sodas, grapes, or some type of junk food to snack on.

When Sally asked me if she could help, I said, "No, I have it under control." There was another girl with Sally at that time. When the girls left, I started unloading my suitcases from the trunk of my car.

If I was going out of town, I had to leave the door leading to the public hall on the basement floor unlocked. Leaving this door locked would be a violation, since the electrical appliances were located on the public hall of the basement floor. If you had to change an electric fuse, the fuse boxes were located on this floor as well. The tenants had to have access to the fuse boxes.

It didn't have to be a blown-out fuse for my tenant Bobo to have a reason to go down to the public hall on the basement floor. Bobo knew that all doorbell wires led from the transformer on the electric meter up to the bell button on the outside, just above the stoop.

What did Bobo do in this case? Bobo went downstairs, located the bell wires, which were connected to the bell transformer, and created a short circuit. That blew out the bell transformer. His bell was not ringing, as well as my bell. At our next court hearing, I had to tell the judge what Bobo had done to the doorbells . . . at my house. What action did the judge take against Bobo? *None.* No comments against Bobo, either. How could I win?

This type of behavior by my tenant Bobo was a form of vandalism. I had no other choice but to buy a new bell transformer. I connected the new transformer, rang Bobo's bell to let him know that his bell was ringing, and disconnected both bells, for the time being. I did not want Bobo to blow out this new transformer.

Several weeks later, I reconnected my doorbell. I figured that Bobo had gotten used to his bell not ringing.

6. Uncapped gasoline in the front room; Bobo's room, which was visible to the eye, but it was capped. Otherwise, I could not have lived there for so many years earlier. Who was I to tell the inspector that the gasoline was indeed capped? I had no choice but to get a licensed plumber to install another gas line from the basement to the top floor.

This was an old house, but a strongly built house. When this house was built, they used gas lights all over the house. But when civilization brought about change, modernization took place at a rapid rate. Old fixtures were replaced by new and modern fixtures. However, I never had any problems with the old capped gas line until my tenant Bobo moved into the room upstairs.

Incidentally, when the plumber arrived to measure the distance that he would have to run this new, independent gas line, I called Bobo to let him know that I, along with the plumber, was coming upstairs. I do not know what Bobo was doing, but he appeared to be very upset. He started to use such abusive language that the plumber did not want go to upstairs. The plumber said, "I can see what you are going through with your tenant." I could see that Bobo was undressed. I did not hear a female's voice, so I could not tell whether Bobo had a date or not. The way Bobo was carrying on, I thought that he was in the middle of a "lovemaking process."

In the past, I had noticed that Sally would be undressed. If I was going upstairs and Sally was undressed, Bobo would yell to her to "put on some clothes, because Mr. B. is coming upstairs."

Since the representative from the Plumbing and Heating Corporation experienced the behavior of Bobo when he came to check the uncapped gas line, I wrote a letter to the corporation requesting a letter from them, on their "letterhead" stationery, mentioning the reaction of Bobo, my tenant, when the representative came to measure the distance that he would have to run an independent gas line from the basement floor up to the top floor. I indicated to him that I was going to apply for a "Peace Warrant" against my tenant and his comment revealing Bobo's behavior when he came to measure the distance that he would have to supply piping to remove the uncapped gas line problem.

I wrote my letter on June 4, 1991, and the reply from the plumbing and heating corporation was dated June 10, 1991, and I quote:

We at the Plumbing and Heating Corporation can sympathize with your plight in dealing with your tenant Bobo. However, since our company's inception we have had certain company policies which we must adhere to. One of these policies is that we cannot place this company, or any employee, into a landlord-tenant dispute.

I am sure you can understand the obvious reasons for such a policy. Therefore, we would not be able to provide you with such a statement either from a serviceman or the company.

We hope that our position on this matter will have no ill effects on our newly developed relationship. Please remember that we are here to service all of your plumbing and heating needs seven days a week.

I could understand the Plumbing and Heating Corporation's policy of not intervening in a landlord-tenant dispute.

It seemed that I was back to square one. Nobody was in sympathy with me. The judge did not listen to what I had to say in court, and my tenant Bobo continued his rampage.

On or about June 13, 1991, we appeared in court as a result of a holdover petition issued by Mr. Jasper. Judge Swan was absent, and the case was heard by a female judge . . . Judge Rono.

Judge Rono let Bobo know that if he did not pay his rent, he could be evicted. "Do you understand that?" she said.

Bobo nodded his head, saying, "Yes, Your Honor."

It seemed that Judge Rono was indeed on my side. She then referred us to a mediator who was located in the back of the courtroom.

The mediator drew up an agreement between the landlord and tenant. In this agreement, it was clearly stated that the tenant would move on September 13, 1991, and the landlord would pay certain bills, like the gas and electric bills, up to that date. Bobo and I both signed that agreement, and the mediator turned that agreement over to the judge.

At our next court hearing, Judge Swan presided, but nothing was said about our agreement. The mediator's agreement between landlord and tenant was completely, ignored. Why have a mediator if the mediator's solutions to a problem are not going to be used? It's just a waste of time.

7. A broken or defective counter balance spring lower sash, front room window, second story: This window was called Bobo's Window, since he used it so much. In the summer months, this window stayed

up all of the time. In the winter and cooler months, this window was up and down constantly, day and night.

These were new replacement windows. They were installed when I had new vinyl siding installed about one year ago, before Bobo moved into the room upstairs.

We have to realize that every product will not last its full cycle if that product is abused, constantly, by an outside force over and over, for long periods of time. This was Bobo's window; he used it to answer the calls of his girls when they came to visit him. Those calls never ceased, day or night.

I did not have to call a contractor to fix the window. Luckily, I was able to reconnect the counter balance spring myself.

8. The nuisance consisting of a concealed water leak in the bathroom ceiling, second story: Since Bobo moved into the front room, I did fix a leak near the hatch door, and later I covered the whole roof with roof coating. Over the years, I learned how to install a new roof, if necessary.

Would you believe that at our next court hearing Bobo told the judge that the water was pouring into the bathroom and in his room as well?

I looked at Bobo in disbelief when he made that statement. It seemed that the judge believed everything that Bobo said against the landlord.

At this court hearing, Bobo had brought Annie with him to court. He had instructed Annie, one of his more familiar girls, what to say, that is, if the judge asked her any questions. The judge asked Bobo, "Who is this female person that you have with you?" Bobo told the Judge that she was a friend of his and she could verify what he said about the water leaks in the bathroom and in his room. The judge asked her if it was true that the leaks continued in the bathroom and Bobo's room? Annie told the judge that it was true that the leaks occurred when it rained.

The judge would give Bobo's female friends a chance to speak. Sometimes it was Annie and sometimes it was Sally. However, the Judge did not listen to what I had to say. Sometimes he would even casually look at a valid receipt that I would present to him, showing him that I had, indeed, removed one of the violations in the house.

Not only did the Judge refuse to listen to me; he would also ignore what Mr. Jasper, my lawyer, was saying sometimes, even if it had a lot to do with my case.

My lawyer was black, and the judge was also black. When the judge ignored what my lawyer was saying, I felt sorry for my lawyer, because it's not nice to completely ignore what someone is saying, even if it's just an average person. Here Mr. Jasper was a lawyer and he was representing me in court, against my tenant Bobo.

After the court hearing, I talked with my lawyer, Mr. Jasper, and he told me that he could report the judge to a "higher authority" for ignoring his testimony in court. But Mr. Jasper never reported the behavior of the judge during the court hearings, against me or him.

After this court hearing, I was anxious to check the roof, since Bobo and his female friend said the roof leaked when it rained. Between the ceiling and the roof was about three and one-half feet. I had enough room to store some five-gallon cans of roof coating for short periods of time. However, it was seldom used.

When it rained, I went upstairs to the area between the roof and the ceiling. I just stood there staring between these two areas. I observed at least five different leaks underneath the roof. I knew right away that this was a form of vandalism. I returned to my living room, on the parlor floor. I just sat there thinking, could anybody in his right mind do such a thing as this? Then I recalled that on one occasion, when I went up on the roof to fix something and returned back down to the top floor area, I was bringing my stepladder downstairs with me, to use to fix something on the parlor floor, which required a stepladder to reach the area to be fixed. I remember Bobo asking me to leave the ladder upstairs, because he might have to use the ladder to go up on the roof himself. I did not give his request for the ladder to remain upstairs a second thought, because—who knows?—there might be a fire and he just might have to use the ladder to go up on the roof to escape the fire, whatever.

As I sat in my living room, thinking, I realized that this was a two-family house and a fire escape was not required for two-family houses. Bobo was only one flight up, and all he would have to do was run down to the parlor floor and go out the entrance door to the stoop. I did not think that way when he asked me to leave the ladder upstairs.

In spite of Bobo's disagreeable disposition, he had a good and cooperative side as well. Maybe the reason that I let him visit my living room occasionally to talk to me was because I felt that I might be able to get on the good side of Bobo by being kind and cooperative to him. Using kindness toward him, I might eventually get to his sympathetic inner feelings toward me. Anyway, it was good to feel optimistic about Bobo changing his way of life.

By letting Bobo into my living room to talk to me, I found out something about his early life. He told me that he was a member of a street gang and he used to get into a lot of trouble with the law. He also told me that his first job was with a roofer. I mentioned this because this part of his life had a bearing on my case with him in court. He admitted that he knew a lot about roofs. Could I charge him with vandalism of my roof, punching holes through my roof? Who would believe me? Certainly not the judge. Bobo knew how to install a new roof. I also knew how to install a new roof. Could I install a new roof for myself? Would the judge accept that? I could not give myself a valid receipt to present to the judge. Therefore, I had to get a professional roofer to do the job so I could get a valid receipt. With a valid receipt, the judge would only casually look at it and give it back to me, and then he would forget that I did remove that violation. How could I win?

In view of all of this emotional trauma, the judge did not forget to remind me that he would charge me with contempt of court and would put me in jail if I failed to remove these violations.

I spoke up at this point, saying, "Your Honor, if you recall, Bobo told you that the roof was not leaking at the last court appearance."

The judge did not offer any answer to this at this point. He simply said, "If you do not remove this violation by the next court hearing, I am going to enforce the contempt of court order, and I am going to put you in jail."

At the next court hearing, there were two orders issued to Bobo. One was an order issued for nonpayment of rent. The second order was a holdover order issued for Bobo to pay up his rent or move out. The judge threw out the holdover order, saying that it was issued because Bobo had filed complaints against the landlord.

The judge warned me that he was coming to my house for a personal inspection of these violations on October 9, 1991.

When the judge arrived, Bobo showed him the refrigerator. It's unbelievable how Bobo could make the refrigerator look so bad. The inside of the refrigerator was virtually pulled out from its original position. He could not have pulled this section out with his bare hands; he had to have used a screwdriver to do such a thing as that. My tenant Bobo is an unbelievable guy. How could Bobo do such a horrible thing as this to my refrigerator? Even if the refrigerator was old, it was working well. All you had to do was defrost it at the proper time. I even offered my service to defrost the refrigerator for him. This was the second refrigerator that I put up in Bobo's kitchen in about two years. Both of the refrigerators had to be defrosted at the proper time. Bobo simply looked at me when I offered my service to defrost the refrigerator.

There were some complaints against Bobo, but whom could I complain to? Not the judge, that's for sure. So I was stuck with Bobo. I could not get him to move, even though he was not paying any rent. He was living at my expense.

The second thing that Bobo showed the judge was the cooking stove. He pulled out the containers that were used to catch spilled-over oils or any other spills from the top of the stove. When you cleaned the stove, you also should clean out these containers. But these containers were filled with debris. I was standing nearby, and I noticed that each container contained something that looked like rat droppings. I immediately yelled out, "Bobo, how can you cook your food on such a mess as this? This stove is filthy . . . even worse than filthy. And you cook your food on this filthy stove?"

The judge just looked at the containers, and said nothing. I knew that the judge had to agree with me, but he appeared to be stubborn, and he refused to agree with me openly.

The third thing that Bobo showed the judge was some old lumber that I had stored at the back of the backyard for future use. This old lumber was stored on a metal rack and covered with an old carpet to help preserve the lumber. Lumber is very high in price today, and you have to save what you can to make ends meet, in the future.

The judge looked at the lumber on the metal rack in the back of the yard and simply said, 'You could get a violation from the fire department for that lumber that you have stored back there."

I looked at the judge, thinking, *What kind of judge is Judge Swan? Anything that's in favor of Bobo, the judge has something to say about, with a positive answer.*

On the judge's way out, I showed the judge a "frostless" refrigerator that I had in my living room. My son-in-law brought the refrigerator to me, at my daughter's request, and I had stored it in my living room. Maybe my daughter was trying to help me out with Bobo's complaints.

The judge looked at the refrigerator and checked with Bobo to see if he approved of this refrigerator, Bobo agreed; then the judge said, "OK, put it up into his kitchen."

The judge's findings on his personal inspection were that I should:

1. Replace the refrigerator.
2. The vermin mice infestation.
3. Patch leak in tenant's room.
4. Plaster holes in the kitchen.

I replaced the old refrigerator with the refrigerator that my daughter had given me, the refrigerator that I had stored in my living room, and with the judge's and Bobo's approval. This made the third refrigerator that I had given to Bobo in two years. For the second complaint, I called an exterminator to take care of the vermin, the mice infestation problem, in Bobo's room. The third complaint concerned the concealed leak in the tenant's room. The fourth complaint, the broken plaster in the kitchen, was caused by the plumber installing the independent gas line in Bobo's kitchen.

When I went upstairs, at Bobo's request, he asked me to stand over near the radiator and look up at the ceiling. I followed Bobo's instructions and looked up at the ceiling.

Bobo said, "Do you see the bulging plaster up there?"

I said, "Yes."

Bobo said, "That hunk of plaster could fall and hurt somebody, and I could be sued for damages."

I told Bobo, "I don't have any money; you do not pay your rent. How can I have money?"

Bobo asked me if I had any insurance on the house.

Bobo is the type of person who would look for something to bring charges against somebody, like his landlord, to sue for damages that he himself caused by his act of vandalism, punching holes in the roof.

At the senior citizens' center where I went for some of my meals, I often saw an elderly lady called Mrs. Jones, who patronizes the center for some of her meals as well. Mrs. Jones was ninety-six years old, and she was considered an adviser to the other seniors at the center. It was easy for me to accept Mrs. Jones as an adviser, because when I was a young boy I liked to listen to my grandmother while she told me about her past, as a little girl and growing up to an adult.

Mrs. Jones would buy a lot of vegetables at a time. I would take her to the vegetable market to buy these vegetables, usually in large quantities at a time, and I would help her take them to her house. I recall that she bought about fifteen pounds of carrots at one time. She told me that she used a juicer to make juice out of them. She would drink a certain amount of different juices a day. Maybe this was why she was able to reach the "ripe old age" of ninety-six.

At other times, we would just sit and talk. She knew a lot about my past, my work in the Political Club. I campaigned for different candidates who were running for public office. I campaigned for nominees for presidents of the United States, as well as other candidates like the governor, the mayors, the borough presidents, and others.

Occasionally I would tell her about my plight with my tenant Bobo. She told me about an elderly man who lost his house to one of his tenants.

I wondered about this statement, because Bobo told me once that he could take my house and not pay me anything for it. Maybe he was trying to do just that. He certainly had the court system on his side. To date, we had appeared in court about twelve times, and Bobo was not paying any rent. He simply ignored the orders to pay his rent that he received! My lawyer issued these orders, but Bobo ignored them. The court system seemed to ignore them, as well. The judge did not enforce these orders, either.

I was beginning to feel like I was the criminal, in this case. Certainly Bobo seemed to have the upper hand in this case. He had taken over the greater portion of my house. I did not use the stoop at all now. Bobo used it at will, with a special cushion to sit on the stoop. What about the law in this case? Would this be a miscarriage of justice? Or were we equal in the eyes of the law? I would say that it was not any of the above. I cannot follow this line of reasoning. Who was I?

Mrs. Jones suggested that with my past work with the different candidates for public office it was time that they should do something for me. She suggested that I write to the borough president and ask him for help in trying to resolve my case in court.

I drew up a letter to the borough president, in pencil form, but I never typed the letter to send to the borough president. I did, however, visit the neighborhood Political Club. I talked with the leader of the club. I told him about the personal visit by the judge to check the different violations against my house as a result of my tenant Bobo. The leader only recommended a man called Jake to do the plastering work, for me.

Jake was not available when I called him to do this work for me. I could not let this bulging plaster remain as Bobo pointed out to me, because Bobo could make it fall. I simply took my six-foot ladder, with the cover from the garbage can to catch the debris, a screwdriver, a putty knife, and a hammer, to break this bulging plaster down. I left a twelve-by-twelve inch opening up where the bulging plaster had been. Now you could see a few lattices up there instead of bulging plaster, and it was safer . . . it would not fall.

When Jake came to do the work, I called Bobo to let him know that Jake was there to do the plaster work and we were on our way upstairs.

When Jake and I reached Bobo's room, Jake said, "Hey, I know you." They talked briefly. Jake said, "What happened to you? You used to be a nice-looking man. What happened?"

Bobo replied by saying, "Problems, many problems."

Jake checked out the area to be plastered and asked if I had any sheet rock. I went downstairs and was able to find a size of sheet rock large enough to cover the area of broken plaster. Jake got up on my ladder to do the work. Jake complained about it being too hot in Bobo's room and said he could not work in such a hot room. He asked me to turn the thermostat to a lower setting. Bobo did not like Jake telling me to turn the thermostat to a lower setting, because Bobo was always telling me that it was too cold upstairs. One reason Bobo would ask for more heat was because when the girls called Bobo from the street he would put the window up to either throw them the key to the front door or give advice to them. The window would be open for several minutes. That would be enough time for the room to get cold again.

There were so many girls coming to see Bobo that it would require him to put the window up several times in one hour. This type of behavior would cause the room to get cold. For instance, if the window was up several hours a day, then the temperature in the room would be just the same as it was on the street. As a landlord not collecting rent, I could not afford to heat the outside, just outside the window. Even if I were collecting the rent on time, I could and would not be able to heat the outside of the window. If I complained to Bobo about him keeping the window up so much during the day, Bobo would pretend that he did not keep the window open that often to make the room cold.

If I did not lower the thermostat, Jake would leave, telling me that he could not work in the room, if it was too hot. Jake would say, "I will be back in two days."

From Bobo's visits to my living room I found out that he needed guidance by a male image. His father was a long-distance truck driver and was away for most of his time, away from home and Bobo.

In observing Bobo's behavior, I found out that he was, in fact, an evil, cunning, and deceitful man. His behavior would change from time to time. When he came down to my living room to talk to me, he usually was on his best behavior. I learned a lot about his background, with his mother, his grandmother, and his Aunt Sarah. Bobo did not talk about his father very much. I do not know why. Bobo must have had a reason for not talking about his father very much. Otherwise, Bobo was very evil, disagreeable, or just a troublemaker.

When Jake returned to finish the job of repairing the hole in the ceiling in Bobo's room, Bobo was willing to let me turn the thermostat to a lower setting so Jake could finish his job. This would have been an easy job for me to repair, but I could not give myself a valid receipt; therefore, I had to get a contractor to do the job so I could get a valid receipt to show the judge, even though he only casually looked at the receipt of any violation removal in my house. The judge would still ask Bobo if the violation was repaired satisfactorily or not.

Even with the contractor, I furnished most of the material to fix the ceiling. It seemed that I could not win, no matter which course of action I took, I ended up as a loser. I did get a valid receipt for the job, however.

In spite of all of this extra expense, I did not collect any rent. It was now approaching 1992, and I had not collected any rent since March 8, 1991. Could you or can you believe that this could happen to a landlord?

The last of the judge's personal visits was for a violation, the water leak from the roof, where the water was pouring, according to Bobo's statement. This water leak was created by Bobo himself, with his own hands. I do not believe otherwise. I have repaired roofs and I have installed new roofs, and I know when a roof is good or bad. Who could I tell, in court, of this experience that I had about roofs or any other repair jobs on a house? Why was this roof so difficult to repair?

It was my tenant Bobo who was creating this long list of violations. He realized that if he had a complaint against the landlord, the judge would not force him to pay his rent or move, just as simple as that. He knew that to create a violation all he had to do was pour surplus cornmeal down the drain. This would cause the water to back up, and that's a violation against the landlord. Bobo could even pour rice grains down the drain. When the rice grains got wet, they swelled, thereby clogging up the water drainpipe.

This next statement might sound fictitious, but it is true. Once Bobo did not have a violation against the landlord; therefore, he created one. He purchased some strainers for the kitchen sink and carried the receipts to show the judge. Bobo also purchased some cheap mice-rat poison and showed the receipt to the judge. This made the type of judge on this case believe that the landlord was negligent in trying to get rid of vermin infestation or trying to unstop the clogged drainpipe.

The next court hearing, February 10, 1992, Bobo was supposed to pay some rent. This court hearing was postponed until February 19 because of the holidays in early February of 1992.

At this court hearing, Mr. Jasper was present; however, the judge did not give Mr. Jasper a chance to speak. The roofer was late installing the new roof because of the rain for a few days. Would you think that the judge would consider an excuse as such it raining for a few days, therefore, the roofer being unable to complete his job of installing a new roof?

The judge did not accept this excuse. He simply enforced his "Decision and Order, Petitioner against the Respondent," and I quote:

> Pursuant to section 756 of the Judiciary Law, this Court, *sua sponte,* hereby punishes petitioner for civil and criminal contempt due to petitioner's failure to effect repairs in the tenant's apartment [the tenant only rented one room in the apartment, and the other part of the apartment was vacant, because I could not rent the other part to someone else due to the behavior of Bobo] from June 15, 1991, to date. The tenant testified credibly at this hearing that petitioner neither further inspected nor attempted to make repairs in his apartment (room) during the last six (6) months.
>
> The Court finds the petitioner Mr. B—— to be in civil contempt of Court's Order dated May 28, 1991. The petitioner is fined $100.00, which is to be paid to respondent on or before February 17, 1992. The Petitioner is also sentenced to Civil Jail for a period not to exceed one (1) week until the petitioner corrects the following:
>
> (1) broken & loose connection-waste line in kitchen;

(2) broken doorbell;
(3) abate the nuisance with respect to uncapped gasoline in the wall of the room, front room of the subject apartment (room);
(4) defective counterbalance spring in window of front room;
(5) refrigerator needs replacement;
(6) insulate all exposed wiring.

Signed February 14, 1992.

I didn't think that I had to explain in detail all of these violations, because I had already removed all of these violations. For instance number one had been corrected March 13, 1991. Number two was repaired a few times, and finally I ran a new independent line for the doorbell, but Bobo found a way to blow the transformer to stop the bell from ringing. Number three: A new and independent gas line had been installed May 29, 1991. Number four was reconnected when the complaint was first mentioned, March 13, 1991. Number five: The replacement of the refrigerator was made two days after the judge's personal inspection date, October 12, 1991. Number six: All wires for the doorbell were insulated wires.

I appeared to be a little stubborn, because I felt, *Why should I pay my tenant Bobo $100 in open court when he, Bobo, owes me $3,392 in overdue rent?* Mr. Jasper apparently knew what might happen to me. He handed me $100 in cash and said, 'Go and give it to your tenant."

To date, I had appeared in court with my tenant Bobo, and sometimes one of his girls accompanying him, about twelve times. After all of these appearances, the judge, who was black, did not recognize any of my lawyer's orders for Bobo to pay his rent. My lawyer was also black.

As a senior citizen and realizing what I was going through with my tenant, my neighbor who was a police sergeant at a different precinct than the one in this area recommended me to the Elder Law Clinic, Legal Assistant Studies, at NYC Technical College, City University of New York, 300 Jay Street, Brooklyn, NY 11201, for help with my ordeal with my tenant Bobo, and the judge as well.

I informed one of the law professors of my difficulty in reaching the judge with my complaints against my tenant Bobo. She, the law professor at the technical college, called me at the East Community Senior Center, where I was filling in as acting director of the center, and suggested that I should give an outline to the judge of my side of the case against my tenant Bobo. She said maybe he would read a short outline of my side of the case.

I made a short outline of my side of the case and gave it to the judge at our next hearing. He read maybe one sentence, put it back in the envelope, and put it on the desk he was sitting behind. After the court hearing, he gave the letter back to me. No consideration of my side of the case in court whatsoever. This was the criminal justice system. What is justice? According to the definition, justice means "the moral principle determining just conduct; fairness, impartiality."

I was at my wits' end. What could I do next. What steps should I take from here to there? Maybe I should try to find something about the man himself, like, for instance, something about his beginning, like how he was raised, how far he went in school, etc.

Since Bobo came down to my living room to talk to me, I thought that this was the route that I should take first.

4
Bobo's Early Life

Bobo appeared to be evil at times, and there were times when he was very accommodating. He appeared to be eager to listen and learn. It seemed to me that he wanted someone to confide in, someone to listen to him. It seemed that he needed guidance by a male image, like a father.

Bobo's father was almost always away. His job was as a long-distance truck driver. His job required him to be on the "go" most of his time. As a truck driver, you have to deliver goods on time, wherever you have to go. It was not in Mr. Ryan's (Bobo's father's) best interest for him to be away for most of his time, away from his son for long periods of time. It was not Mr. Ryan's choice to accept a job as a truck driver; it was the only job that he qualified for at the time.

When Mr. Ryan was scheduled to report to work, he reported on time. He believed in being the best that you could be at any job that you qualified for. He soon developed a record as a good truck driver, one that you could depend on in the absence of the boss. This type of record by Mr. Ryan inspired his boss.

Mr. Ryan knew that he had to have a job; therefore, his policy was to be the best he could be, and the dividends would pay off in the end.

Mr. Ryan did get some time off at times. When he was at home, he devoted some of his time with his son, Bobo. Then Mr. Ryan would rest for the next trip. He knew that to be a good truck driver you could not be tired.

This was why Mrs. Ryan had to devote most of her time to supervising Bobo, her son. She knew that there was a void in Bobo's life in bringing him up; that's why she devoted most of her time to him. Some parents do not realize the void in the family when one parent is absent most of the time. A child needs both parents to raise him or her adequately. Good parents realize this need early in life and take steps to correct that void.

Bobo's visits to my living room were when he thought I had time to talk to him. I think that he tried to judge when I was available to talk to him. When he heard classical music being played on my "rack system," he felt that I was available at that time. This was, however, not always true, because I could work while I listen to music. I could even read while I was listening to classical music.

Even though Bobo had bad manners at times, I accepted him whenever he came down to my living room to talk to me. Maybe listening to classical music made me a good man. Nevertheless, I enjoyed listening to classical music almost always.

My interest in classical music started when I was a small boy. My mother had only one record that could be classified as classical. It was titled "The Persian Market." We had the old type of record player. You had to wind it up with something like a crank. When you wound it up, that would cause the spring to tighten up, which gave power control when it was released. The tension in the spring caused the disk to turn; thereby, the needle traveling through the grooves caused sound. This sound came out as a musical sound, as it was recorded in the studio. Here the arm controlling the needle, and its going through the grooves as the disk was turning, produced sound, which came out as vocal or instrumental music playing. Whatever was recorded came out in this manner. The old record player was called a Victrola. I used to play this old musical instrument over and over.

My father knew how to read the notes of a scale of music. He used to sing with a tenor voice, the old barbershop type of singing. My father had a good voice, and he sang solos most of the time at different functions. He taught me how to read music from the scales like:

My father did not know anything about the C, D, E, F, G, A, B, and C scale. They learned the old-fashioned scale: do, re, me, fa, so, la, ti, and do. They used to sing by notes. That is, whatever notes appeared on the line or in the space. Like, for instance:

me - me - fa - fa - me - me - so - so,

They would pronounce so as "sol," etc., while singing.

It was when I moved to Savannah, Georgia, that I was exposed to all aspects of the musical world. I studied music the right way. I also sang with the young choir members at the church. The choirmaster said that I had a good second tenor voice. He selected one of his favorite songs and asked me to learn the words to that song.

The choirmaster at the church was also the music director at the high school. He gave a concert at the school to raise money for the school athletic teams. He put me on his program to sing a solo. I was a little nervous when I walked on the stage and saw all those people sitting in the audience. I thought about my father and said to myself that my father would not want me to be nervous. I composed myself and sang the song that the choirmaster had assigned to me to sing. The people in the audience applauded for a long period of time.

My next move was to New York City. I was introduced to radio stations like WQXR, WNYC, etc. Listening to these stations, I learned about Bach, Beethoven, and Brahms. There are a lot of other good composers that I like as well.

When Bobo would come down to my living room to talk to me, he had no choice but to listen to my program of classical music.

One day when I was returning home, I met a neighbor who said, "I thought that you were at home because I heard your favorite music being played."

As I got nearer to the house, I could tell that the volume was very high. I do not turn the volume up high when I listen to classical music. From the high volume it was easy to trace the direction that the music was coming from. It was Bobo's radio playing. He was tuned to WQXR. I guess that Bobo wanted me to know that he could listen to classical music on his radio as well, not the jazz music that he was accustomed to listening to.

On, I would say, about the fourth visit to my living room, Bobo appeared to be in a very good mood. I wondered what he wanted to talk about today. First he said, "The other day when you heard your type of music coming from my radio I just wanted you to know that I can get the same radio stations that you get on your radio."

I simply said, "That's good that you can; then you don't have to listen to jazz music all of the time."

This time, Bobo wanted to talk about his mother. I was listening to classical music, as usual. After Bobo composed himself, he told me that his mother used to talk about her mother and how she was raised. Bobo said that his mother talked so much about how she was raised, along with her brothers and sisters, that what she talked about started sounding like fairy tales. She did not read bedtime stories to him; she would talk about her past as a girl.

Bobo's mother told him that during those days life on the farm was not easy. You had to perform your chores, no matter what they might be.

Mrs. Ryan told Bobo that her grandparents owned their own farm. She said that her great-grandparents inherited land from their slave owners. When the slaves were freed, the slave owners divided up land and gave land to all of their former slaves. Her great-grandparents told her that their former slave owner divided up the land among the most faithful slaves on the farm. Her great-grandparents then passed the land down to her grandparents.

Bobo's mother told him that if you owned your own land, you had a better chance to prosper in life.

Mrs. Ryan continued saying that her great-grandparents used to say that after living and working for the slave owner for a long period of time came a time when you felt that you could not live without the guidance of your slave owner. You became like a child depending on his or her parents for guidance.

When a slave wanted something or needed something, he or she would go to his or her slave owner and ask him for what he or she needed or wanted.

Mrs. Ryan said, "If you own your own land, it is not easy to survive. There is a lot of work to be done on the farm, and you have to be able to manage your profits wisely in order to prosper."

Bobo's mother told him that her grandparents were able to send her mother to school, where she took up a trade as a seamstress, along with the required courses to matriculate.

Mrs. Ryan continued saying that after her mother finished school she was able to get jobs making new dresses for whoever needed a new dress. She was able to supplement the income from the farm. She had customers like the doctors' wives who lived in the nearby town. This outside work enabled her to get the things that were needed for the family.

She made dresses for the girls who were graduating from high school in the area. She made dresses for the brides and the bridesmaids as well. Her parents did not have a telephone; therefore, messages had to be delivered by someone. Mrs. Ryan's mother's name was Sally Ann Watts. Mrs. Watts was given a message that the doctor's mother-in-law wanted a new dress made and wanted to know if Mrs. Sally Ann could come to her house and make her a new dress on her sewing machine.

The nearby town was about two miles or so from Mrs. Sally Ann's house. Usually Mrs. Sally Ann would carry her daughter, Callie (Mrs. Ryan), with her when she would walk to the nearby town. Callie was about seven years old at that time. She was the baby daughter, and she was next to the baby son, who was about five years old at that time.

When Mrs. Sally Ann reached the doctor's mother-in-law's house, the mother-in-law would give Callie some type of game to play with while her mother would be working, making the new dress for the doctor's mother-in-law.

In addition to making dresses, Mrs. Sally Ann could decorate a coffin with black material. During those days, if someone died the community folks would get together and pool their money to help with the funeral. There wasn't very much money in the community during those days; that's why it took cooperation with the neighbors to help put someone away, or bury someone.

A job for Mrs. Sally Ann like decorating a coffin was a charitable contribution to the bereaved family. The men in the area would make the coffin and the box to put it in, and they, too, would have to pool their money to buy the lumber, nails, and black material to cover the coffin. They did not have insurance policies in those days to defray the expenses of a funeral.

Most people referred to those times as "hard times." When Callie (Mrs. Ryan) related these stories to her son, Bobo, she would always emphasize the importance of learning a trade or something else that would help you get a job. This way, he would be able to support his family, as well as himself, when he reached that stage of life.

Callie said that her mother was always telling her to learn a trade like she did when she was in school. You were lucky if you could go to school for the full semester, because in rural areas, schools were a distance away from where you lived. Schools were like two or three miles from where you lived. You had to walk to school.

There was no school bus service during those days. You had to walk, You had to accept what you had; there were no choices. You either walked to school or did not go to school at all.

Many young children did not have the opportunity to go to school for the full school year, because they had to do work on the farm.

Callie (Mrs. Ryan) recalled that when she was in the tenth grade a new teacher came to her school. She taught English and History. One day, she advised her class that she knew how to type. She told her class that when she was in high school she took up typing, as it was offered as an extracurricular course. The course in typing was not a required course that you had to take. She took the course because she wanted to learn how to type. She continued, saying that she received a diploma in typing, in addition to her college degree.

She informed the class that if the school would get the typewriters, she would teach the class how to type. She asked, "Are you interested in learning how to type?" The class was unanimous in their decision to take the typing course. Callie knew that this would be a trade like her mother had always said to learn. Callie was the first to stand up in agreement that the course in typing should be taught in their school. Other students stood up after Callie had stood up. Even if the typing was not a lifelong job, it was good to know how to type.

Callie believed that it's better to know how to do something even if you don't need it than not to know how to do something if you need it to make ends meet.

Ms. Singer, the new teacher, informed the students that the board of education was not going to pay her for this service. She informed the class that she was entering into this extra service for the class of her own free will. She continued, saying that she had submitted a request for new or used typewriters, as long as they worked, from the board of education and she was waiting for a reply from the board of education.

At this point, Callie informed Ms. Singer that her mother and father were active in the PTA at the school. Mr. Watts was invited by the school by the teacher, Ms. Singer. An additional request was made by Ms. Singer and given to Mr. Watts. Mr. Watts told Ms. Singer that he would deliver her request to the board of education in two days. Ms. Singer emphasized that if the typewriters were not new, they should be usable old typewriters.

Within a three-week period, the board of education gave the school twenty-three old but usable typewriters and two new typewriters. Some of the old typewriters needed new ribbons. Ms. Singer told the class that she knew how to replace the ribbons on the old typewriters.

Ms. Singer informed Mr. Watts that she needed a classroom to be able to set up the typing class.

The board of education sent a box of new typewriter ribbons. There were forty new typewriter ribbons in the box. Ms. Singer was now waiting for a room to set up her new class for the students to learn a new trade at the school.

Mr. Watts stopped by the school and checked with the school board regarding an empty room that could be used for Ms. Singer's new typing class. The school board informed Mr. Watts that there was a vacant room in the back area of the school building that was currently being used for storage. The members of the school board said that the room was large but would have to be cleaned up and painted.

Mr. Watts arranged to have a meeting with the members of the PTA to get their help in preparing this room for Ms. Singer's class. Mr. Watts invited the members of the school board, as well, to attend this meeting.

There was a large turnout at this meeting. It seemed that everyone in the area was interested in Ms. Singer's new program at the school. Mr. Watts was able to get a lot of help from the PTA members, as well as some of the members of the school board itself.

Due to the immediate response of the PTA members and the school board of directors, the room was ready in one week. Ms. Singer stopped by with Mr. Watts to check the room for her new class. When Ms. Singer entered the room, she said, "This is a nice area for my class. But not yet. We need tables, a blackboard, chalk, erasers, and a ruler. Oops! Chairs, please."

Mr. Watts spoke to some of the officials of the school for this last request by Ms. Singer. These supplies were forthcoming, and Ms. Singer began setting up her new typing class.

When everything was in place, Ms. Singer invited the class, during one of the rest periods, to the room set up for the new typing program.

When the students sat down in the chairs facing the typewriters, Ms. Singer was surprised by a visit by the principal of the school. The principal spoke to Ms. Singer and the class, looked around the room, and said, "This is wonderful; it is marvelous. Ms. Singer, maybe I can recommend you for a raise." Ms. Singer and the class were smiling with joy.

Ms. Singer informed the principal that she needed some more supplies, like typing paper, carbon paper, "and please, if you will, a desk and desk supplies." The principal promised that she would get those things that she needed in a few days.

Mr. Watts stopped by to check on the new class and to see if Ms. Singer needed anything else. Ms. Singer told Mr. Watts that the principal of the school had stopped by and promised a few more supplies that we needed for this class. Mr. Watts asked Ms. Singer for a list of all the things that she needed. She gave Mr. Watts a list of the things that she needed for the classroom and the students.

Ms. Singer gave Mr. Watts the same list that she had given the principal, adding pencils, some typing charts, and liquid paper.

When Mr. Watts returned with the rest of the supplies, he, along with some of the male students, put up the charts, prepared a section in the back of the classroom for the supplies, and put everything in place.

During a vacant period, Ms. Singer invited the class back to the typing classroom and in a thrilling voice said, "Please sit down." The students sat down and positioned themselves, then looked at Ms. Singer. Ms. Singer threw up her hands above her head and said, "Thank you, God. This is what I always wanted, since I completed my typing course, several years ago."

Ms. Singer continued, saying, " 'Seek and ye shall find, knock and the doors will be opened unto you,' " and she said, again, "Thank you, Lord."

Ms. Singer put her whole heart and soul into the teaching of her new typing class. It was now up to the students to do well learning how to type professionally.

After several months of typing instructions, the students started competing with one another. Ms. Singer gave each student a paragraph of about 120 words and said, "Practice this paragraph over and over until you can type it with speed." She said, "When you can type with speed, then I will give you a time limit in which you should be able to type this paragraph."

The students continued to compete with each other. After about two more months, they felt that they were ready to take the test. The students had already timed themselves to see how long it would take to type the paragraph. Callie was considered more advanced than the other students. When Mr. Watts was getting the typewriters for the class, Callie's father also got a used but usable typewriter for Callie. Callie would practice at night; that was why she was more advanced than the other students.

Callie, being the spokesperson for the class, approached Ms. Singer and asked her to give them the typing test. Ms. Singer told Callie, "Today is Friday, and I would rather give the test either on Monday or Tuesday of next week."

Callie informed the class of Ms. Singer's decision. Ms. Singer told the class that she did not have a gavel but would try to get one by next week. "If, however, I am not able to get a gavel, I will use my ruler to do the job of a gavel."

On Tuesday, Ms. Singer gave the rules to the class. She said, "I will strike the desk with my ruler to start, and I will strike my desk on the side when the minute is up, OK?"

The class, in unison, said, "Yes."

"Listen carefully, because I will count like one, two, three, and I will strike the desk at the count of four." Ms. Singer started counting and when she reached four she gave a striking bang on the side of her desk. The students started and they typed away. When the minute was up, Ms. Singer struck the desk and said, "Time is up."

The typewriters were ringing. Ms. Singer hit the desk indicating that the minute was up. When she looked over the class, she saw four hands up. They were the hands of Callie and three others. Some of the students said that when the typewriters started ringing it made them nervous and they thought that they were typing slowly.

Ms. Singer informed the class, "When you are competing with other students, all you have to do is think of what you have to accomplish and not pay any attention to the noise of the other typewriters. That is the key in typing. Try it and you will see that it's true. Next time, try that scheme, and you will find that you can type faster."

She asked, "How many of you finished the paragraph?" Out of a class of twenty-three, eighteen had finished the paragraph. She emphasized her scheme and said, "Try harder next time. Try not to be nervous."

Ms. Singer walked over and asked one student, "Why were you nervous?"

She and the rest of them said that the typewriters' bells were ringing and that made them nervous and they felt that they were typing slowly.

Ms. Singer said, "This is not a test to give you a grade; it's only to give you some confidence in typing skills." She said that she would give a few more typing skills tests before the examination was given. "I will let you know in time when I am going to give the grade-rating test."

The end of the semester was only one month away when the teacher informed the class that in view of the fact that there are only sixteen students out of twenty-three that were active, she was going to give the typing examination earlier. Just about all of these students were farmers' children, and had to perform chores on the farm, almost always daily. Some of the students lived near the school, and they could get home in time to take care of some of their chores before dark.

Some of the farmers owned their own land, and it was these children that could spend more time in the classroom. Fortunately, the high school had a teacher like Ms. Singer who was willing to impart some of her knowledge to her students. Ms. Singer, from the beginning, wanted to relate to the students something that she felt would help them in many ways in the future. There was no other school in this community or nearby that offered such a course for black students. The technique that Ms. Singer used was to accomplish her aim by volunteering her service for free.

Bobo in telling this story about his mother said that his mother told him that her father did not own his own land at that time, but he was able to buy land later. He was a sharecropper, and they had to work very hard to make ends meet. As a sharecropper, you had to produce enough harvest to divide with the owner of the land. That meant that you had to work harder to produce enough harvest to divide with the owner of the land and have some for yourself as well.

Callie said that one of the reasons that she could spend more time in the classroom than some of the other students was because her mother and father were well-known in the community, her mother as a seamstress and her father for being active in the PTA and performing chores for the school.

Bobo continued telling me that his mother told him that a sawmill had opened up or, you might say, moved to the area where there were a lot of pine trees. The owner of the sawmill was looking for men to work at the sawmill. Their chores would be cutting timber and helping to cut the logs up into lumber.

Bobo's grandfather, Callie's father, applied for a job at the sawmill. He was hired right away, because he was a tall man and weighed about two hundred pounds. The sawmill owner classified Bobo's grandfather as a good man for the job. His job was turning logs to be cut into lumber. Mr. Watts had a long reach because of his long arms. These logs were riding on a carriage, back and forth. Callie described this carriage as going fast in one direction and then returning back to the original position at a fast rate of speed.

Mr. Watts was using some type of hook with a long handle. When this hook was put in the right position, Mr. Watts was able to turn the log to be cut on the other side. You had to know exactly how to gauge the hook to be accurate for different sizes of lumber. Mr. Watts told his daughter that when you were used to doing this, you could work fast, which was needed for this type of job. The hook had a sharp spikelike point on the end. The arm of the hook was curved to form about a 135-degree angle and this curve could be hooked over the log by a flexible hinge.

The spike with the point pointed inward forming an angle of about ninety degrees with the end of the arm enabled the log turner to hook the log on the opposite side of the log with the 135-degree-angle curved arm properly attached, allowing the log turner to pull down the handle, thereby turning the log to its proper position, and the other side.

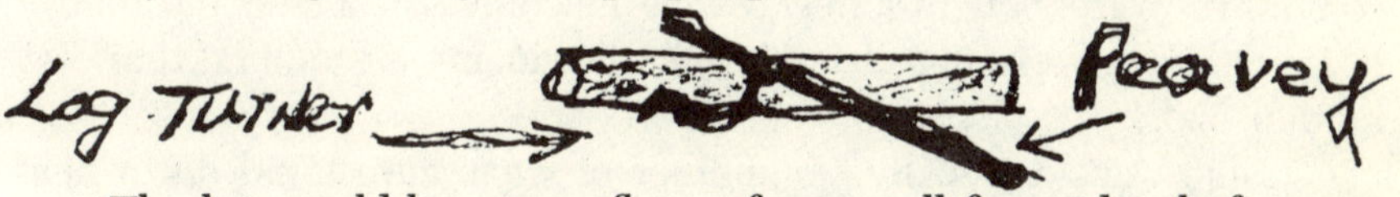

The log would become a flat surface on all four sides, before you could gauge the size of the lumber that you were supposed to cut. In other words, each side of the log would be a huge parallelogram with all its angles right angles. Then you could cut the size of lumber boards that you had to cut.

At this point, another lumberjack would pull a horizontal handle that was calibrated to move to a designated distance as wanted, in this case one-inch width for each lumber board.

As the carriage would repeat its path, moving back and forth, the lumberjack would pull the horizontal handle for each lumber-board.

These lumber-boards could be one inch by four inches, one inch by ten inches, one inch by fourteen inches, etc., depending on the size of the log, or parallelogram, if you will.

As the carriage would be moving back and forth, the saw would be doing its part by cutting each board as needed. This was done by the person controlling the carriage.

Bobo said that his mother told him this story so many times that he could almost remember every detail.

Callie, Bobo's mother, advised him that if you made up your mind toward a goal that you wanted, you could reach that goal, if you stuck to it.

Mr. Watts, after working at the sawmill for three or four years, was able to put a down payment on his own farm. Meanwhile, his children were running the sharecropper's farm. They had a good year and were able to divide their produce with the landowner at harvest-time.

The composition of Mr. and Mrs. Watts's family was four boys and three girls. Callie was the baby girl; she was two years older than the baby son. They all lived in harmony in the small town of Avon, Georgia.

Callie during her time home on the farm was the only child that was very devoted to her mother. Callie was with her mother most of the time. She used to go with her mother whenever she had to go to the small town to make dresses for her customers. Callie became a seamstress by being taught how to sew by her mother. When Callie was eleven years old, she could make dresses as well as her mother could. Mr. Watts bought a new sewing machine so Callie could relieve her mother in making dresses for the many customers that her mother had.

Callie was advised by her mother of what she should do to help her in planning her future. This was when Callie's mother told her to learn other trades if she was exposed to any other trades even if she did not use that trade to support herself in the future.

Callie was one of the original students striving to learn how to type when the new teacher came to the high school. Mr. Watts, on one of his days off from the sawmill, stopped by to see how Ms. Singer was making out with the typing class. Ms. Singer responded by saying that the students, especially his daughter, showed a lot of interest in the class and they said that they were happy that she had volunteered to teach this typing class.

Mr. Watts said, "That is good. I will suggest the Parent Teachers Association and the school board of directors help in making this typing class a part of the high school curriculum for next year." Mr. Watts was now the president of the school board of directors as well as a member of the PTA.

Ms. Singer said that she would be very happy if the high school would include the typing class as part of the curriculum. Then Ms. Singer, looking at Mr. Watts while smiling, said, "Then I will get paid for my new typing course."

Mr. Watts, also smiling, said, "You deserve all of the recognition for this new additional course in typing as a standard part of the high school curriculum."

Mr. Watts continued, saying, "You are the only one who has even attempted to do and did something for the school here. No other school in the nearby counties offers such a course for the students, especially the black students in our community. You did it for free. Now I think that you deserve to get paid for your dedicated service for the students here at the high school." Mr. Watts returned home, carrying his daughter's typewriter, which he had repaired for her. Mr. Watts figured that since his daughter was interested in typing, she should try to be one of the best typists at the high school.

Mr. Watts was preparing to move his family to their new home on their own farmland in about one week. Callie's mother was getting orders to make the dresses for the graduating class in about five weeks, when the high school was scheduled to close.

The family was rushing to move and get settled down long before the high school closed. Since Mr. Watts bought a new sewing machine for his daughter Callie, she could help his wife make the dresses for the graduating class this year. In two more years, Callie herself would be one of the graduates. One of her sisters was graduating this year.

The junior-senior prom this year was being given at a new location. The gymnasium was new to the school; however, this was an old building, once owned by a large moving company, and they used this building to store furniture for their customers. It was renovated and now it looked like a new building. The new gymnasium for the high school had just completed one month ago and was one block from the high school building.

Callie would not attend the prom this year. She would be a junior next year, but she was making the dress for her sister, who was graduating this year.

When Mr. Watts paid a down payment on the land it was in April, around Eastertime, and the seller had already started his crops for the year. Mr. Watts also had planted his sharecropper's farm as well. However, the house was vacant and the Wattses were able to move into the house early, before harvesttime. The seller and the buyer understood this waiting period, and there were no objections to this plan. Mr. Watts was happy that he was able to buy this land near the high school.

Callie would be a junior in high school when her father was able to plant seeds in the fields on his own land. Planting seeds in the fields was not new to Mr. Watts; however, planting seeds in the fields on his own land was new to him and, of course, was new to the whole Watts family.

The only problem that Mr. Watts would have was what to plant here and what to plant there? His choices were good.

Next year would be the first year that the family would be able to gather their own produce, and for the first time he did not have to divide the produce with a landowner as a sharecropper.

Callie's sister that graduated last year was engaged to get married by June of next year. Callie would be expecting to get promoted to the twelfth grade next year, one month before the wedding of her sister.

This would be the first girl of the family to get married. Her husband-to-be was working for the sawmill. He was planning on buying his own land after he got married. The Watts family would have two occasions to celebrate next year, and they planned to combine the two events to be given at the same place at the same time.

The two events were, first, the first girl in the family getting married, second, the first year that the Wattses would be able to gather their own produce at harvesttime.

Mr. Watts had filed an application to rent the high school gymnasium to give this historical affair, and they were working and planning a first in renting the high school gymnasium in this area to give an affair of this magnitude in this small town of Avon, Georgia.

Callie was handling the invitation list. They expected at least 300 to attend this affair, the first wedding in the Watts family. Sarah, a cousin who lived in Brooklyn, New York, was expected to attend this affair. Callie's mother was asking some of the PTA members to help in preparing the food.

In this small town of Avon, Georgia, you did not have any big affairs to be given, that is, when you could invite the whole community to attend. That's why it was so important to everyone in the community and there were some outsiders who were asking if they could attend the affair, along with the ones that were invited. Mr. Watts felt that everybody who would like to attend should be invited.

Callie concluded her invitation list and realized that some type of entertainment should be added to the program, but what? Professional musicians in Avon, Georgia, did not exist. She recalled that when she was in the ninth grade their teacher gave a play consisting of sixteen girls. The play was a success; everyone said that they enjoyed the play. Since that time, the girls had organized a club called the Jolly Sixteen Girls, but would it be appropriate for this affair? Since Avon, Georgia was so small, there was nothing that the girls could do, so they abandoned the club. Callie was just being optimistic, thinking that they could reorganize themselves in time to practice the play to be presented at this affair.

Someone at the Methodist church suggested looking for someone who could play the piano, you know, someone who could play jazz music. The organist at the church, could only play sacred songs; Callie wouldn't even mention it to her.

It was through the Baptist church that they found someone who could play the piano, his name, as they called him, "Mr. Jazz Man." He did not play by reading notes, he played by ear, but he could play all of the jazz music that you would want.

Two of the brothers of the Watts family set out to find this Mr. Jazz Man. They found him, but he had an excuse. He said, "I have not played the piano in one year, and I am out of practice."

The piano player was almost always playing for charity and decided that he would retire from playing the piano, as it was not profitable in a small agricultural town.

The brothers did not accept that excuse. They said, "We are going to pay you for playing for this affair."

This was all that the piano player wanted to hear . . . to get paid for his service. The Jazz Man said, "OK, I am going to start practicing right away."

The brothers, in unison, said, "You have two months to practice."

The brothers returned and told Callie that the piano player had promised that he would play for the affair, but they had to pay him. Callie asked, "How much?"

The brothers said, "We do not know, but whatever amount it is, we have to pay him for his service."

Callie said, "I have a few dollars that I made helping Mom to make the dresses for the graduating class at the high school."

The elder son, who had been working for his pop while he was sick, said that he would help pay the piano player for his services.

Callie said, "Whatever he charges, we will pay him for his services."

Callie, who had been taking her final examinations, asked if the piano player was dependable. Could they depend on him to keep his promise?

Callie said, "We only have two more weeks before the wedding and the wedding reception and our first harvest on our own land is gathered, so I will write a letter to him and I will send a self-addressed stamped envelope for his reply. We don't want to be disappointed; this is important." The piano player answered telling them that he would keep his promise and that he would come at least two hours before time to assure them that he would not disappoint them.

Early this historic Saturday morning, the family members of the whole community, it seems, were up and doing their shopping chores early, so they could participate in this historical wedding and wedding reception, which was being held in the high school gymnasium, a first in this small agricultural town.

The wedding was scheduled to start at 1:00 P.M. At 3:00 P.M., the motorcade would proceed to the high school gymnasium, which was about two miles from the Methodist church. There would be a pause to give everyone a chance to meet the bride and groom. At 4:30 P.M., the food would be served. While the food was being served and the participants were eating, the organist from the Methodist church would be playing the piano, some of her sacred songs. The jazz part of the program would begin at 7:00 and would last until 10:00 P.M. At this time, the bride and groom would leave for their honeymoon.

At 10:00 P.M., closing time, everybody was still dancing, laughing, and talking. Even the little children were jumping up and down and running about the gymnasium. The piano player, I was told, had a few highballs, and it seemed that he didn't want to stop playing. The Jazz Man was still ringing those piano keys with joy.

Mr. Watts asked the management for permission to end the affair at 11:30 P.M. That would be the deadline, because at twelve midnight it would be early Sunday morning, and that could not happen. It was lucky that they were able to clear the gymnasium by midnight. This affair would be in the minds of everyone for many years to come.

Callie finished washing the breakfast dishes and was looking for her mother. Callie had a break from class for three days. It was early in January, and the whole twelfth grade was taking a break while formulating their plans for the last semester at the high school.

Callie found her mother just outside, standing in the front yard. The front yard extended out from the front of the house, oh, about fifty feet and about forty feet wide. The yard was covered with white sand. They swept the yard occasionally to free the yard of leaves and other debris.

The broom used for this chore was made of some type of wild-growing bush; it was about four feet high, and the stalks were about three-quarters of an inch in diameter. They tied several of these stalks together, and the limbs, about five per stalk, were spread out, creating the broomlike effect, about two and a half feet in diameter. With this awkward type of broom they were able to sweep the yard, thereby freeing the yard of leaves and other debris.

Callie walked outside and stood near her mother. She noticed her father standing diagonally across from them, near the left corner of the yard. He was holding a pad in his hand and appeared to be writing something on the pad. Callie asked her mother what her father was writing on the pad. She told Callie that her father had been writing down how much produce was gathered last year from the farm. He also was planning what he was going to plant for this season and what fields he was going to use for different seeds, like corn, peas, beans, potatoes, etc.

Her father was walking toward Callie, still holding his pad in his hand. Callie said, "Dad, what are you doing?" He answered, saying, "It's time to start planning for this year's crops. It's almost time to start planting the fields with your choice of seeds that you are going to plant in each field."

"Do you know that it's only January fourteenth?"

He said, "You can start tilling the soil."

"How are you going to do the work, this year, on the fields?"

"Well, Buba will be working at the sawmill, since I am not able to do that type of work anymore. I want Son to stay in school. Remember, he is the only one in the family who is attending college. I want him to finish college. So I guess I will have to till the soil in the fields myself."

Callie asked, "Do you think that you will be able to do all of that work, Dad?"

"Yes," he said. "It's been a long time since I did any plowing in the fields, but I think that I can handle it OK. Remember, when you are plowing all you have to do is walk behind the plow while you are guiding the plow and old Mance, the horse, will be pulling the plow and you as well. All you have to do is keep up."

Callie's mother said, "Jacob thinks that he can do the same things as he did when he was younger."

He said, "I know that I cannot do all of the things that I used to do, but I am willing to try. If I cannot manage, I will look for other options. I am not as strong and I am weaker than I used to be. That is why I turned my job at the sawmill over to Buba, because I know that I cannot turn logs like I used to do. Owning my own farm, I can piddle around the farm like I want to do. Nobody to tell me what to do or what not to do. I make all of the decisions myself."

Callie was returning to school. The school break was over, and now the twelfth grade class had to get down to business. Callie's brother Jacob, Jr., Son, was also at home on his school break as well. Now he had to return to classes at the college. He was due back on the campus by tomorrow to resume his classes. Callie had decided against going to college, since she had lost so much time in high school during the semester. She from time to time had to perform chores on the farm, since she was a sharecropper's daughter. She was two years behind her grade level in school.

This unfortunate way of life, as sharecropper's children, meant a lot of children lost time from their studies. The Watts family was no exception, at that time, because they were sharecroppers. About 60 percent of the children lost time from their studies because they had to leave school before the semester ended. They had to perform chores on the farm.

Son also lost time in school. He was about two years behind his age level in college. Son just decided that he wanted to finish college and registered for college late, but next year would be a junior in college.

Callie's future interest in life was in leaving Avon, Georgia, and moving to New York and living with her cousin Sarah until she could settle down, and make her future decisions from or based on a different lifestyle. Callie had always said that she did not want to marry a farmer;

that's final. She felt that she had already contributed enough of her life as a farm girl. Now she wanted to live a different life for the rest of her life.

"Mother! Mother!" Callie was calling her mother. As she looked out of the back window, she saw her mother walking toward the house. Callie noticed that she had a long pole in her hand like a walking cane. She asked, "Mom, why are you walking with that whatever it is in your hand?"

Mom answered, "You see, when you are walking through tall grass you might see a snake or something that you have to hit with a pole or something to protect yourself from anything that can hurt you. Do you remember when you were going to the field to take your father or your brother fresh water while they were working in the fields in the hot sun?"

"Yes Mom," Callie said.

"I told you to look under your feet. Remember that?"

Callie said, "Yes, Mom."

"That meant that you should always look to see where you are going and not see anything in your way as you walk in a path surrounded by tall grass. These creatures called snakes can slip up on you. You have to protect yourself."

"Yes, Mom," Callie replied. "I just wanted to know why you were carrying that pole, that's all."

"Now you know," Mom said to Callie. "Callie, you should see the plants that your father planted in the fields. . . . They are up and growing. I carried your father fresh water, and I was amazed when I saw how beautiful those plants are. He certainly has a beautiful crop this year. He should be able to produce just as much or more this year than he did last year."

"Then Dad is stronger than what we thought he was at the beginning of the year."

Mom said, "Well, he complains at night of how weak he is feeling, but he gets up in the morning and he goes to work and he works all day, except for lunchtime. After lunch, he goes back in the fields and works until dark. He simply leaves then because he cannot see to work any longer.

"Your father said soon he will be able to start to lay by his crops. Then he can rest until harvesttime. You will have graduated from high school by that time. I am getting orders for the graduating class already, to make their dresses. You can make your own dress for graduation."

"Yes, Mom," Callie said, adding, "I will be happy to be able to graduate this year."

Callie said that she was going to make a new dress for the junior-senior prom this year. "I cannot wear the same dress that I wore last year. I want a new dress. I can wear the same shoes. They still look like they are new.

"The only problem that I have this year is that I don't have an escort to take me to the prom. I don't have a boyfriend, because I am planning on going to New York soon."

"What happened to your boyfriend that you had last year?"

"He was too serious, he wanted to get married."

"Well, don't you want to get married?"

"Not to a farmer. I've had enough of the farm life. I want to do something else."

"Do you want to be a seamstress, like your mother?"

"That's OK. I like sewing very much."

"Lenny is always asking about you when I see him."

"Oh, I had forgotten about Lenny. Where does he attend church? Do you know?"

"He attends the Baptist church near the grocery store. Do you know where that is?"

"Yes, Mom. I will attend the Baptist church next Sunday. Maybe I will see Lenny there."

"Son will be at home in two weeks. He is going to escort Sarah to the junior-senior prom. Cleo wanted Son to escort her to the prom."

"It's too bad that you cannot escort two girls to the prom."

"Well, there are not enough good men to go around these days."

"You are right, Mom."

* * *

"Callie, I see that someone brought you home after church."

"Yes, Mom, that was Lenny."

"Oh, you did see him."

"Yes, Mom, and he is still as accommodating as ever. I am surprised he did not get married yet."

"Maybe he is waiting for you, Callie."

"Oh, Mom, I hope he is not waiting for that to happen. Lenny is still a farmer. Anyway Mom, he is going to take me to the prom."

"Well, at least you don't have to worry about that, not having an escort to take you to the prom. I feel sorry for Cleo. Why don't you and Lenny take her with you all."

"We could do that, because Lenny and I are not courting. We do not have any secrets that we cannot share with Cleo. I will get in touch with Cleo."

* * *

"Good morning, Mama."

"Good morning, Callie."

"Where is Son going in the old car, Mom?"

"He is going to get some gas so he can take his father to the hospital for a checkup."

"Dad is not feeling well?"

"No, he did not rest well last night and I suggested that he go to the hospital for a complete checkup."

Callie said that she wanted to move to New York after she graduated from high school. "I am late graduating from high school because of having to work in the fields before the semester ended each year. My last birthday I was twenty years old. That's why I did not want to go to college. I would have been older than my classmates in college."

"I am glad Son did not think that way, Callie. Now Son will be graduating from college in about two more years."

"My preferred lifestyle is different from Son's lifestyle. I guess that all I want to do is go somewhere else, get a job, and get married later in life."

"Well, Callie, I hope that you are not disappointed in your plans. Life is beautiful if you live it the right way."

"I cannot go anywhere since Dad is not well. I will have to put off going to New York for another year or so, to see how Dad is going to get well and be able to run the farm like he likes to do. So for now, I am still a farmer's daughter.

"I will get myself a boyfriend and try to live a peaceful life until I am able to leave home for a while. Cleo did not have a date for the junior-senior prom, but someone told me that Cleo met a man who is working at the sawmill."

* * *

"Look! Harvesttime is almost here. This year will be the second year gathering our own crops. Doesn't time fly? If we have a good year, that will make Dad feel better, because he did most of the work on the farm himself. Since I cannot leave now, I think that we should gather the crops ourselves and let Dad rest and just be able to check on what we are gathering . . . the amount, that is. He likes to do that, because if the year is good, it means that we are succeeding, not regressing, as independent farmers.

* * *

Oops! It's near Halloween time. That meant they gathered some pumpkins as well. The kids could make their jack-o-lanterns early this year. That would enhance their game of "Trick or Treating."

Callie stayed two more years, and she helped on the farm each year, as well as helping her mother to make dresses for the town folks. Before this harvesttime, her father expired. Callie was then twenty-two years old. After her father's funeral, Callie decided to stay two more years so she could help her mother deal with her father's absence.

Callie was able to get a couple boyfriends to take her out from time to time, but she did not get serious with either of them.

After Callie thought that her mother could live with the void of her father's absence, she packed her things, not too many things, to say the least. Callie was now twenty-four years old. The other children at home had dwindled down to three children, two boys and one girl. Callie notified Sarah, in Brooklyn, that she was leaving in two weeks and wanted Sarah to meet her at the train station.

5

"A Trip Toward My Future"

Callie asked her brother, Son, to take her to the train station. She was leaving for New York. Son told Callie that he would take her to the station.

As the time was approaching when Callie had set to leave to go to the train station, Callie did not see her brother Son. Callie started running about the house, and she went outside, looking for and calling her brother. A neighbor heard Callie's voice calling her brother Son. She went outside and yelled to Callie, "Your brother is over here, visiting my brother. I will tell him that you are ready to leave."

Callie yelled back, "Thanks!" to the good neighbor.

Son came to pick up Callie. Callie was arguing with her brother, because she did not want to miss this train. Son said, "I thought that you told me that the train would arrive by two-thirty P.M."

"Yes, I did," Callie said, "but I want to get to the train station before train time."

Son said, "It's only twelve noon, now."

Callie said, "Don't forget that it's six miles from here to the train station, and I want to get to the station a while before the train comes. I would rather wait for the train, because the train will not wait for me."

"OK," Son said.

Callie said good-bye to her mother and sister, who were standing outside nearby. They said, "Good-bye, Callie; have a good and safe trip to New York. We will be waiting to hear from you as soon as you can write to us to let us know how you are doing."

As the car left, Callie looked out and was waving good-bye to her mother and sister as they were standing nearby.

Callie also waved, as the car left the area, to her home, the farm, the hogs, the chickens, and the dogs. They had three dogs. Son and his brothers used the three dogs as hunting dogs during the deer season.

Callie remembered the game that her brothers used to play during the hunting season. That was part of home life in the country type of living.

About two miles away from home, the car started saying, *Putt! Putt! Putt!* Soon the old car started slowing up. Finally, it stopped still.

Callie seemed to be in a rage. "What is wrong with this old car?"

Son did not say anything; he simply got out, walked to the front of the old car, and put the hood up. He looked the motor over but did not see anything wrong.

By this time, Callie was out of the car and she was also looking at the motor. She would not see anything wrong with the old car, anyway. It was a good gesture for her just to look at the motor, just because her brother was looking at the motor.

The old car had gotten very hot. Callie heard a car coming, and she told Son that she heard a car coming. She said that she would ask them to take her to the train station. As the car approached, she noticed that the car belonged to their good neighbor whom Son had been visiting before they left. It was Chuck. Callie called Chuck and asked him to take her to the station.

Chuck asked, "What is wrong with the car?"

Callie said, "It said, *Putt! Putt!, Putt!* and just stopped."

Chuck got out of his car and walked over to the other car while asking Son, "Did you identify anything wrong with the car?"

Son said, "Not yet."

Chuck noticed that the car was very hot. He asked, "Were you driving fast, Son?"

Son said, "Not really. Just at average speed."

Chuck looked under the hood, and he saw right away and pointed out that the fan belt was off.

"Is it broken?" Callie asked.

Chuck reached under the hood and pulled the fan belt up, saying, "No, it is not broken, it's just old and stretched a little more than it's supposed to be."

Chuck put the fan belt back on and told Son that he should buy another fan belt after he left the train station. Chuck told Son to get some more water for the car but first check to see if the motor was not too hot before he poured the water into the radiator. Son got an old bucket from the car, went to a nearby ditch, and filled the bucket with water from the ditch. Son then poured the water into the radiator very slowly. Chuck said that you should never pour water into a hot radiator, because that would damage the radiator. The radiator would crack on the side, and that would create a leak in the radiator.

Son said, "Good. I will remember that in the future."

Chuck was older than Son and was considered a good mechanic in the neighborhood. You might say a manmade mechanic. You will find a few manmade mechanics in the neighborhoods in and around the countryside. It is what you might say you learn to do what you have to do when you cannot afford to hire a real mechanic.

Nevertheless, Callie was able to reach the train station on time or before time, thanks to a good neighbor like Chuck.

After Chuck helped Son start the car, he followed them for about one mile. When he reached the road to his father's house, he turned off the main road.

Son and Callie reached the train station about 1:30 P.M., one hour before train time.

Callie said, "I do not mind waiting for the train."

Callie appeared to be nervous.

Son told Callie, "Just relax. Why are you nervous, anyway? You are here one hour before the train is scheduled to arrive."

Callie said, "When the old car stopped, that made me nervous, because I thought that we would not get here at all. We were lucky that Chuck was leaving just about the same time as we were leaving."

Son told Callie that the train was coming now. They carried Callie's luggage near the train tracks and stood there waiting for the train to pull up alongside the waiting area.

When the train arrived, it remained there for about one half hour. It appeared that the trainmen were fixing something on the train. Finally, Callie heard the old familiar: "All aboard!" Just a few people were waiting for the train. The conductor put the old familiar stool-like step down near the steps on the train. Each passenger carefully stepped on the makeshift step and then got on the train. As they were in line, Callie asked Son to run to the car and get her lunch, which she had forgotten and left on the seat of the car. She thanked Son for getting her lunch, and then she said, "Good-bye, Son, and thanks for bringing me to catch the train."

Son waved and said, "Enjoy your trip to New York."

When Callie sat in her seat, she noticed an old metal wood or charcoal-burning heater standing in one corner of the coach. It was not cold; therefore, they did not need any heat. The heater was just there if needed to furnish heat for the coach. Callie continued looking around in the old coach for the bathroom. She found the rest room at the end of the coach. She did not have to use the rest room; she just wanted to know where it was just in case she had to use it later. She had her own lunch, so she did not have to worry about whether she would be able to eat or not. She realized that she would be riding for a long, long time and she did not want to starve, although, she almost forgot and left her lunch in the old car, for her brother to eat on his way home, because she knew that her brother would not be able to catch the old train if he chased it so he could give Callie her lunch. In spite of Callie's nervousness as a result of the old car stopping, she was able to compose herself in time to remember that she did not have her lunch before boarding the train.

What do I have to look for? Callie asked herself. She remembered: water. What about water to drink? She looked around again, and she saw a water fountain near the end of the coach. *Now,* she figured, *that is all that I will need on this trip.*

No, that's not all that I need. I need someone to talk to while we are traveling. She looked around, and she saw an elderly lady sitting about two seats above where she was sitting on the left side of the coach. Callie was sitting on the right of the coach. Callie noticed that there were several vacant seats on both sides of the coach. But there were several more stations where the train would be stopping, and it was possible that the coach would be filled up after a few more stations.

Callie said to herself that she should not be too hasty to meet anybody so soon, because it might be somebody to share her lunch with. *After all, it's going to be a lot of hours before I get to my destination.* Callie recalled that the old car had stopped on their way to the train station and God forbid, the train could also stop somewhere along the way to New York. *Before we left the station, the trainmen did have to do some repairs on the train. It could happen again, to delay the time of our arrival.*

Callie had just heard that the train would not go beyond Washington. She would have to catch another train from Washington to New York.

Callie noticed that the elderly lady was eating some of her lunch. She seemed to have a big box of lunch. Watching the elderly lady eat her lunch made Callie feel hungry. Callie reached in the lunchbox and got a piece of chicken and a slice of bread to eat herself. Callie did not have to worry about sharing her lunch with the elderly lady, because the elderly lady has enough lunch to share with someone else.

Eating something made Callie feel thirsty, and she went to the water fountain for a drink of water. On her way back, she stopped by the elderly lady's seat and spoke to her, starting a conversation with the elderly lady. Finally, Callie sat down besides the elderly lady.

In talking to her, Callie found out that the elderly lady was coming to the state of New Jersey and was from the state of Florida. The elderly lady told Callie that she had been to the state of New Jersey many times, visiting her elder daughter. She said that she had three daughters and four sons. Callie laughed and said that her mother had three daughters and four sons, too. The elderly lady, smiling said, "Even though we did not know each other, we were counting together, still smiling."

At this point, Callie knew that she had a good person to talk to on their way "up north."

At Washington, in transferring from one train to another, Callie and the elderly lady were unable to find a seat where they could continue sharing the same seat, but they would visit each other and talk briefly.

At Washington, they spent twenty-five minutes transferring from one train to the other. In the northern-bound coach a different atmosphere existed. In this coach, there were no segregated seats. All shared the same coach, white and black. You sorta had a feeling that you were accepted even before you reached the northern states. Now, as this was her first trip to a northern state, Callie had to start readjusting herself to a different lifestyle. Callie recalled reading a passage that said: "When in Rome, do as the Romans do," or something to that effect.

Callie started observing how other people reacted, and she would try to imitate the actions of northerners.

Callie felt that she had to assume the identity of someone else . . . not Callie from Avon, Georgia, the girl from the country.

Callie leaned her head back on the seat and dozed off. She was interrupted when the passenger sitting to her left wanted to go to the rest room. Callie knew that the other passenger would be coming back in a few minutes, so she remained awake until she returned. Then Callie dozed off again. This time, she was able to sleep for about two hours.

While Callie was asleep, the train traveled several miles, passing several stations in the process. The conductor walked down the aisle of the coach saying, "Next stop will be New Jersey." Callie realized that this was the stop where the elderly lady would get off. Callie stood up quickly and attempted to look for the elderly lady. *Where is she sitting?* Callie asked herself. She looked around, but to no avail. It was too late for Callie to locate the elderly lady so she could say good-bye to her. The aisle of the coach was full of passengers getting their luggage so they would be able to get off when the train stopped at the New Jersey station.

Callie did not see the elderly lady anymore. She looked out of the window, but to no avail. She could only think of her as a nice old lady who reminded her of her grandmother. The elderly lady was gone but not forgotten.

* * *

Callie was now waiting to hear the conductor announce, "The next and last stop will be New York." Before the conductor announced the New York stop, Callie saw a few passengers getting their luggage from the luggage carrier above them. Callie knew that it was time that she got her luggage down as well. The conductor had problems getting through the aisle because of the number of passengers standing in the aisle.

Callie was thinking to herself that she hoped her friend Sarah would be on hand to greet her when she got off the train. Sarah was there waiting with open arms to greet Callie when she got off the train.

As the two ladies emerged from the lower level to the waiting room section, Callie observed that there were people all over the area, and as she and Sarah walked toward the subway entrance, Callie noticed that people were going from her left to her right, from her right to her left, and she was facing people, as well as seeing people going in the same direction as she and Sarah were going.

Callie asked Sarah, "Do they, the people, know where they are going? Because they are going in all directions, as if they are confused and do not know where they should be going."

Sarah pointed. "You see, some are going to pick up their luggage over there, some are going to buy their tickets to go to New Jersey or somewhere else, some are looking for their relatives or friends that they came to meet at the station, some are going to the lunchroom, some are going to the rest rooms, and some are going to the subway, like we are going. Each of them has an objective to fulfill. It's just that there are a lot of people mingling together with a purpose in mind. You will get used to it, Callie, in time, if you are here long enough.

"Now, you see people are leaving the subway station and some are going to the subway station, only two directions at this point. We are going to the subway station. At this station, some trains are going uptown and some are going downtown. We are going downtown. Do you see that train leaving? The train is going downtown; we just missed it. Now we have to wait for the next train."

"How long?" Callie asked.

"Oh, Sarah said, "about ten or fifteen minutes. The trains run more often during the rush hour. We will wait here. You see that train over there? It's going uptown.

Sarah said, "Our train is coming now. When you see me get on the train, you get on at the same time, Callie."

"OK," Callie said.

As the two ladies got settled in their seats, Sarah told Callie, "We are leaving the borough of Manhattan and we are going to the borough of Brooklyn." Sarah continued, saying, "Our stop in Brooklyn will be Nostrand Avenue at Fulton Street."

Callie was silent as they rode the train from station to station. Callie was silent, but she was observing the action of the train and the doors of the train as they stopped at each station. Finally, Callie said, "Sarah, I notice that each time the train stops, the doors open and close by themselves."

Sarah answered, saying, "There is someone controlling the doors, but you just do not see him. We will be getting off at the next station." Sarah took Callie's suitcase and told Callie, "Hold on so you won't lose your balance as the train stops."

As they walked out on the platform, Sarah said, while pointing, "Callie, look, do you see that man leaning out of the window?"

Callie said, "Yes."

"He is the one that is controlling the doors of the train."

"I see," Callie said.

As the two women came up to the street level, Sarah pointed. "You see, this is Nostrand Avenue and there is Fulton Street. We go in this direction to Halsey Street, the street where I live."

Callie said, "It seems to be very complicated to remember all of these directions and places where you have to go."

"It will take a little time, but you will learn how to travel as you go from place to place."

When Sarah reached her house on Halsey Street, the first thing they did was sit in the living room and discuss their past together in Avon, Georgia.

"But, Callie, you are in the state of New York, now. What are your plans for your future? I know one of your plans would be to find a nice boyfriend, one that you can trust, one that you can put confidence in, one that would make a good father."

With both ladies smiling, Callie said, "The last statement you made, one that would make a good father, is the most important aspect in a boyfriend that I would want at this time."

Sarah emphasized the fact that Callie was indeed in the state of New York and she had to start looking for these things in life. "Do not start looking for a job, as yet. Give yourself a little chance to just relax and adjust yourself. I can afford to support you for a while. I have a good job, and it pays well. Be sure, however, to write to your mother and let her know that you arrived here safely and that you are still excited from the sudden change in your lifestyle."

Sarah called Callie and showed her the room and bed she would be occupying while she was here. Both ladies appeared to be anxious to get into bed; why? Because it was two o'clock in the morning.

Sarah said, "I am glad that it is Saturday, because I don't have to go to work today."

Each lady gave a sleepy and tired smile and departed for bed.

* * *

Callie, after she got up from bed, heard Sarah in the kitchen preparing breakfast. Callie yelled, "Sarah, what time is it?"

"It's ten o'clock."

"OK," Callie said as she went into the bathroom.

After Callie left the bathroom, she went into the kitchen, talking as she walked into the kitchen. She told Sarah that she had an extensive dream the few hours that she slept.

Sarah asked, "What was the dream all about? Do you remember?"

"Yes," Callie answered. "When I got on the train, in real life, I was looking for someone to talk to. I noticed an elderly lady, sitting alone, just diagonally across to my left. I went over and spoke and introduced myself to her. She looked up at me and introduced herself to me as Sue Ellen Baxter, from Florida, and she was going to New Jersey. We talked as we sat together, until we got to Washington. We had to change trains in Washington. Because of the confusion, we sat in different locations and we did not see each other anymore. She reminded me of my maternal grandmother. You remember my maternal grandmother, don't you, Sarah?"

Sarah said, "Yes, I remember her. She was very caring and wanted you to be comfortable and happy."

"That was my Grandmother," Callie said. "This elderly lady was the same way, it seems.

"I dreamed that we were, apparently, in Avon, Georgia, and walking through some tall grass. She was holding my hand, and she was talking as we walked along the path. She was telling me to be careful, because something could jump from the tall grass and bite me. That would cause me to grasp her hand tightly and walk close to her side, for protection. I remembered that my maternal grandmother used to talk like that.

"As we walked, she suddenly stopped. She spoke softly, saying, 'I think I saw a snake or something on that little bush up there.' She was pointing in that direction. As we walked slowly, I saw a long green snake sorta inside the branches of that little bush. I told the elderly lady that I saw the snake on the branches of the little tree. She said, 'Where, child? I showed her where the snake was. She said, 'Yes,' just like I told you. You can see better than me, because I could only see the branches move, but I could not see the snake. The snake is green and the leaves are green; you have to look very closely to see the snake."

"It was after it had rained and the frogs were singing. We heard different voices. The elderly lady said, 'Listen. Do you hear that fine voice? That's a small frog; now that voice that you hear now is a larger frog. Listen; that very heavy bass voice is what you call a bullfrog. Frogs won't hurt you, but don't trust anything, just be careful.' "

Callie said in her dream she saw a little puddle of water right in the path where they had to walk. "I said, 'Uh, I don't know what to call you, by your first name, or—'

" 'Well, child,' the elderly lady said, 'just call me Grandma.'

" 'You do remind me of my maternal grandmother.'

" 'Well then, just call me Grandma.'

" 'OK,' I said. 'Grandma, there is a puddle of water in the path up there. We have to look to see if we can go around that puddle of water. 'Oh!'

" 'What now, child?'

" 'There is a fish in that puddle of water. Look; he is swimming around in the puddle.'

" 'Are you sure, child?'

"There was a man standing over there. He spoke to us: 'Good evening, folks.'

"The elderly lady said, 'Good evening, mister. I heard the child say that she saw a fish in that little puddle of water.'

" 'It rained very hard yesterday, and when it rains that hard it floods this area. Over there,' he was pointing, 'is a pond, and when it rains hard the fish swim away from the pond and they don't have sense enough to swim back to the pond before the water runs off the higher areas. They get stuck and can't get back to the pond. I catch them all the time when this happens.'

" 'Well,' the elderly lady said, 'I have never heard of this happening before . . . out of all of those years that I lived on the farm.'

"I woke up at this point. It seemed to have been very real. Maybe it was because I did not get a chance to see the elderly lady anymore and I was thinking about her. . . . I won't forget about her . . . ever," Callie said.

Sarah told Callie that the way she told the dream it seemed to be real, as if it occurred in real life, and she was able to remember it all the way through.

"Breakfast is ready; let's eat. Callie, there are a few places that I would like to take you before you get a job and settle down."

"OK, Sarah."

"Maybe you heard of the Apollo Theater?"

"Yes," Callie said.

"I heard Jim talking about the Apollo Theater. . . ."

"Ol' Jim they used to call him."

"Why did they call him Ol' Jim, Sarah?"

"Because he used to act like he was old, that's why, Callie."

"Oh."

"Anyway, the Apollo Theater is located in the heart of Harlem. It's on one-hundred-twenty-fifth Street. Last year, 1931, was considered one of the best years at the Apollo Theater as far as selecting good talent in singing and dancing. I did not go to the Apollo Theater in 1931. It was in 1930 the last time that I attended one of their talent shows. I thought it was good at that time. Maybe I am not a good judge in selecting good talent. Anyway, we will go next week . . . on Thursday night. You have a good voice, Callie; why don't you sign up for a test of your voice?"

"No, Sarah, I only sing church songs in a choir. Seldom do I sing a solo part in the choir."

"In that case, Callie, you can join the choir of the Methodist church."

"Now, Sarah, I will take you up on that suggestion."

"When we attend church Sunday, Callie, I will introduce you to the choirmaster."

* * *

"OK, Callie, I am not going to rush you into anything yet. I am not going to introduce you to the choirmaster today. You can just be a visitor today so you can observe how the choir sings; then you can make your comparison with the choir back home."

Callie agreed with Sarah. Callie became so engrossed in what she was hearing from the choir, that she was virtually singing along with the choir while she sat among the congregation.

"Callie, you don't have to tell me that you enjoyed the choir singing, because I saw you singing with them."

"Yes, Sarah, I enjoyed the whole service. In Avon, Georgia," Callie said, "The Methodist church back home cannot afford to buy an expensive organ like they have here at this Methodist church. The quality of music coming from an expensive organ enhances the value of the choir. It just sounds better with a good organ."

"You are right, Callie. That organ here cost a lot of money. They told us how much, but I do not remember how much they said. It was a lot of money."

"The choirmaster can play the organ as well as direct the choir. He is a good musician. That helps to make a good choir," Callie said.

"This week, Callie, we are invited to attend an affair at the Savoy Ballroom in Harlem on Friday night. You remember that we are going to the Apollo Theater on Thursday night."

"I remember, Sarah."

"Can you adjust to all of these affairs, Callie?"

"Yes, Sarah. It's you that have to work."

"Oh! I have two days off from my job this week . . . Thursday and Friday."

"Good for you, Sarah."

"Anyway, Callie, you will have a chance to meet some people at the Savoy Ballroom . . . maybe a new boyfriend."

"Good, Sarah, as long as he is nice-looking and very intelligent."

"Well, Callie, you have to make that determination for yourself."

"Sarah, I saw a lady at the church that reminded me of the elderly lady I met on the train."

"Did you have any more dreams, Callie?"

"No, I was just thinking about her."

"I can see that she left a lasting impression of herself with you."

"Yes, she reminded me of my maternal grandmother. I cannot forget that. She said that she visits her daughter in New Jersey every two years. This year, she said that she was late with her visit because of the deaths of some of her old friends and she wanted to attend their funerals. She said that the last time that she visited her daughter was in 1929, May of 1929. 'Now,' she said, 'that it is in June of 1932 how many years ago was that? About three years or so since I visited my daughter. My daughter will understand, because she knew those people who were my friends.' I am sorry that I did not get her address. We might not ever see each other again.

"What should I wear to the Apollo Theater Thursday night, Sarah?"

"Never mind about what you should wear Thursday night. . . . You can wear almost anything to the Apollo Theater; it's what you should wear to the affair at the Savoy Ballroom. Anyway, Callie, it is not a formal affair; you just can wear a nice party dress."

"Sarah, you have to remember that I am recently from Avon, Georgia . . . a small country town. But I do have a party dress that I made about two years ago."

"That is OK, Callie, as long as it fits. Did you gain any more weight, Callie?"

Smiling, Callie said emphatically, "No!"

"Then," Sarah said, "you do not have anything to worry about."

The next day, Sarah was on her way home from work and then announced, "Callie, I am home," when she arrived.

"OK, Sarah."

"Did I get any mail today?"

"No, but I received a letter from my mother."

"Any good news?"

"My brother Son seems to be engaged to a Sarah Sheds. Do you know her, Sarah?"

"Sarah Sheds? No. Where does she live?"

"She lives in a section called Deep Creek. Do you know where that is, Sarah?"

"Yes, I know where Deep Creek is, but I do not know any Shedses."

"Son escorted her to the junior-senior prom about two years ago."

"Oh, and he sorta got hooked?"

"Yes, it seems so."

"Sarah, I tried my party dress on today and I found that it was a little tight . . . more than I wanted it to be, so I cut a piece from the belt and let the dress out about two and a half inches . . . see?"

"Oh, Callie, you cannot even tell that you let it out any."

Callie, with her chest sticking out, boastfully said, "That's because I am a seamstress."

"Excuse me!" Sarah replied. "I'd better try my party dress on to see if it fits OK . . . My dress fits just right," Sarah said. "Then we are off to the party tomorrow night."

* * *

"How did you classify that talent show last night, Callie?"

"Based on my knowledge of music, Sarah, I would say that five of the contestants should do a lot of practicing before they even attempt to compete with anybody else on a talent show again."

"How about the girl who attempted to sing 'Blue Moon'?"

"Sarah, I am glad that you said *attempted* to sing 'Blue Moon.' They should not have put her on the program at all. Why put a person in an embarrassing situation like that, before a large audience? That will give that person an inferiority complex, and that person may never be sure of herself anymore. She may withdraw herself from society forever. That is not a good policy to do that. If a person does not measure up for a talent show, she should not be put on the program and she should be told to practice some more before applying for another tryout on a talent show.

"If a person is not qualified, tell her that she is not qualified. Otherwise, she will appear and be booed off the stage, and that is very embarrassing to anybody. A boy who got out of his seat, walked over to the aisle, and leaned over to her and said, 'Boo! Boo! Boo!' was very uncouth. I wanted to smack him myself."

"You are right, Callie. The girl who won first place and was crowned Miss Apollo of 1932 had three other tryouts, or appearances, in 1929, 1930, and 1931. It was time that she won the title of Miss Apollo. . . . She had previous experience.

"Callie, let's see how we make out tonight at the Savoy Ballroom. I asked a casual acquaintance of mine to escort both of us to the Savoy Ballroom. His name is Mack Webb. He is one of the supervisors on my job. He has a car, and that will be better than taking the subway over to Harlem. Especially when we leave at maybe two o'clock in the early morning, returning to Brooklyn. He lives in Brooklyn, and he won't be going out of his way. As far as I know, he does not have a girlfriend."

"Maybe he has his eyes on you, Sarah."

"Oh, I don't think so. He is just a nice guy."

"That's good. It's better than two ladies riding the subway in the early morning hours and then having to walk from Nostrand Avenue to Halsey Street by ourselves."

"You got that right."

"What time will he pick us up?"

"He said about eight thirty P.M."

"OK, I had my bath already. All I have to do is dress."

"It's seven P.M. now, Callie. I am going to take my bath, and then I will start dressing myself."

* * *

"How do I look, Sarah?"

"My . . . you look like a model, smiling. Are you going to model that dress tonight?"

"Well, I hope that this dress looks good to the audience."

"It will, Callie. I am glad that we do not have to wear coats."

"Yes, it's nice and warm outside."

"That's the doorbell now."

"I will get it, Sarah."

"Hello! You are Callie, yes?"

"Yes; how are you?"

"Sarah told me about you. . . . You look like Sarah's sister."

"No, we are just cousins."

"How do you like being in New York City?"

"Well, it's very exciting . . . there is much going on . . . all of the time."

"You can say that again."

"Hello, Mack."

"Hello, Sarah."

"I guess you two have met?"

"Yes, Sarah. I told Callie that she favors you a lot."

"We are old friends as well as cousins. It goes back a long way. Oh, good, I have the tickets for the Savoy Ballroom. Do you have your ticket, Mack?"

"Yes, I do."

"Then we're off to the dance."

* * *

"Oh, there is a spot where I can park the car. That's because we are early. We do not have too far to walk."

"Yes, Mack. It's good to be early. I see members of the band coming now. We should be able to get good seats near the stage."

"Yes, we are lucky. Well it's good to be early. Can I get you ladies something to drink?"

"Not yet, Mack. Let's wait until a lot of people come and we're seated. You can get something for yourself, Mack."

"OK, Sarah.

"The band members are tuning up. Callie, I want you to have a good time. . . . Just let your hair down and enjoy yourself . . . to the maximum."

"Oh, Sarah, you sound like you had a drink or something."

"No, Callie. I refrain from drinking. I only drink sodas, but I can pretend that I am getting high."

"I am the same way, Sarah."

"It seems that the band is ready to start playing. I am lucky I have two ladies to entertain tonight. I hope that I can do a good job."

"You do not have overexert yourself, Mack."

Mack dropped off Sarah and Callie exactly at 2:00 A.M. He said, "Good night, ladies, and have a restful night." In unison, with Callie trying to open her eyes, they said, "Good night, Mack, and get home safely."

* * *

"Oh, Sarah, I feel like I can sleep two days."

"I know, Callie, that you are not used to this fast life here in New York City. I was the same way, when I moved here several years ago. You will get used to measuring your ability of how to cope or deal with any situation that might exist with your lifestyle from day to day in the future."

"I hope so, Sarah. O-o-o-o-h."

"What is wrong, Callie?"

"This bed feels so good."

"Yes, have a restful night, Callie.

"OK, Sarah, I will."

Later that morning, the doorbell rang.

"I'll get it, Sarah."

"You mean that you are up?"

"Yes. I had to go to the bathroom. What time is it, Sarah?"

"It's nine-forty-five A.M."

"That late? Yes, it seems that I was the one anxious to go to bed."

"Not you Callie."

"Well, we both were tired at that time in the morning."

"That guy that you were dancing with so many times . . . did you like him, Callie? I mean like a boyfriend?"

"*No!* After he found out that I just came to New York City, he apparently thought that he could lead me on with his fast-talking schemes. Not so. I know how to judge a person's behavior after I am with him for a short while."

"That is very good, Callie. Then you won't be misled by a braggart, who pretends to be more than what he is actually."

"Last night, Sarah, everything that he was connected with was good. He was the greatest; he was the supervisor on his job. I found out that he was not a homeowner; he was a roomer, and he does not own a car. He said that he came here by subway. The suit that he was wearing had a few patches where he had his pants repaired."

"Oh, Callie, you are the one to observe his attire, since you are a seamstress. I probably would not have noticed that his pants had been repaired."

"After he described himself as a supervisor, I asked him what he did. He said that he was a supervisor over several machine-operating pressers at a shirt laundry."

"Yes, Callie, I remember seeing several shirt laundries in different locations in Brooklyn. Well, at least, he brags about his job.

"Callie, there is one more place where I want to take you: Radio City Music Hall. We will wait until near the Christmas holidays, so you can see the Christmas show with the Rockettes."

"That's good, Sarah, but don't you think that I should start looking for a job?"

"Well, Callie, I guess this is where your vacation and your trip toward your future ends. We will start looking for a job for you next Monday, Callie. Would you like to get a job at the shirt laundry?"

"No, Sarah, because I might end up working for the fast-talking man."

Both ladies were smiling.

6

Callie's Future Depends on How She Manages Her Present Status

"Sarah, it seems that we are always discussing something that happened in our hometown, Avon, Georgia. Now let's talk about looking for a job. I have chosen the course that I should follow in my plans: first, the type of job and how I might prosper and second finding someone, a male companion."

"Callie, it's not that I did not think about you and your future plans, I submitted your name to my boss before you came to New York City, and he has your name on his 'most wanted list.' He is just waiting for someone to retire or leave for some other reason; then you are hired."

"Where do you work, Sarah?"

"I work in a factory where they make electrical parts like switches, outlets, and other electrical parts that are used in an apartment or house. It's a good-paying job, and you do not have to be an expert to get a job there. I have been working there for about six or seven years now. I like the job, but different people like different jobs."

When Sarah arrived home the next day from work, she and Callie, as usual, started talking about old times back home. These conversations were somewhat spontaneous. They always, had something to talk about. Sarah was very happy that Callie was staying with her. Sarah and her husband had separated about one year ago. Sarah's two children, a son and a daughter, ages twelve and ten, respectively, were staying with their grandmother in Avon, Georgia.

While Sarah and Callie sat in the living room talking, Sarah mentioned that her boss was still waiting for a vacancy to occur at the factory so he could call Callie in for an interview. Sarah knew that back home in the country you did not have much of a chance to take up a trade or anything that would prepare you for the future.

Laughing, Sarah asked Callie, "What can you do? Besides make dresses?"

When Sarah said that, Callie remembered what her mother had told her about learning a trade, any kind of trade, even if she did not plan to use that trade for a lifelong job. At that point, Callie jumped up and threw up her hands and said, "Sarah I am a typist."

Sarah responded, "You a typist? Where did you learn to type?"

Callie happily said, "At Pope's High School."

At this point, Sarah stood up waving her hands and saying, "Callie, I am six years older than you, and when I was attending Pope's High School there were no course in typing at that time anywhere in Avon, Georgia."

Callie stood up, so both ladies were standing up at this time, and said, "You see, we got a new teacher; her name was Miss Singer. This was about two years ago, and she turned out to be a typist. She volunteered to teach the class how to type if the school would supply the typewriters for the class." Callie continued, saying, "My father was a member of the PTA and the school board of directors. He helped Miss Singer to get whatever she needed to operate the class. My father was also instrumental in getting a room for the typing class. While this was going on, he bought me a good used typewriter, so I could practice at home. This enabled me to become one of the best typists in the class. I made the highest marks on the typist test, Sarah."

"Oh, I did not know that. . . . That's good, Callie."

"It was very fortunate for us that Miss Singer devoted her personal time to teaching us for free. That is why I am a typist, Sarah. I am not just a typist; I am a *good* typist."

"Well, it's good when you can pat yourself on the back and say that you are good. I am happy for you, Callie.

"Incidentally, Callie, about two weeks ago I was reading in the *Chief* newspaper where I saw an ad for typists." Sarah said that she would look for that newspaper. Sarah continued, saying that when she came to New York City she had a difficult time finding a job. "I was lucky to find this job at the factory. We get good health benefits, which is very important today, and we also get our retirement benefits.

"Callie, I hope that I can find that newspaper. If you can get a job typing you will be lucky. Because of the depression, there are a lot of people out of work. Even some of the banks are closing. I heard that a lot of people were laid off, starting in 1929."

"Sarah, listen to this. I just read in the letter I received from my mother that Ms. Singer's typing class was accepted as part of the Pope's High School curriculum and Ms. Singer is getting paid to teach typing in the school."

"That is very good, Callie. Even though I do not know her, I am happy for her, because that means so much for the children at the high school."

"My mother continued, saying that the reason was because the state of Alabama, which is just across the border, heard about Miss Singer's new typing class and that she had volunteered her service for free and offered her a job just across the border in the state of Alabama, and they will pay her a good salary if she accepts the offer.

"The board of education heard about this offer from a different state to hire Ms. Singer, so they called her in and offered her a good salary to stay at Pope's High School and to continue her typing class. Everyone at the school is happy that Miss Singer stayed at the school."

Sarah called Callie from the back room of the apartment and told her that she found the newspaper with the ad for typists. Sarah said, "Here it is, Callie. They are looking for typists at the Department of Welfare and the Department of Sanitation." Sarah pointed out that the Department of Sanitation was on Worth Street in Manhattan and the Department of Welfare was located in Brooklyn.

Callie said that she would like to check out the Department of Welfare there in Brooklyn. Callie called the Department of Welfare on Friday about 2:30 P.M., and she was invited to come by the office on Monday at 10:00 A.M.

Callie, feeling that she was out of practice, asked Sarah if she knew someone with a typewriter. Sarah checked with three of her friends and came up with a friend who had a friend with a typewriter. Sarah was able to locate that person with a typewriter, who was willing to let Callie practice on her typewriter over the weekend. Sarah contacted her friend (male) and asked him if he would take her and Callie to this person's house to pick up the typewriter. This was about 6:00 P.M. Friday. Callie practiced typing from Friday night to Sunday A.M. They returned the typewriter to their good neighbor by Sunday night.

Sarah took Callie by the Department of Welfare office just to show Callie where she should go Monday for the interview.

Sarah did not have to wake up Callie Monday morning, because Callie was already up and getting dressed for her appointment at the

Department of Welfare. Sarah wished her good luck and warned her not to get nervous, but just be calm. Callie said, "That's easier said than done."

Callie left the house shortly after Sarah left to go to her job at the factory. Callie arrived at the Department of Welfare's office at 9:30 A.M. She was sitting and waiting for her appointment when the supervisor arrived. Callie nervously waited, which is not an unusual type of reaction when you are waiting for a job for the first time in a new place or a new setup.

At 10:15 A.M., someone came by and informed Callie that someone would see her soon. Callie waited and waited. Finally, at about 11:10 A.M., someone came by and ask Callie for her credentials. Callie had her high school transcript, and she presented that. The person that was supposed to interview Callie looked over the transcript, gave it back to her, and walked away without saying anything to Callie. A few minutes later, another lady came by and invited Callie to come with her. Callie followed the lady to a room that was virtually full of typewriters and almost full of typists, and they were busy typing. This made Callie nervous for a while. Callie recalled that when she was taking typing, back home, the noise of the typewriters distracted her. Callie had learned how to deal with that type of situation, so her nervous emotions soon calmed themselves and Callie was now ready to take a typing test if given one.

Callie was seated by the senior typist's desk to observe how to type up the forms necessary to relay information from this center to the Main Welfare Center in Manhattan.

The senior typist showed Callie the forms that they used and the information sheets that they used to type up the forms. The senior typist continued telling Callie part of the operation of the center. She pointed out that there were social investigators who interviewed the clients who came to the center for assistance and told Callie about the different types of cases and that the information that the social investigators got was put together and the typists typed up this information for the main center, which was located in Manhattan.

At this point, the senior typist wanted to go to the ladies' room. She invited Callie, but Callie did not want to go to the ladies' room at this time. The senior typist left Callie sitting beside her desk. While Callie was sitting there, she noticed that the senior typist had put the form in the typewriter with the information sheet nearby. Callie sat there for a while, waiting for the senior typist to return. Apparently, the senior typist had stopped to gossip with one of her friends. Maybe eight minutes passed. Callie got up and sat in the senior typist's seat and typed the information from the information sheet onto the form, which was in the typewriter.

The senior typist returned, sat down in her seat, and positioned herself to type the information on the form in the typewriter, but she noticed that the information was already typed on the form. She said "Did I type this information on the form before I went to the ladies' room?"

Callie said, "No, I typed the information on the form, while you were in the ladies' room."

The senior typist looked the form over and said, "You do not need me to show you anything, because you already know how to type up these forms."

The supervisor came and invited Callie to go with her to a desk just a few steps away from where they were. The supervisor pointed with her left hand, saying, "You may sit here; this is your desk." The supervisor left and returned a little later with some material to be typed up. She gave this material to Callie, said, "Good luck," and left the area.

When the senior typist saw the supervisor leave, she immediately went over to Callie and said, "You are a good typist, Callie, but don't overdo it. That is, we limit ourselves to a special number of cases to be typed up each day. We want you to stay in line with us. . . . You won't be getting a gold medal for this work."

Callie said, "Thanks. I will comply with the regulations of the typists."

Callie was not used to this type of setup, yet she knew that she could, in fact, type. As Callie was sitting at the desk, looking around, the senior typist returned to Callie's desk and gave her some typing paper and said, "You can type anything on this typing paper; it's just to give you a chance to get used to your new Underwood typewriter." She smiled and walked away.

When the supervisor returned, this time she said, "It's time for lunch. You may go out for lunch and return in one hour."

While Callie was out, she met some of the other typists who were also out for lunch. One of the other typists told Callie that she was hired because they saw that she could type better than some of the typists that were there now. "You see," one of the girls said, "if you belong to a political club, you can get a job as a provisional. I know that you do not know about being a provisional worker or typist. That means that you can get employment on a temporary basis. If, however, you take the examination and pass the typist test while you are a provisional, you will become a permanent typist, which means that you qualify for the job as a typist.

"Some of these girls are connected with some of the political clubs, and they got their jobs through some of the politicians they campaigned for while they were running for public office of some kind. What is your name again?"

"My name is Callie, Callie Watts."

"Well, Callie, have you voted yet?"

"No, I did not register to vote as yet."

"When you register, no doubt you will join up with some of the political clubs, and this is when you start campaigning for someone who is running for public office."

"Do you have to join the political clubs when you register to vote?"

"No, Callie, it's only when you are looking for a job and they can help you to find a job, that's all."

"So you do not have to join the political club, when you are eligible to vote?"

"Right, you do not have to join; it's only when you want to join for a reason, like I just told you."

"OK, I am not joining the club when I register to vote."

"That's your option, Callie.

"Even though, Callie you know how to type, you might have to take the typist test, which is scheduled by the city to be given next month. There are other girls here that are scheduled to take that exam. . . . You will be with that group."

Callie was relieved when the girls said that she was hired. Lunchtime was over and all of the girls returned to the Department of Welfare office. Callie returned to her newly assigned desk and sat down. Callie was thinking of all of the confusion that occurred when one of the girls tried to explain how some of the girls got their jobs.

Callie sat at her desk doing nothing for about an hour. Finally, the supervisor came with a handful of papers and gave them to Callie. She said, "Look over these papers, and if at any time you do not understand something, all you have to do is come to my desk and I will explain whatever it is to you. I know that you are new here and I know that you cannot come to grips with everything without some help."

In about another hour, the supervisor returned and sat down beside Callie and reached for the papers that she had given to Callie. She explained to Callie how she should type them. She pointed out in detail how Callie was supposed to type them. She asked Callie a few personal questions and then said, "In forty-five minutes you can leave for home. Tomorrow morning you can report to work at nine A.M."

"Thank you," Callie said.

"These papers you can type up tomorrow morning and give them to me at my desk." Pointing to the direction of her desk, she added, "Over there near the window. A telephone is on my desk."

Callie, smiling, said, "OK," and asked, "Do I have to bring anything with me tomorrow morning when I report for work?"

"No, just yourself, Callie," and she walked away, saying, "I will see you tomorrow."

Callie nodded with a smile, saying, "OK."

The supervisor did not know that the girls had heard that Callie was hired and broken the news to Callie while they were out at lunch. Callie did not let the supervisor know that she had already heard that she was hired earlier.

Some of the other girls greeted Callie as she was leaving for the day.

Callie walked outside and looked around to see which direction she should go to get home. She remembered passing some of the buildings to her right and said, "This is the direction that I should go home."

Callie stopped by one of the corner grocery stores on her way home to buy food to take home with her. As Callie walked down the aisle looking for something to buy, she saw Sarah coming from the other direction. When they focused their eyes on each other, they spontaneously ran toward each other, grabbing each other with a bear hug, a very clumsy or rude hug. Callie blurted out, "I am hired. . . . I have a job." Sarah was also overjoyed, because they had an inner feeling for each other. After they finished that episode of joy, Callie promised Sarah that she would give her the whole story when they get home.

Since Sarah was the "lady of the house," she did make all of the selections of what type of food they should buy. They returned home after their purchases.

After Callie had settled herself down at home, she explained in detail the reaction of the supervisor and the procedure that she used in interviewing her for the entire day. Callie said that the reaction of the supervisor was very stern and she was the same way for the whole day as Callie sat at her newly assigned desk. "I only typed a large paragraph from a sheet that she, the supervisor, had given me to type. I gave the typed sheet to the supervisor; the supervisor left without saying anything about the typed sheet that I had given her. It seems that she accepted the manner that I typed the paragraph as she watched me type it."

Callie suddenly said in a loud voice, "I have a job." They both laughed and laughed with enthusiasm. Callie said that she would not make any future plans until she got her first salary check. "I will, however, write a few letters to my mother and some friends back home."

Callie's money was just about gone. She was wondering whether she should ask her mother to send her a few dollars to tide her over until she got paid from her job. Sarah was always asking Callie, "Do you need anything? Money or otherwise?" Callie realized that she had been living off Sarah for some time now and was not able to offer any financial support as yet. She, also, realized that her mother had only a small income now that she was not sewing like she used to when someone was getting married. These days, they simply went to the department store to buy their dresses.

Callie realized that just a few years ago her mother, it seems, was the only source for people who needed a new dress. They would always go to her mother. "My mother has a lot of competition, now. With cars people can go to the nearby city, where they can go to the department stores to buy any type of dress that they need. So far my mother has only the high school graduating classes to make dresses for their junior-senior prom. Seldom does she get customers for a wedding ceremony these days."

Callie did chores around the house but did not help to pay the bills, like food shopping, the phone bills, the electric bills, and the gas bills. Sarah owned a small car, and she had to pay for the maintenance of the old car. Callie realized that she had only a few weeks before she could offer some help to Sarah and to her mother. Now that Callie had a good job, she could build up her independence after a few paydays—that is, financially.

At this point, Callie stood up, braced herself, and said to herself, *I'll be able to operate on my own after a few paydays.* She heard Sarah coming in and prepared to greet Sarah as she came into the apartment.

Callie greeted Sarah as she entered the room with a few packages in her arm. It seemed that Callie and Sarah were very compatible. It was like this with their relationship with each other since Callie arrived a few weeks ago. Sarah opened a package that she had brought with her. Sarah had purchased a lot of cosmetics, mostly the kind that she saw Callie using. Sarah said, "I have your brand of cosmetics, Callie." Sarah continued, saying, "Since I have been using your brand of cosmetics, Callie, I find that I like your brand better than the brand that I used to use."

"You are welcome to use some of these cosmetics. After all it's your brand of cosmetics now."

Callie knew Sarah bought her brand of cosmetics because she knew that Callie only had a little or a small amount left. Callie thought to herself, *What else did she buy for me? It seems that Sarah can read my mind, at times, and that is often.*

Sarah, with her cunning self, knew that Callie had met a new guy on her job and felt that Callie wanted to use some makeup, as most ladies like to do, to impress, in this case a new guy. Finally, Sarah said, "Callie, don't you have something to tell me?"

Callie said, "Sarah, I knew that you had something up your sleeve. You want to find out about the new guy that I met at the office. Well, I will have to find out more about him myself. Anyway, Sarah, I will owe you a lot of money when I get paid. You have been like a sister to me since I have been here with you."

"I might surprise you when I say that you do not owe me anything, Callie."

Callie said, "Oh." Putting her arms around Sarah and hugging her, she said, "Sarah, you make me feel so good. I am grateful to have someone like you to share an apartment with. You are very kind to me, and I really appreciate it very much, more than words can express my inner feeling toward you."

Sarah, with her cunning smile, walked over to Callie and gave her a big hug saying, "You are my sister."

Callie looked at Sarah, realizing that they did favor each other and a lot of people had referred to her and Sarah, saying, "I saw your sister the other day at the grocery store," or sometimes, to Sarah, "I heard that your sister is going to join the choir." Callie walked over to the mirror hanging on the wall and looked at herself in the mirror. . . . Then she looked at Sarah again. Sarah said, "I'll tell you the whole story one day. . . ." Then she asked Callie, "You never heard that we are sisters?"

Callie said, "No."

Sarah said, "During those days, people kept a lot of secrets to themselves. You see, when your mother gave birth to your brother Jacob, she became ill. She was sick for a long period of time. Your older brother and older sister were in school. There were good neighbors, at that time, and they would offer their services, if needed. When some of the other neighbors were unable to offer their services, they would notify my mother and ask her to help out, those days when they were unable to give a hand to help with the chores at the house. Your father would pick up my mother and carry her to the house. Many times, my mother would go with your father to shop for the groceries and other things that were needed in the house.

"It was told to me that my mother would go over to help out with the chores of the house, in addition to helping your father to do the shopping, my mother would help with the changing of the bedsheets, and she would help wash the dirty clothes, and she would help in cooking of the meals. My mother even helped your mother with her baths and kept her on schedule taking her medicine.

"It seemed that your father needed other favors during the long period of time that his wife was sick. I think that my mother was the youngest neighbor helping out, at that time, and since your father was with my mother more than the others while doing the shopping his attention was drawn to her. It was during that time when my mother got pregnant. My aunt said that I was born nine months later.

"It seems that my features favor yours but not your sisters' and brothers'. On the other hand, your features favors mine, as well as, my sisters' and brothers'."

"It was my aunt that revealed this secret to me," said Sarah. "It was after my aunt insisted that my mother admitted to me that I could be your father's child. I knew about this before you came to live with me, Callie."

"Why you did not tell me, Sarah?"

"Well, I figured, in time I would tell you, now you know that we are, in fact, sisters."

Callie and Sarah hugged and hugged and cried and laughed.

"These type of stories you do not go around telling people; you keep them secret, like my mother and your father did for a long time. It was my talkative aunt that broke the story, Callie."

"I am glad she did, Sarah. I had noticed that a lot of people asked me, 'How is your sister?' I would always say, "She is fine.'

"Sarah, since I have been here with you I noticed that you treat me like a sister. Now I can say we are sisters."

"Aunt Mamie's son, Joey, who lives on Macon Street told me that his mother is coming to visit them when his wife gives birth to their third child. If she does come, Callie, I will invite her over and she can verify what I told you about our close relationship. . . . We are sisters."

7
Finding a Reliable Male Companion

Callie, with a smile on her face, approached Sarah saying, "Sarah, I will use some of that makeup that you bought the other day on my face tomorrow morning before I go to work."

Sarah, in a moment of silence, with a smile thought to herself, *I knew that Callie needed some more cosmetics so she could decorate her face like ladies are accustomed to doing. That's why I bought a new supply of cosmetics.* Callie gave her reason why she wanted to look her best at work the next day, because the new guy she met a few days ago would, instead of looking at her, approach her to start a conversation, which would eventually lead to a date.

Sarah said, "You are a nice-looking your lady without the make-up, Callie."

Callie said, "Sarah, why do people shine their shoes?"

"So they will look better, of course."

"Then if I make-up my face I will look better, yes?"

"Yes, Callie, you got a point there. Use whatever you want, Callie. That's why I bought the cosmetics in the first place, so you could use whatever you wanted to use."

Sarah got home a while before Callie arrived. Sarah was waiting for the good news from Callie. Callie came in and threw her handbag on the chair. Sarah said, "Well?"

Callie, with a snap in her voice, said, "That guy did not even show up at work today. . . . I like his nerve. After I went to all of this trouble trying to look nice for him, he did not even show up for work today. I only wanted to impress him."

Sarah said, "Callie, maybe he was sick."

Callie said, "He'd better be sick."

Sarah knew that Callie was upset, but those things were expected in life.

Callie said, "Maybe it's because he is the first man I met since I am here that I like."

"You will have a chance to meet a lot of them in the future, Callie."

One of the most important aspects of Callie's future was finding a male companion, Someone that was reliable, trustworthy, understanding, and cooperative. She could be too hasty in relying on one guy. She had to compare a lot of them.

When Callie returned home the next day, she did not appear to be frustrated; she was, apparently, sure that he was sick. This was Friday and Callie had received her second check from her new job as a typist. "Can you imagine that I have been working for two months as a provisional employee?"

How could Callie call this guy her new boyfriend? They only met about two days ago. Maybe it was because Callie was very anxious to have a boyfriend of her own. This guy had a line, and Callie accepted him on the spot. She would think of what Sarah said then and not be too hasty. There were no background checks on this guy at all. He did not know where Callie lived, and he did not know anything about Callie's background, either.

From her past experience with these so-called city slickers, Sarah felt that it was time that she warn Callie to be on her guard at all times. Sarah, the consoler, told Callie not to fall for these guys on the spur of the moment, because some of them might have a false affection for someone like her, especially if they know that she was new here. "You should talk to them and listen to them closely to see and hear what they are saying. Don't you remember the bragging guy that you met at the Savoy Ballroom affair? Well, there are a lot of them around. Just be careful, Callie.

"When you listen to them talk, you should also watch their reactions. It seems that when you meet a guy from the South, most times he changes his behavior. They, apparently think that if they change their behavior, then they are acting like a New Yorker."

Sarah's suggestion was to go with the guy for a while, like several months. "Give yourself a chance to learn what the new guy is interested in, what he does for a living. What about his past? If you follow these guidelines, you can sorta figure them out. What they do now possibly will be what they will do in the future. Do not take anything for granted.

Sarah continued, saying that some of these guys only wanted to take you to Lovers' Lane. "Remember, Callie, that you are my sister and anything that hurts you, hurts me as well."

"OK, Sarah, I will follow those guidelines."

When Callie reported to work Monday morning, she noticed a group of provisional workers had been invited into a side room. Here they were given applications for the typing exam. The exam was scheduled to take place on Worth and Church Streets in two weeks. Callie was wondering why they did not give her an application to take the exam with the group of provisionals.

The supervisor gave the exam takers the rest of the day off, and as they were leaving, she said, "Be on time for the exam, and good luck."

The supervisor explained to Callie later that she would not be ready to take the typist exam until the next time that the typist exam was given. The supervisor further stated that these provisionals had been here a long time and their typist exam was long overdue.

Later that day, Callie looked around in the large office to see if the new guy she had met was at work today. She did not see him anywhere.

Callie brazenly walked over to the supervisor and asked her if Mr. Kemp was at work that day. The supervisor told Callie that Mr. Kemp had been transferred to another office. Mr. Kemp was a social investigator. Callie said, "Thanks," and started to walk away.

The supervisor said, "Wait a minute, Callie."

Callie returned to the supervisor's desk and stood for a while. Finally, the supervisor turned around in her swivel chair, and as she faced Callie, she asked, "Callie, did Mr. Kemp persuade you to fall for his cunning, persuasive technique, luring you to go out with him on a date?"

Callie said, "No, because we only talked for a short period of time."

"Well, that is the reason he did not persuade you to go out with him on a date." The supervisor continued, saying, "He has persuaded several of the new female workers here to go out with him on a date in the past two or three years. He is classified here in the office as just a flirt. You should be happy that he did not get the chance to talk to you a second time. Otherwise, you would be like some of the other ladies here beguiled by Mr. Kemp."

Callie rushed into the apartment upon arrival from work. Sarah could see that something was on Callie's mind and it was not good. Sarah did not wait for Callie to say anything. Sarah said, "What happened today on the job, Callie?"

Callie responded saying, "One thing that was not good for me, yet it seems that it did happen for the best way out of it."

Sarah said, "Oh."

Callie continued, saying, "You know that new guy that I told you I met on the job?"

"Yes," said Sarah.

"Well, he turned out to be just a flirt. The supervisor told me that he lured several of the new female workers out on dates in the past two or three years and he just walked out of their lives without any remorse whatsoever, and he had the nerve to come and talk to them as if nothing had happened between them in the past."

"Remember I said not to rush into any situation, especially if it's with a male companion, Callie?"

"Yes, Sarah, I can see that some of these warnings are true. I will be more careful in the future."

Tuesday, Callie came in almost like she had come in on Monday. Sarah was waiting, and she again asked Callie, "What happened on the job today, Callie?"

Callie responded in a positive way this time. She said, "The supervisor gave our applications for the typing exam scheduled to be given in two weeks."

Sarah said, "Are you happy about that, Callie?"

"Yes, and I will have to practice on some of the questions that they might ask on the exam."

Sarah said, "That's better news than that new guy who would have lured you out on a date and then would have walked out of your life like he did to the other ladies."

"You are right, Sarah, and do you know that he knew that he was going to be transferred and he did not tell me anything about it?"

"Now you can see the type of guy he is. . . . All he wanted to do was take you to lovers' lane. That would have been his objective, Callie. I am glad that he is out of your life, Callie.

"Anyway, Callie, what type of work did that guy do at your office?"

"He was a social investigator. My job is to type up cases as a result of his investigations with his clients and the other social investigators' clients."

"At least, he had a good job, but his character was not good for you, Callie."

Callie said, "Now I can concentrate on the typing exam, which is scheduled to be given in two weeks."

While Sarah was in the kitchen preparing her shopping list, Callie was waiting for her in the living room. Callie's mind was not idle; her mind was in a state of recollection of past events regarding how easy the typist exam was back home in Avon, Georgia. She realized that here in New York City the typist exam would be more difficult. It's not the typing part, per se; it was the other questions that they might include on the exam.

Callie arrived at Worth and Church Streets about forty-five minutes before the exam was scheduled to begin. Callie remembered how Miss Singer, who taught her how to type, had told her how to prepare herself before taking an exam. Callie did compose herself, but when she saw such a large group gathering for the exam, Callie got nervous. She turned around and walked about a block away. She stood there for a while. Finally, she blurted out, "How can I ignore this huge crowd here to take the exam?"

Nevertheless, Callie walked into the building with the crowd of about two hundred applicants. Callie settled down in her seat assigned to her for the exam. Each applicant was given instructions for the exam. The lady in charge said, "Good luck."

Callie was one of the first to pass her typing papers in to the lady in charge. The monitor had clocked Callie at 122 words per minute. Callie did not know this until she received her results, about one week later. Callie said to Sarah, "It's time for me to celebrate. . . . I am now a permanent worker. I can now do some of the things that I wanted to do a long time ago, like buy some new clothing, shoes, coats, or whatever I want to buy."

Callie told Sarah that she made the highest score in the group from her office. The runner-up made 119 words per minute.

Callie, in a happy state of mind, told Sarah that she was going to buy herself a new wristwatch. She said that she was ashamed of her old wristwatch and that was why she did not wear it to work.

Callie took a few days off from her job. She told Sarah that she was going shopping in downtown Brooklyn. Sarah laughed and said, "Do you need me to help you carry all of your packages when you finish shopping?"

Callie laughed and said, "I don't think that I will have that many packages, Sarah. There will always be other times when I can go shopping; I do not have to buy everything on this one trip."

Sarah said, "OK."

Callie started her shopping spree at one of the department stores in downtown Brooklyn. There is a saying "shop until you drop." This was what Callie was doing. It was more cosmetics, rings, a new watch, three pairs of earrings, something for her hair, etc., etc. Callie had several packages to take with her to the subway She could hardly carry everything. She stopped inside the subway station, took out the box with her new wristwatch, took the watch out, and put it on her left arm. She could hardly wait to display her new wristwatch on her arm.

The merchant had set the wristwatch before he put it into the box when she bought the watch. After looking at the watch on her arm for a while, she proceeded to go home on the subway.

After the train reached Nostrand Avenue and Fulton Street, Callie got off the train and proceeded up to the street level. Callie backed up to let a few cars pass, then started to cross the street. When she reached the north side of Fulton Street and Nostrand Avenue, Callie dropped three of her packages. She then threw the other packages to the ground. Callie appeared to be very irritable.

From diagonally across the street from where Callie was standing a young man started walking across the street toward where Callie was. As he approached Callie, he said in a soft-spoken voice, "Miss, you seem to be having problems carrying your packages."

Callie looked at the young man in a dazed-looking condition. She appeared to be confused. However, she recalled Sarah asking her, "Do you need me to help you carry your packages?" She realized that she had purchased too many packages on this one shopping trip. Then she asked herself, *Why did I buy all of these things?* Then she convinced herself that she needed all of these things that she had bought.

Meanwhile, the young man was still standing there to offer his help. Callie said, "I am sorry, mister. I just had my mind on something that happened to me lately."

The young man asked, "Is it serious?"

Callie said, "No, it's just that I let myself buy too many packages on one shopping trip, that's all. Oh, mister, it's a long story. Maybe I am silly for acting like this. Mister, I am sorry. I will feel better when I get home, where I can relax for a while."

"Where do you live, miss?"

"I live on Halsey Street, near Nostrand Avenue. That's not too far," he said. "Can I help you carry those packages, miss?"

She said, "Yes."

The young man started picking up the packages, and when he saw that one box was opened he asked, "Did you lose something from this box?"

She said, "No," showing him her new watch on her arm.

After picking up the packages, they started walking toward Halsey Street. Callie felt that she should explain to this young man why she had so many packages. She said, "Mister, you see, I have two days off from work and I decided to go shopping. It was not my intention to buy so many things on this trip, but I guess I got excited and bought the things that I needed, that's all."

The young man said, "You are lucky that you can buy this much at one time, miss. There are a lot of people that cannot buy half as much as you bought, miss."

Callie said, "I agree with that statement, mister."

"What kind of work do you do, miss? "I work for the Department of Welfare."

"Oh, that's a good job," the young man replied. He said, "I am a long-distance truck driver."

Callie said, "That must be exciting. Where do you go?"

"I go as far as California, Arizona, and Ohio, to mention a few places that I go."

"Is that exciting, going to all of those different places?"

He said, "Yes, but you soon get used to it. Then it's just a job that you have to do."

They were approaching Callie's address. Callie said, "This is where I live with my sister, mister."

Callie opened the door and asked the young man to put the packages, pointing, "Over there."

He said, "My name is Bobby Ryan."

"And my name is Callie Watts. Nice to meet you."

"Same here."

"Thanks a lot, mister, or Mr. Ryan. Can I give you a drink or something?"

He said, "No thank you."

As he left, Callie said, "Thank you very much for the help that you gave me."

When Sarah came home, she noticed that Callie had all of the things that she had bought spread out on the bed, even the shoes. Sarah walked into the room saying, "My, what a shopping spree you had today. How did you bring all of these things home, Callie?"

Callie answered, saying, "A young man that I met helped me to bring them home."

"You mean that you met another man . . . another new man?"

Callie said, "Yes, but he only helped me bring the packages home."

Both ladies smiling, Sarah picked up some of the things with a gesture of admiration.

Callie said, "I *could* have used your help, Sarah.

"You know Sarah, when I came upstairs to the street level at the Nostrand Avenue subway station, I dropped three of the packages and I threw the rest of the packages to the ground, laughing. This man walked over to me saying, 'Miss, can I help you?' You know that I did not say anything. I guess the man thought that I was crazy. I stood there for a while before I answered him. I think that he asked me twice, 'Can I help you?' I said, 'Yes, thank you.'

"I was very rude. Anyway, we talked as we walked home. He is single, and he described himself as being on the road most of the time. He named a few more places that he goes, in addition to California, Ohio, et cetera. I told him that I work for the city Welfare Department as a clerk typist. I also told him that I was single. The man, after putting the packages that he was carrying down, simply turned and walked away. In a way, Sarah, I wanted him to flirt with me. If I had been in a better mood, maybe he would have flirted with me, like Mr. Kemp did. I might not even see him again."

Callie was thinking that she was her own worst enemy when it came to meeting a nice male companion. She was thinking that she turned them off with her attitude at times. Callie promised herself that she was going to try to be more careful in the future.

Callie turned over in her bed, saying, "What is for you, you will get. All you have to do is be patient and wait for it to happen."

Sarah heard a loud noise outside, and she went to the door to check to see what it was. Whatever it was, by the time Sarah opened the door it was not there anymore. Sarah said to herself, *That was strange.* Whatever it was, it had disappeared. While Sarah was looking around, she saw Callie coming home from work. Sarah noticed that Callie appeared to be in a jolly mood.

As Callie entered, the house, Sarah said, "My, you look to be very jolly, Callie. What happened to you today at work?"

Callie said, "Wait. I have to go to the bathroom, and I will tell you all about it . . . after I use the bathroom."

Sarah sat down and waited for Callie to come out of the bathroom. Callie came and plop, she sat down in a nearby chair.

Callie related her story about what happened when she arrived at work today. Callie started by saying, "When I got to work today or this morning, one of the girls told me that the supervisor was waiting for me. . . . She wants to see me in her office. I am thinking now, *What did I do wrong?* I had two days off last week, Thursday and Friday, but I had permission to be off. That was part of my annual leave."

Callie had braced herself and walked into the supervisor's office, where she said, "One of the girls said that you wanted to see me." The supervisor said, "Yes. Sit down," pointing to the chair. The supervisor asked, "How did you enjoy the days off from work last week?" Callie responded by saying that she enjoyed those two days and wished for some more days off just to relax.

The supervisor said, "I have some good news for you."

Callie said, "Yes," and waited for the supervisor to speak of the good news.

Callie, while squirming in her seat, was eager to hear what the supervisor had to say. Meanwhile, the supervisor was looking over some papers that were on her desk. It seemed that the supervisor was only concerned with her daily work routine.

Finally, the supervisor looked up and said, "I am sorry, Callie. Look at all of this work that I have to do, possibly today." Then the supervisor said, "The good news is that you are in line for a promotion."

Callie said, "A promotion? I am eager to hear what it is."

The supervisor continued. She said, "You made the highest typing score on that examination from this office. Congratulations."

Callie jumped up and said, "Thank you, because I worked very hard preparing myself for that examination."

The supervisor continued, saying, "The supervisor over in the typist section is leaving, or rather, she has already left, and we have to get a replacement for that position." Looking at Callie, the supervisor said, "Would you accept that position, Callie?"

Callie now jumped up saying, "Yes, yes. I will accept that position."

Sarah said, "How many supervisors do you all have in that office, Callie?"

Callie said, "There is a supervisor over each section, like in this case over the typist section, one over the social investigators, one over the recording section, and we have the main supervisor over the whole office. He is sometimes called the head supervisor."

Sarah said, "You deserve a celebration. In only six months you are a supervisor, Callie. Congratulations. You need a man to take you out to dinner, Callie."

Callie was in favor of Sarah's suggestion and said that she would settle with Sarah and her friend and a few other friends to take her for dinner. Sarah told Callie that she would pursue that celebration in the near future.

* * *

It was Sunday morning and Callie looked like she was partying all night. Sarah came into her room and quickly observed that Callie was in no mood for conversation. Sarah, being alert, said, "Oh" as if she had forgotten to do something before coming into Callie's room. She backed up and went into the living room.

Meanwhile, the telephone rang and Sarah answered the phone. It was for Callie. After Callie answered the phone, she remained in the living room with Sarah. Sarah sat silently waiting for Callie to speak. Callie appeared to be searching for the proper words to tell Sarah about how she felt about her new appointment as a supervisor. Finally, Callie spoke out.

Callie told Sarah that she felt a little depressed because on Monday she would be assigned to the position as supervisor over the typist section, the same section where she worked with the girls that she would be the supervisor over. But she emphasized that it was not that causing her to be depressed; it was because the former supervisor left hastily and she did not have anybody to break her in on the new job.

Sarah said, "You should feel happy, being promoted to a supervisory job in less than one year." Sarah continued, saying, "I know that you are concerned about the other girls, but it comes a time that you have to think about yourself. To be promoted to supervisor over the typing section in just six months you must have had something going for you to be qualified for that big step in your job. You had something for them to select you over the other girls who were working there before you came. I know that you made the highest score on the typist examination, but you have other qualities that played an important part in this selection, Callie.

"Callie, forget about what people think. If I were you, Callie, I would rejoice and let the chips fall where they may. . . . There's a possibility, that the chips will fall in your favor."

"It won't be easy. You see, Sarah, I did not realize at the time that I would not have anybody to break me in on the new job. The supervisor, or rather the former supervisor, of the typing section left rather promptly . . . without a going-away party . . . nothing; she just left."

"Well, Callie, I guess she must have had a reason for leaving like that."

"Only she knows, because she certainly did not tell anybody that she was leaving at this time, Sarah."

"Let's go to church this morning. Maybe you will feel more secure after you listen to a good sermon by the preacher."

* * *

"Good morning, Callie. I enjoyed yesterday, Sunday, but it seems that we are not satisfied . . . we want two Sundays to rest, but you cannot have everything you would like to have; therefore, you have to settle for what we have. Have a good day, Callie. I will see you when I come home from work."

"OK, Sarah, same here."

* * *

"Good morning, Miss Supervisor."

"Good morning, Sue," Callie answered. Callie was wondering why Sue spoke to her like that. Was she being sarcastic? *Maybe she thought that I would take it as a joke . . . Speaking to me like that. Anyway, I will ignore it and treat her the same as I did when I was her coworker and not her superior in the office.*

Later, the head supervisor came by Callie's desk and gave her some transmittal sheets. He explained to her that the transmittal sheets are used to send the typewritten material to the central office.

Callie felt relieved, because this was part of what she would have been told by the former supervisor in breaking her in on the new job as supervisor of the typist section.

Callie compiled all of the typewritten sheets that the typists had typed up last Friday, prepared the transmittal sheets, which were easy to follow, and attached the transmittal sheets to last Friday's work and put everything into the outgoing basket, which would be picked up later. Callie felt more confident in her duty as a supervisor.

Callie recalled that the former supervisor used to give them work to be typed up during their assignment for the day. Callie collected the material to be typed up and distributed those sheets to the typists and explained what should be put on the sheets. Callie, knew how to type up these forms from her past experience typing them up when she was one of the typists in the section. Callie did not have to emphasize how these forms should be typed, because the girls, like Callie, knew how to type them up.

The day passed without any confusion whatsoever. This made Callie feel more sure of herself in performing her duties as a supervisor. Now she could hardly wait to tell Sarah about her first day on the job as a supervisor.

When Callie reached home, she found Sarah sitting in the living room, waiting for her to arrive. When there was something to be discussed by Sarah and Callie, they usually ended up in the living room. Now they spoke a little but did not say anything much, because it was obvious what the discussion was to be about.

Sarah asked, "Do you have to go to the bathroom, first?"

"No," said Callie.

When Callie and Sarah were discussing something about each other, they tended to evaluate each point carefully. They tried to be precise on each point, as if they were obligated to make a high score on an examination, etc. If, however, they found that one of them needed to improve herself in her social behavior, appearance, promptness, character, or anything that applied to decorum, the other helped her to make those corrections. They listened to each other as if a mother was advising her daughter to make certain adjustments. It worked both ways; that is, Sarah advised Callie and in some cases Callie advised Sarah. They always listened to each other.

In this case, it was Callie's responsibility to report to Sarah on how she handled her new position as supervisor over the typist section where she was one of the typists.

Callie told Sarah that she would start from the beginning of her first day on the job as a supervisor. Callie told Sarah that when she reached the typing section she was greeted by one of her former coworkers, who said, "Good morning, Miss Supervisor!"

"I did not expect that type of greeting and I took it as a sarcastic gesture on her part, because we were coworkers before. I simply took it as a joke and ignored the possibility of her being sarcastic, because I am now her superior.

"The next episode was that the head supervisor came to my desk and gave me some transmittal forms that I had to use in sending the typewritten work to the main or central office. That was a relief, because I knew then that this was part of my duty as a supervisor. . . . That made me feel happy, because it seems that I can rely on the head supervisor for guidance.

"Sarah, I am just going to take it one day at a time."

"That's the right attitude, Callie. I am sure that you will find that everything will fall into place. If not, just ask your head supervisor for help."

"I have a suggestion, Sarah."

"What is it, Callie?"

"I was thinking that I should invite my mother to come and spend some time with us."

"That's a good suggestion, Callie."

"What about this suggestion, Sarah? . . . I am thinking that I should get my own apartment."

"Now, Callie, I do not agree with that suggestion. But if your mother would not like sleeping in the back room, Callie, I could rent a room from Gail next door. Gail lives alone, and I bet she would be happy to have your mother live with her for a few months."

"Yes, Sarah. Gail seems to be a nice person. Anyway, I have to write to my mother and ask her if she would like to come and spend some time with us.

"The last letter that I received from my mother, she seemed to be depressed. She needs a vacation. Maybe that's easy for me to say. My mother may think differently. She is like that you know, Sarah."

"Yes, Callie, I know a lot about your mother's ways. To help her to decide, I will send her a note in your letter, Callie."

"OK, Sarah."

During the day, Callie felt that something was going to happen to her. It was Thursday, and Callie was preparing the work for the typists to do on Friday. Callie had to attend a meeting first thing when she arrived at work Friday morning. On her way home, she changed her mind about stopping at the store, because she felt that Sarah might join her when she went shopping at the store near the house.

As she walked slowly, she noticed two men in her path up ahead. The men were engaged in conversation. The men were near the corner of Nostrand Avenue and Halsey Street. Callie did not pay any attention to the men as she passed.

One of the men said, "Hi, Miss Watts."

Callie said to herself, *Oh, he recognizes me.* As she looked around, she recognized one of the men as Mr. Ryan.

As he, Mr. Ryan, walked toward her, he said, "How are you?"

"I am fine," Callie responded.

Mr. Ryan told Callie that he had been on a trip to Ohio and a few other places in that vicinity and he just returned yesterday, which was Wednesday.

Callie said, "How have you been doing?"

"Fine," he said, "except that I have been working steady for the last few months." Mr. Ryan asked Callie, "How have you been for the last few months? I think that's when we met for the first time, wasn't it?"

Callie said, "I believe so."

Mr. Ryan asked, "How are you doing on the job? You are a clerk typist, are you not?"

Callie responded by saying that she was a clerk typist at that time, but since then she had been promoted to supervisor over the typist section.

"Oh," he said, "congratulations. That means that you are doing or have been doing a good job, to warrant a promotion."

Callie said, "I guess so."

"Did you celebrate your good fortune yet?"

Callie said, "No, not yet." Callie continued by saying that she was inviting her mother to come and spend some time with her and her sister.

"That's very good," responded Mr. Ryan.

"I expect to have my mother share in my celebration when she comes to visit us."

Mr. Ryan asked Callie if he could walk her home.

She said, "Yes."

Mr. Ryan turned and waved to his friend, standing on the corner, to let him know that he had another assignment to fulfill at this time.

Mr. Ryan commented "You do not have a lot of packages that I can help you to carry home this time?"

Both smiling, Callie said, "No, not this time."

As Mr. Ryan and Callie approached the house, Mr. Ryan asked, "When can I see you again?"

Callie said, "Today is Thursday. What about the weekend?"

Mr. Ryan said, "That will be fine with me. Maybe we can go to the movies either Sunday or Saturday."

Callie said, "Saturday, because I am going to church on Sunday."

Mr. Ryan as he walked away stopped, turned around, looked at Callie, and said, "Why don't we start calling each other by our first names?"

Callie said, "My namc is Callie."

Mr. Ryan said, "My name is Bobby, Bobby Ryan."

They agreed not to be too formal the next time they were together.

Bobby took Callie home after the movie and informed her that he would be back next Friday. Callie said, "OK, I will be waiting."

* * *

As Callie and Sarah sat in the living room, Sarah said, "Looks like you will have a male companion to take you out to celebrate your promotion after all, Callie."

Callie said, "Yes. But my mother said in her letter that she would not be able to come to visit us at this time, because her church is having a fund-raising campaign. My mother is a person very dedicated to the church. However, she hopes that she will be able to come in the near future."

Bobby returned by the weekend. That was a short trip. The first question that he asked Callie was: "Did your mother come to visit you-all?"

Callie in a low tone of voice said, "No." She said that her mother was part of a fund-raising campaign currently and she was part of that committee to raise money to do some needed repairs on her church.

Bobby said, "In that case, we can celebrate ourselves." Bobby told Callie that the reason that this last trip was short was because he had to attend a meeting of the long-distance truck drivers. He continued, saying that he was elected president of the Long-Distance Truck Drivers Association.

Callie said, "Congratulations. Now we can celebrate our promotions together."

Both smiling, said in unison, "Yes."

"It seems that we have something in common. Sarah and her friend said that they could join us in celebrating our good fortune."

"That will be fine," Bobby said. Bobby told Callie to set the date, because he had the next four days off work and would have to report to work on Monday.

Both agreed on Saturday and Sunday, the Saturday date scheduled to begin at about 2:30 P.M. Bobby told Callie to let Sarah and her friend know the time would be Saturday. He informed Callie that they would be going to a restaurant in Manhattan, the same restaurant where he was nominated president of the Long-Distance Truckers Association. He continued telling Callie that they were famous for serving good food. At this point, Callie left everything up to Bobby. Yet Bobby was thinking that he was taking Callie and Sarah over to Manhattan, yet he didn't know anything about Callie's likes or dislikes. He wanted to impress Callie on their first "big" date.

Bobby hesitatingly asked Callie, "Would you like for me to call a taxi to take us over to Manhattan?"

Callie, not familiar with the distance from Brooklyn to Manhattan, said, "No, that would be too expensive. Let's go by subway."

Bobby said willingly, "OK by me."

They, Bobby, Callie, Sarah, and Sarah's friend, walked to Nostrand Avenue and the Fulton Street Station, where Bobby remembered seeing Callie with a lot of packages and helping her to carry those packages home.

Bobby said, "I'll never forget this section, because this is where I saw you for the first time . . . remember? You had all of those packages."

Callie laughed and said, "There is a long story of why I had all of those packages at one time. That was my first shopping spree after I got the job working for the Department of Welfare. Those were much-needed things to replace the old things in my wardrobe. Usually, I do not buy a lot of things on one trip, but I needed those things and I bought them, not thinking that I had too much for me to carry at one time. Luckily, you came along to help me carry them home. As a rule, I shop very moderately. I shop when my needs are not so great." Smiling, Callie said, "In the future if I buy a lot of things at one time, I might not be so lucky as to meet another Mr. Ryan, or Bobby to help me carry my packages."

While both of them were laughing, they, along with Sarah and her friend, went down the stairs to catch the subway.

When they reached the restaurant, they seated themselves and placed their orders. Sarah's friend ordered champagne and proposed a toast to Callie and Bobby for their promotions.

After they returned home, Sarah thanked Bobby for selecting such a nice place to celebrate their good fortune of being promoted to a higher level. Sarah and her friend went inside, leaving Callie and Bobby outside.

Bobby told Callie how much he had enjoyed the outing, being with her, and informed her that he would pick her up tomorrow, which was Sunday, about the same time that he had picked her up today, Saturday.

Callie asked, "Where will we go tomorrow?"

Bobby replied, "To dinner, and if you wish, we will take in a movie."

Callie said, "OK."

Sarah's friend was leaving at this time, and both men left together.

8

Callie's New Male Companion

Callie felt that after accepting Bobby as her new male companion this changed her lifestyle, because now she felt that she had accomplished her aim in finding a reliable male companion. Now Callie turned over a new leaf in her new lifestyle, from day one to the inevitable lifestyle yet to come.

You can believe that Sarah was waiting for Callie to come inside so she could find out if Callie was satisfied with Bobby, if it would last, and if so, how long. Only Callie could give good answers to those questions.

Callie came inside and commented on how elegant the restaurant where Bobby took them was and how Bobby appeared to be a perfect gentleman. Callie continued, saying, "Do you remember when Bobby took me over to meet a couple that he had recognized sitting not far from where we were sitting? The gentleman was also a truck driver. The food was delicious. Do you remember when we walked around Times Square and he pointed out the various buildings and famous theaters to us?"

Sarah replied, saying, "Yes." Sarah, changing the subject, said, "Callie, I noticed that you do not use a lot of makeup. like you used to use."

"No," Callie said. "The reason is that Bobby mentioned or indicated in one incident that some ladies could use too much makeup. I took that as a cue not to use too much makeup on my face. Especially if Bobby is around."

Sarah said, "I think that you look better with little makeup on your face."

Sunday morning, Callie was ready and waiting for Bobby to come to pick her up so they could go on their second meaningful date. The doorbell rang. Callie opened the door and said, "Hi," as Bobby stood outside. Callie invited Bobby in for a moment. Bobby spoke to Sarah. As Bobby and Sarah talked, Callie finished what she had to do before leaving. Sarah informed Bobby that where he had taken them to celebrate was a very good restaurant. Bobby responded by saying that he took or selected that particular restaurant because it was like a landmark. His boss had taken them there when he was nominated as president of the truckers' association. This was when he discovered that they served good food. He continued, saying that when people discovered a good place they returned at a later date. "This is good business for them; if you serve good food, people will patronize your business more frequently. People like to enjoy themselves, and they go where they can enjoy themselves."

Sarah, while smiling, said, "Enjoy yourselves today like you did yesterday."

All were smiling at this point.

Both Callie and Bobby said, in unison, "OK," as they left the house.

As Bobby and Callie walked to the subway station, Bobby asked Callie, "Have you heard from your mother lately?"

Callie said, "Just a few a days ago I heard from my mother."

"How is she?" Bobby asked.

Callie told Bobby again that her mother was very active in the church and they were currently ending a fund-raising campaign."

Bobby replied, "For renovation, no doubt?"

Callie said, 'Yes, and they want to buy a bus for the church to take short trips for the members of the church."

Bobby told Callie that he was taking her to the Winter Garden Theater. He said that he heard that there was a good movie on the screen at this time. Callie, the girl from the country, was very excited. She did not show her emotions to Bobby. She simply acted as if she were familiar with New York City's majestic theaters.

After they left the theater, Bobby took Callie to a restaurant nearby. He warned Callie that he was not familiar with the restaurants in this area. It turned out to be a good restaurant. He then returned Callie home safely. After bidding Bobby good-bye, Callie checked to see if Bobby had left before rushing in to tell Sarah about her second outing with her new male companion.

Callie was very enthusiastic in relating to Sarah what she had experienced with Bobby on the theater party and dinner date. Callie literally hugged Sarah as she explained to Sarah what she had experienced on the second date with Bobby.

Sarah said, "You just wait until Bobby takes you to Radio City Music Hall, especially at Easter time or during the Christmas holidays. I am glad that you are enjoying yourself, Callie."

Callie responded by saying that she did not know that people could enjoy themselves going to these places. "I did not even realize the enjoyment one could have by going to these places. It's truly amazing that this type of entertaining can be developed in such a way as to be presented for entertainment purposes."

Sarah said, "Wait. What about Bobby's reaction toward you?"

Callie humbly said, "He hasn't kissed me as yet."

"Then," Sarah said, "you have to kiss him."

"No," Callie said, "I am too timid for that approach, Sarah. I do not want to be too aggressive. I will take it one step at a time, Sarah."

"I guess that it is better not to rush things. . . . Take your time."

"For one thing, Sarah, he is not a flirt . . . like one of my previous boyfriends."

"I know who you are talking about."

"I will wait to see what Bobby's next moves are. He seems to show his affections by assisting me when I am going up the stairs. He shows his interest by asking, 'How are you today? Do you feel well? How was your day at work?' He has not hugged me as yet. He does have a gentle touch when he catches my arm to assist me while I am going up the steps. Give him time, Sarah. I hope that everything will fall in place as time goes on.

"The next time Bobby is in town, I am going to invite him to one of our affairs. I will introduce him to some of my coworkers and friends."

Sarah replied by saying, "That is a nice gesture."

"We are planning on going on a long weekend trip Labor Day weekend for Saturday and Sunday, leaving Friday evening and returning on Monday. I will not invite him on that trip, because I feel that my exposure to him on such a trip for three days would be or might be too detrimental to our good relationship."

"Not so," Sarah said. "That exposure of yourself to him might be the right thing to do. Why don't you try it and see for yourself, Callie? You do not have to expose yourself to him every moment while you are there. Let him spend some time with the fellows who will be on the trip as well."

"You see, Sarah, how I was raised; girls do not expose themselves to men in a disorderly manner. They should continue to maintain their virginity as long as possible." Callie continued, "Bobby is due in town in two more days. I will set-up the appointment."

"I am in your corner," Sarah said.

Bobby contacted Callie about two hours after his arrival. Callie informed him of the weekend trip to Liberty, New York. It was called "The Welfare Center Personnel Weekend Trip." Bobby told Callie that he would stop by to see her in about two hours. Callie told Bobby, "OK."

Bobby was on time, as he had promised Callie. Callie showed Bobby the brochure. Bobby read it and said, "This is good. I will go with you-all on the trip. The only thing is that I have to have my suit dry-cleaned. When do I have to pay for the tickets?"

"When we board the bus," Callie replied.

Bobby said, "OK."

* * *

Bobby and Callie joined the group at Fulton Street and Stuyvesant Avenue, where they boarded the bus. Callie told Bobby that she had already paid for her ticket and all he had to do was pay for his ticket. Bobby paid the person who was in charge, and they left for Liberty, New York.

Upon arrival at the Liberty Manor, the men were shown the section where they would be staying, while the women were shown the section where they would be staying. They were given instructions to meet at the Social Hall at 8:00 P.M. for a little snack and to learn what the weekend at Liberty would consist of: Saturday morning at 9:00 A.M. breakfast in the dining room, lunch at 1:30 P.M., dinner from 7:30 to 9:00 P.M., social gathering (dancing) at the Social Hall from 10:00 P.M. to 1:30 A.M.; Sunday, same hours for the meals and at 9:30 P.M. a lecture on the purpose of the welfare system. Monday, after breakfast, the bus left for New York City. When the bus arrived at Fulton Street and Stuyvesant Avenue, Bobby and Callie boarded the trolley car that carried them to Fulton Street and Nostrand Avenue. They walked two blocks to Callie's address, on Halsey Street. Bobby explained to Callie how much he had enjoyed the trip with her to Liberty, New York, Callie said, "Same here."

Sarah was not at home when they arrived. Callie invited Bobby in for a while. Bobby complied and they talked and talked.

After about fifteen minutes, Bobby told Callie that he was leaving on another trip and was scheduled to leave next Tuesday at 9:00 A.M. This trip, he said, would last seven or eight days. He assured Callie that he would miss her very much. He continued, saying that she had become part of his life and he dreaded having to leave her behind. It now seemed he thought about her constantly and wished that she was near him.

Bobby stood up and said, "There is always a first time."

Callie was wondering what Bobby meant by making that statement. Then Callie said to herself, *Maybe he has more to say by that statement.* As she stood silently looking at Bobby, she found out very soon what Bobby meant by saying, "There is always a first time." Bobby pulled Callie up close to him and kissed her on the cheek as a starter. He then apologized to her for being so rude and backed up, away from her. Callie, looking as if she was in a daze, said, "That's OK, Bobby."

After a few moments of silence passed, Bobby approached her again and again kissed her on the cheek. Then the final blow came instantly. He kissed her again, but this time it was not on the cheek. Callie was almost breathless but not surprised. It seemed that they had gotten used to each other while they were dancing, that is, the feel of each other's flesh.

At this point, Bobby was overstaying his time. At a time like this, you can lose track of the time. Bobby knew that he had to leave. He backed up again, telling Callie that he was going to miss her very much. Callie said, "I will miss you, too, Bobby." Callie wished him luck on his trip and said she would be waiting for him when he returned.

Callie undressed for bed. Sarah came in with her friend. She spoke to Callie and remained in the living room, entertaining her friend. When Sarah's friend left, Sarah went into Callie's room to find out about the weekend in Liberty, New York, with the personnel of the Welfare Department. Callie told Sarah that Bobby appeared to be out of place in the beginning, but he soon fitted in with the fellows who had gone on the trip.

Callie outlined everything that happened on the trip: the meals, the activity, the sleeping quarters, and, in general how Bobby had reacted to her. Callie told Sarah that Bobby was a changed man now. "He is just now showing his affection for me. He hugged and kissed me tonight.

His reaction toward me makes me feel that he is the only man that I would want in my life for the rest of my life."

"My," Sarah gestured, saying that it took him a long time to reach that stage in their life.

Callie agreed and said, "I think that it is better to measure your next move. It is better to not be too hasty. I like it that way, Sarah."

"It seems that you are right, Callie."

Callie admitted to Sarah that this was the best time in her life. She was now beginning to enjoy her life on earth. "With this inspiration in life, Sarah, it makes me feel like I want to live forever."

"Oh, Callie, what did Bobby do to you? Anyway, I am happy for you. You deserve a change in your life." Sarah said, "The way you feel now, Callie, I am sure that you will rest well tonight." Sarah said, "Good night," and she went to her room.

As Callie adjusted herself in bed, she realized that her lifestyle was changing as a result of her friend Bobby and she said to herself that she had to turn over a new leaf and began to adjust herself to those inevitable changes in her life.

Callie returned to work with a lot of energy and more enthusiasm about her daily chores. Even the girls, the clerk typists, noticed Callie's behavior since the trip last weekend. The girls whispered to themselves but did not let their supervisor know that they noticed a change in her attitude since last week. Callie even typed up a few forms that normally the other girls would type up. Sarah noticed the change in Callie's behavior around the house. Sarah said, "God bless her, because she is living in a dreamworld."

The next day, Sarah reached home before Callie. Sarah took the mail out of the mailbox, and she noticed that the letter was from Bobby. Normally, Sarah left Callie's mail on a table near the door of the living room. Today Sarah held the letter in her hand until Callie arrived. Callie came in and looked on the table, but she did not see any mail for her. She spoke to Sarah, and meanwhile Sarah gave Callie her letter.

Sarah did not interrupt Callie while she read her letter from Bobby. When Callie finished reading the letter, she simply sat there speechless, emotionless, and without the knowledge of Sarah being present in the room with her. Then she stood up, threw up her hands, ran over to Sarah, and hugged and kissed her.

This gesture surprised Sarah.

"What is it, Callie?"

Sarah said. "Quickly."

Callie said, "Wait. I will read this part to you. Bobby did not hesitate to let me know that it had been or will be one year and two weeks since we began dating each other. He said: 'I am not a coward, but I feel to break the ice it's better by letting you know how I feel about you . . . as a lifelong companion . . . or a wife, if you will.' Anyway, he continued: 'You can think about that possibility by the time I return to New York City.'

"Oh, Sarah, can you imagine how I feel at this moment?"

"Yes, Callie, I know how elated you are. Just remember to take it one step at a time and between those times formulate your plans in a way to make him happy, always.

"If you need my advice, Callie, I would suggest that you start making plans for a wedding."

"I hope that my mother is not helping in a fund-raising campaign this time, because I cannot get married if she is not here to witness the marriage ceremony."

"To be on the safe side, Callie, I will help you select the bridesmaids, help you select the type of dresses to be worn, and help you with the whole program to follow the wedding ceremony."

When Bobby returned to New York City, he stopped by to see Callie. After they had decided on where they wanted to get married and how soon, Bobby bought the engagement ring. The date was set for September 15, 1933. Bobby told Callie that since it was the middle of September she would be his early Christmas present . . . a long-lasting Christmas present . . . for the rest of his life. Bobby told Callie that he was leaving in a few days, but he would take about a month off from work for the wedding. "Meanwhile," he said, "you can start looking for an apartment where we will live."

Sarah and Callie started looking for an apartment two days after Bobby left to go on another trip, on his job. They were lucky to find an apartment on Herkimer Street, near Ralph Avenue. Bobby had given Callie some money to make a down payment on some furniture. Callie, with Sarah, selected the furniture and paid a deposit on the furniture. Then Callie requested that the landlord paint the apartment before she requested delivery of the furniture. Callie even started staying in the new apartment for a few days before Bobby returned to Brooklyn. Sarah stayed with her in the new apartment.

Sarah along with Callie set up the furniture arrangement in the apartment, which consisted of the main bedroom, the living room, the hall bedroom, the kitchen, and the bathroom. Callie figured that to persuade her mother to come and not ask her to stay with them for a long period of time, she would send a round-trip ticket. This way, Callie said, her mother would come, realizing that she would not be forced to stay for a long period of time.

Sarah asked Callie if she was going to stay in her new apartment after she (Sarah) left after spending a few days with Callie to break in the new apartment. Callie said "No, I am going to go back to your apartment with you. Remember, Sarah, Bobby and I are not married as yet."

Callie said that the next night that she stayed in her new apartment would be with her new husband.

Sarah said, "Excuse me. I see that you have already made your plans on how you are going to approach your future, staying with your new husband."

"Yes indeed," Callie replied.

Bobby had something that he wanted to tell Callie before he left to go on his last trip before their wedding, but he could not remember what it was. Now he had returned two days before the wedding date. He contacted Callie, saying, "I remember what I wanted to request of you; invite your mother."

"I have already invited her. I sent her a round-trip ticket so she would not refuse to come to our wedding."

Bobby said, "You know when I want to ask you to do something I find that you have already done it. I like how you think, Callie, and how you respond to different situations. It seems that you can read my mind and do the things that I want you to do. That's good; that's very good, Callie. You are the woman that has captured my heart and self-esteem."

Bobby later called Callie to inform her that he was on his way over to Sarah's apartment. He also informed Callie that he rented a car, so they wouldn't have to walk to the apartment and could do some shopping. Callie and Sarah were ready and waiting for Bobby to arrive.

Callie opened the door to the apartment.

Bobby walked in behind Sarah and Callie. Bobby looked around and said, "This is amazing, such beautiful furniture, and how neatly it is arranged." Bobby knew that the furniture was expensive, so he asked Callie, "Do you have the bills?"

"Yes," Callie responded. Then she explained that she had put a down payment on the furniture or, rather put a deposit on the furniture and arranged to make monthly payments until the whole bill was paid off. She gave him the balance to be paid and the time limit left to pay it.

Bobby realized how efficient his wife-to-be was; he told Sarah to excuse him. He walked over to Callie and hugged and kissed her. Bobby then said, "I want both of you to know that I am very happy."

Sarah responded by saying, "We want you to be happy, Bobby." He then kissed Sarah on the cheek. Both ladies had tears in their eyes. They could tell that Bobby's eyes were also tearing. All three of them were very happy of how everything was progressing for a better future for their lives . . . together.

The wedding was set for September 15, 1933, Callie, it seemed, was the child most devoted to her mother and felt obligated to follow her mother's request, even in marriage. It was Callie's mother who had advised her to learn a trade. As her mother emphasized, even if you did not pursue that trade as a lifelong job, you should learn it anyway. Callie already knew how to sew, taught by her mother. When the neighborhood school in Avon, Georgia, hired a teacher who offered her services in teaching typing for free at the school, Callie was one of the first to register for the course. Callie's mother believed in the principle of "it's better to know it and not need it than to need it and not know it." It was for that reason that Callie, when she came to Brooklyn in 1932 and needed a job borrowed a typewriter, so she could practice her skills in typing, applied for a job as a typist, took an examination, passed the examination with the highest score of the whole group, and in six months was a supervisor of the typing section at the office where she worked. Part of her success was, however, luck. The former supervisor resigned her job, leaving that spot vacant. Callie was qualified to fulfill that position, and she was lucky to get the job . . . as supervisor over the section where she had been one of the clerk typists.

The other advice that Callie's mother insisted on was, "If you are to get married, get married in a church." Callie had attended service at one of the nearby Methodist churches, and she had met the minister of the church, the Right Reverend Charles Few, on previous visits to the church. Now, remembering what her mother had advised her to do, Callie had already arranged the wedding plans with the minister of the church, so everything would be in order when Bobby returned to Brooklyn for the wedding. Callie was, however, late in making her request for a big wedding at the church, but the minister assured her that he could arrange for a small wedding in the church September 15, 1933.

This was how the wedding plans were set up by the officiating minister, the Right Reverend Charles Few.

The Wedding Party

Matron of honor: Sarah Smalls
Maid of honor: Dolly Smith (a friend of Callie's from the Center)
Best man: Bill Burris, Sr.
Flower girl: Chessie Dol
Ring bearer: Bill Burris, Jr.

From Sarah's record collection she was able to furnish the music, while her male friend controlled the record player for the bridal procession with "The Bridal Chorus" by Richard Wagner and for the recessional the "Wedding March" by Felix Mendelssohn. Joe Smith, Dolly's husband, would act as Callie's father, giving her away.

Since the wedding was not a big wedding, there would not be any: bridesmaids, groomsmen, or a Bible bearer. The wedding would take place at night, and only a few close friends, relatives, and other onlookers would be present to witness this "historical wedding."

Bobby, the president of the Truckers' Association was called by his boss to return on the job to outline the essential parts of the job that the new truck driver who would be filling in for Bobby while he was off for his wedding. Bobby would be back in plenty of time to get married to Callie.

Meanwhile, Callie was scheduled to meet her mother at Penn Station on September 12, 1933. Miss Sally Ann, Callie's mother, arrived on time at the station. She was greeted by her daughter Callie and Sarah. Miss Sally Ann did not hesitate to let her daughter know that she needed a new dress. Miss Sally Ann was an experienced seamstress, and Callie thought her mother would have made her own dress before coming to attend the wedding. Callie told her mother that she was getting married, not her (Callie's mother).

While the ladies were laughing, Miss Sally Ann said, "Yes, but I need a new dress to wear to your wedding, Callie, and I want one not made by my own hands. I have a few dollars in my purse, Callie."

Callie said, "OK, Mama, we are near Gimbel's Department Store, and we will go there to look for a new dress, and I will use my credit card to pay for it, Mama."

As the ladies walked across the street to Gimbel's Department Store, Miss Sally Ann looked up at the huge store and said, "This is a large building, Callie. You mean that you have credit at this store, Callie?"

"Yes, Mama, I have had an account here for several months now."

Miss Sally Ann looked down at her feet and said, "Maybe I need some new shoes as well."

Callie stopped and said, "Mama, do you need a whole new outfit?"

Miss Sally Ann said, "No, just a new dress and a pair of new shoes. After all, I want to look good at your wedding. Besides," she added, "I might meet a new boyfriend."

The ladies just laughed and laughed at Miss Sally Ann's remarks about finding a new boyfriend.

"I am available you know." As Miss Sally Ann admired the huge store, she said, "This is nothing like what we have back home in Avon, Georgia."

"Mama," Callie said, "this is a big city, the largest of all cities here in the United States of America."

Miss Sally Ann agreed, and they proceeded to look for the new dress and new shoes for her.

As the ladies shopped for the new dress, they came to the shoe section first. Callie said, "No, we'd better buy the dress first, so we can match up the color of the shoes.

"Here they are," Sarah said.

Callie called her mother over to the rack where the dress was.

Miss Sally Ann spotted a dress that she liked and held it up against her body, "How does this look?" she asked.

Callie assured her mother that the dress that she selected was beautiful. Sarah admired the dress as well. Callie produced her credit card and paid for the dress.

Miss Sally Ann said, "What about the shoes? I could use a new pair of shoes with this pretty dress."

Callie said, "OK," and went to the shoe department and purchased a new pair of shoes to match the dress.

Callie paid for the new shoes with her credit card. When Callie and Sarah started leaving the store, they noticed that Miss Sally Ann was lagging behind.

Callie turned around and asked her mother, "What now?"

Miss Sally Ann said, "In Avon, Georgia, they wear hats to a wedding."

Sarah and Callie agreed, and they went to the hat department and bought a new hat for her mother to wear with the new dress and new shoes.

As the ladies were leaving the store, Miss Sally Ann said, "With the new outfit that I will be wearing at the wedding, I know that I will look attractive. I want my picture made. I believe that I may be able to find a boyfriend in this outfit." While the ladies were laughing, Miss Sally Ann said, "You know that your father has been dead for several years now, Callie. Don't you think that I should start looking for another husband?"

"Are you lonesome at home now, Mama?"

Miss Sally Ann said, "Yes. I would appreciate having a new friend visit me from time to time. I am not dead as yet."

The ladies continued laughing.

The ladies returned to the waiting room where Sarah's friend was watching Miss Sally Ann's luggage. They gathered the luggage and boarded the subway for Brooklyn.

When they arrived at Sarah's apartment, Sarah looked to see if her old camera was in good working order. She did not want to disappoint Miss Sally Ann by not being able to take a picture of her in her new outfit.

* * *

The ladies were busy preparing for the wedding and checking to see if they were leaving something out that should be included. Sarah suggested that Miss Sally Ann try on her outfit to see if there were any adjustments to be made before the day of the wedding. That suggestion was favored by Miss Sally Ann until Sarah mentioned taking her picture while she was checking to see if her outfit fit her OK.

Miss Sally Ann said, "No. I cannot let you take my picture, because my hair is not groomed."

When Miss Sally Ann made that statement, Sarah looked at Miss Sally Ann, and Callie looked at both of them. All three ladies agreed that all three of them should go to the beauty parlor to get their hair groomed for the wedding.

Callie informed the other ladies that they would have to make an appointment with the beautician; they could not just go to the beauty parlor to get their hair done. They had to make an appointment first. Sarah assumed that responsibility and went to the beauty parlor and made appointments for all three of the ladies.

The ladies, after having their hair done, returned home. Miss Sally Ann tried on her outfit. Sarah took her picture and said, "You look beautiful in your new outfit. You might just attract some of the men who will be attending the wedding."

The ladies laughed.

Miss Sally Ann said, "I am in favor of that."

At this point, Bobby called Callie and told her that he had just arrived but would not stop by to see her, because he was scheduled to stop by the tailor to try on his new tuxedo.

Callie said, "OK," and told him that her mother had arrived and bought a new outfit and was ready for the wedding. Callie also told Bobby that she had made all of the arrangements for the wedding with the pastor of the church. All they had to do now was make sure that the photographer got there on time, before the wedding started.

When Bobby came by to see her, Callie informed him that she could only get a date at night for a September 15 wedding. Bobby expressed his disapproval, but Callie told him that she felt that it was all right, because there were some weddings that took place by the river, on a train, on a street, or even in a public park. Bobby had no other choice but to agree with Callie.

Bobby said, "I will see you tomorrow."

Callie said, "Tomorrow night," because she had to work until 5:00 P.M.

Bobby said, "In that case, OK."

Bobby came by to see Callie the next day, and Callie told him that there were only two more days before the wedding and that she would be in isolation and he wouldn't be able to see her until the night of the wedding.

"Where will you be staying?" Bobby asked.

Callie informed him that she would be staying with a friend from the office.

Bobby called Sarah and asked to speak to Callie, but Sarah said, "Sorry, Bobby, you won't be able to see Callie until the night of the wedding." It seems that Bobby could not understand that ruling. Reluctantly, Bobby had to accept that ruling, as a permanent decision.

Bobby was only thinking of Callie, because he felt that she needed him for something. Yet he realized that Callie was capable of handling anything, where a decision was to be made.

The day of the wedding night, Sarah secretly picked up Callie, and carried her to her apartment so she could dress for the wedding, and the three ladies were together again, and they could see that each of them was dressed properly. When they were finished dressing, Sarah carried them to the church. They met Reverend Few. They discussed, briefly, how they should start. They were in the pastor's study room. Sarah gave her record albums to her friend, and the pastor instructed him as to how he should play the records for the wedding.

They all agreed that the starting time would be 7:30 P.M. Sarah dropped Callie off at her friend's apartment. Miss Sally Ann returned with Sarah to Sarah's apartment. Nearing the starting time, the small audience was seated as they were coming in. Reverend Few noticed a few ladies coming in without hats. Reverend Few, realizing that this was an old tradition that all ladies attending a wedding must or should wear hats, said, "This is 1933, and the ladies over there," pointing in one direction, "should have hats on their heads. I know," Reverend Few said, "you are here and you do not have a hat and what can I do. Well, you can improvise by getting a handkerchief and tying it at each end. You can place it on your head. This will be sufficient for the wedding ceremony."

The ladies were able to get some of the men's handkerchiefs and tying each, as the minister suggested, were able to comply with the old tradition of wearing a hat while attending a wedding ceremony. After the ladies placed the handkerchiefs on their heads, Reverend Few said, "That's good. Now we will proceed with the wedding."

Bobby, the groom, came in looking for Callie, but Callie was not there yet. Apparently, Bobby was not familiar with the wedding ceremony procedure. Bobby stood wondering when she would appear.

At the appropriate time, Sarah's friend played Richard Wagner's "Bridal Chorus," Everyone was standing up and looking and looking at the entrance door; Bobby realized that this was when his wife-to-be would be coming in to join him.

The guests saw Callie dressed in her beautiful wedding gown as she marched in holding to her friend's husband's arm. Joe Smith was acting as Callie's father. Bobby, seeing his wife-to-be for the first time in three days, was almost breathless as he stood there, thinking, *Callie, in a matter of minutes, will be my wife.*

The nuptial ceremony began. The ceremony took about forty-five minutes, and relatives and friends witnessed the ceremony as they passed through the nuptial procedure.

The reception followed, in the Methodist church's Assembly Hall. The photographer continued taking pictures as each new development took place.

Callie suggested going to Fulton Street and Nostrand Avenue to have some pictures taken. Bobby said that it was strange that she would want some pictures taken there.

Callie, smiling, said, "Don't you remember that this is where we first met?" Bobby, remembering, said, while smiling, "This is where I saw you drop all of those packagers, on this corner . . . the same side that the Brevoort Bank is located."

Callie said, while still smiling, "Isn't that enough to want to remember this corner where that incident took place?"

Bobby suggested writing all of this down in their diary. "Then we could show it to our children."

Callie, still smiling, said, "Let's not rush having children at this time . . . because I want to serve as supervisor over the clerk typist section for at least one year before we start raising a family."

9

"I Am Bobby's Wife, Forever"

After the wedding, Bobby jokingly addressed Callie as "Mrs. Callie Ryan" and said, "You have to get used to your new name." Callie acknowledged what Bobby was saying to herself; that change in name would not be a problem for her. Only, however, the clerk typists in her section would have to change her last name from Watts to Ryan (Mrs. Ryan). She thought that they could deal with that without a problem.

Bobby and Callie selected Washington, D.C., to spend a few days on their honeymoon, because he had to return to the city to instruct the truck drivers who were assigned to transport a cargo of Christmas toys to Ohio, Arizona, and Nevada in time for the Christmas holidays.

The newlyweds spent the rest of their time decorating their apartment, putting up curtains at the windows, installing a telephone in their bedroom, and just shopping for things for the house. In their conversation, Bobby promised to take Callie to Radio City Music Hall to see the Christmas show on Christmas Day. Bobby informed Callie that she could invite some of her friends to come and spend some time with them during the holidays. Callie informed Bobby that she would prepare a nice meal for them.

Time passed and it was about three weeks before Christmas Day. Dolly, one of Callie's friends, was visiting the newlyweds. As Callie was cleaning and arranging things in the living room, Callie almost lost her balance at one point. As Dolly observed Callie, she noticed that Callie looked a little pale in her face, as if she were going to faint. Dolly said, "Callie, are you all right?" Callie responded by saying that she felt a little weak. Dolly did not hesitate to suggest that maybe she was pregnant.

Callie said, "I think that I *am* pregnant."

"Then be careful, Callie," Dolly told her.

Dolly continued, saying "You told me that you were going to start your family in about one year's time, Callie."

Callie said, "Yes, but Bobby . . . I think that he did this on purpose, Dolly."

"How many months, Callie?"

"It's about three months now."

"That means that you were pregnant before you got married?"

"Yes," Callie responded.

"Well, in that case, Callie, you have to deal with it . . . you cannot turn the clock back."

"I realize that, Dolly."

"I wish you luck, Callie."

"Thank you, Dolly."

During the Christmas holidays, the Ryans carried out their plans for the holidays, since this was their first Christmas as husband and pregnant wife. Being pregnant reduced the enjoyment of Christmas for Callie, but maybe she would rejoice when her first child was born.

Bobby returned to work and was away for about one month. Callie's mother had returned to Avon, Georgia, for her Christmas holidays with the members of the Methodist Church. This was an old tradition, for the members of the church to spend the Christmas holidays together.

Callie remained on her job until the month of April. At that time, Callie applied for "sabbatical" leave from her job. Callie informed her mother and invited her to return to Brooklyn, so she could be with her during and after the birth of her first child. Callie was advised to go to the library and get some books on giving birth to a child. Older women at the Methodist church lectured Callie on giving birth to a child. Miss Sally Ann, Callie's mother, replied telling her daughter Callie that she could not return to Brooklyn until the month of June 1934. Callie informed the faithful members at the church of her mother's decision, and the same old members who had advised Callie on giving birth to a child told Callie not to worry, because one or two of them would be by her side.

Finally, the month of June was here. Sarah, along with some members (ladies) of the church, came over and cleaned the apartment for Callie, because they were expecting a new member of Callie's family to arrive in about twelve more days. The ladies also did some shopping for Callie. Meanwhile, one of the ladies from the church carried Callie to the hospital just to get a checkup. Callie's doctor came out and checked Callie. The doctor advised the lady that had brought her to the hospital that he would recommend Callie to remain in the hospital for a few days for further checks on her condition.

The nurse brought Callie a gown to wear while she was in the hospital. The nurse gave Callie's clothes to the lady who had brought her there and instructed her to take them back home.

Sarah and another member of the church were surprised to see another member returning with only Callie's clothes and not Callie herself, as expected. When the member of the church gave Sarah Callie's clothes, they knew that the waiting period of nine months had been cut short, for some unknown reason.

"Why did they keep her?" they asked.

The lady said, "The doctor said that there was some type of complication and that he would keep her for a few more days, just to check further to be sure."

The next day, all three of the ladies went to the hospital to check on Callie. When they arrived, they were surprised to find out that Callie had given birth to an eight-pound, eight-ounce baby boy. The doctor told the ladies that Callie had some complications giving birth and that he would not advise her to have any more children for several years hence. They saw the baby but not Callie. She was in the intensive care unit.

The ladies were happy that Callie was going to be OK.

Bobby arrived home. He contacted Sarah to find out about Callie's condition. Sarah brought Bobby up-to-date on Callie's condition, and Bobby and the three ladies returned to the hospital the next day to bring Callie home with the baby.

Before they left the hospital, there was a brief discussion about what to name the baby.

Bobby said, "He will be named Junior."

Callie said, "I do not want to call him just Junior. I will name him Bobby Ryan, Junior, and call him Bobo."

The ladies agreed with Callie, and Bobby finally said, "OK Callie, if that's what you want."

They all returned home and rejoiced because "a child was born!"

The ladies had already purchased a crib, linen for the crib, and a few outfits for the baby as gifts for the newlyweds. Callie thanked the ladies for their generosity.

Bobby and Callie discussed how they would raise the baby. Bobby, realizing that he would be away most of the time, knew that Callie would have most of the responsibility for raising their son. But, for now, Callie knew that she would be on sabbatical leave from her job for at least, one year, taking care of and raising her little boy, Bobo.

When they attended church, they arranged with the pastor to have little Bobo christened. The pastor gave them a date when he would be christening a few more babies in the church. At this point, Bobby knew that his wife, Callie, was capable of raising their son in the proper direction.

A few years passed, and Bobo was waiting to celebrate his fourth birthday. He was attending Sunday school, and he was going to celebrate his fourth birthday in the church's Sunday school room with his Sunday School teacher and others in his class.

One day when the nursery school was closed, Mrs. Ryan carried Bobo, her little son, with her to work. The ladies in the clerk typist section admired Bobo so much, they literally stopped work and were playing with little Bobo. Mrs. Ryan did not want to stop the girls from playing with Bobo; she knew that was not the proper decorum in her office and it was her son who was captivating the girls in her office. Mrs. Ryan said, "It looks like I will have to take my son home. Otherwise, I won't be able to get the work done in the typist section that's required for today."

Some of the girls were single and they were looking for a reliable male companion as Callie had been looking for when she was single. One of the girls in her office brazenly asked Mrs. Ryan, "Where did you find Bobo's father?"

"That's a good question," Mrs. Ryan replied. Mrs. Ryan continued, saying, "I guess that you have to be lucky to find a reliable male companion. I would suggest, however, that you go to church and go to other functions where you might meet a reliable male companion. Try that and you might be lucky to meet a man of your choice."

Since Bobo was four years old, Mrs. Ryan was thinking that she might take him south to see his grandmother . . . and to receive his first bicycle from Santa Claus this Christmas. Christmas was next month. Bobby would be off from his job, and he might be able to join them during the Christmas holidays. Mrs. Ryan continued to have Bobo participate in some type of activity in the Methodist church. He now served as one of the acolytes every Sunday morning . . . lighting the candles at the beginning of service and extinguishing the lights at the end of the service.

Bobby had been helping Callie, to pack the things that they were carrying with them to Avon, Georgia.

Mrs. Ryan prepared her son for his first trip south to see his grandmother and to experience living in the country. Mrs. Ryan told Bobo a bedtime story after he had prepared himself for bed. It took Mrs. Ryan three nights to complete her story to her son of a girl growing up in the South and her first experience in a big city, Brooklyn, New York.

Mrs. Ryan explained to her son that when she was single and her name was Callie Mae Watts. Callie revealed her first experience riding on the subway for the first time. Callie repeated her experience as a little girl until she married her son's father, Bobby. Bobo remembered these stories of his mother's past, almost verbatim. Callie informed her son that she was inspired about her past from a little girl to where she was today.

While smiling, Mrs. Ryan told her son that she was going to take him to her hometown and the farm. She said, "You will see a lot of land and a lot of open spaces around you."

Bobo was four years old at that time. He asked his mother what produce was.

She said, "Produce is what you raise on the farm, like corn, beans, peas, potatoes, and pumpkins, to name a few products. She continued, saying, "You also raise vegetables like collards, cabbage, onions, and even squash."

Bobo asked, "What is squash?"

"Squash is a fruit that grows on a vine. You can see them as they grow larger on the ground, as they grow larger and larger.

"The first time that we owned our own farm, we planted cotton. We had to pick the cotton, and it's back-breaking; you are bending over the stalks as you are pulling the cotton out of the burrs. You are also pulling a sack full of cotton behind you, which is heavy. We only planted cotton one year, and we were glad our father did not plant any more cotton. We planted other products which were easier to gather.

"Dad was working on an outside job, and the children ran the farm. Our father was able to buy the extra things that the family needed. When you own your own farm, you can live independently. You do not have to listen to the owner of the land as you would have to listen to him when you were a sharecropper. When you own your own land, you do not have to divide your produce with anybody else. . . . It's yours to keep."

Mrs. Ryan continued explaining to her son what it was like living on a farm. "You have a lot of space, no lights at night outside. It's real dark outside at night."

Bobo interrupted his mother at this point and asked, "You mean that you cannot see anything outside at night?"

"No Bobo, only images. We had lanterns that we used to produce light at night. But the light from the lantern only projected light to about eight or ten feet on each direction away from you. We stayed home most of the time at night.

"On Sundays, we went to Sunday school, when we were small, and after Sunday school we stayed for the morning service at the church. The preacher would preach to us. In his sermons, he tried to explain how we should live and get along with one another as family members. That is, he explained to us how we should live with our neighbors and friends, as well as with ourselves.

"At our church, we only went to church once a month. We could, however, go to other churches in the surrounding area. We did visit other churches, to have someplace to go on Sundays.

"During the summer months, we gave picnics in the park. The parks were several miles away, but we had an old car to take us to the park and back home. The beaches were farther away than the parks. Therefore, it was very seldom that we went to a beach. We found other things to do instead of going to the beach.

"The people in the country should be healthier than the people living in the city, where there is so much smog encircling you on the street . . . whereas when you are in the country, with all of that open space around you, you inhale fresh air most of the time. This is good for your lungs. We also have a lot of time to rest in the country. This is one of the reasons that people in the country have more children than city folks. Since the people living in the country have more time on their hands, they engage in different types of activities to break the monotony wherever it prevails. This is just a way of life in the countryside.

"When we grew up under these conditions, we accepted this type of life, because we did not know any better. We thought that this was how it should be in life. When we got older and wiser, we then took steps to better our lifestyle."

Mrs. Ryan insisted that her son, Bobo, learn something about the country lifestyle before he visited the place. She continued telling Bobo that he would be able to see for himself how the people lived in the countryside, because he would see how things existed in the farmland area.

* * *

Bobo was now five years old and his mother felt that he was able to understand more about life and how people live with one another. Mrs. Ryan told her son that she had planned to take him to Webster County when he was three years old, but now he was five and he would understand more about how people live in the different areas of the country.

Mrs. Ryan went to the window and called Bobo and asked him to come inside. She informed her son that she had planned to take him south when he was three years old, but now that he was five years old he would be able to understand what she had been telling him to be true and how he could deal with the change in the different lifestyles of the people.

Now that Bobo was five years old, Mrs. Ryan told him that her trip south was scheduled to take place next month. Bobo told his mother that he did not want to go with her to her hometown. Mrs. Ryan asked him why he did not want to go with her.

Bobo said, "Because there is nothing to do there."

"Who said that?" Mrs. Ryan asked.

Bobo answered, saying "You told me that in your stories about how you grew up on the farm."

Mrs. Ryan said, "Oh, well, I could take you for a ride in the country and let you see the animals, the chickens, turkeys, and you might see squirrels and rabbits."

Bobo said, "I see a lot of squirrels all the time here in the trees."

Then she said, "You will see horses, cows, hogs, and even goats."

Bobo said, "Can we go somewhere else?"

Mrs. Ryan could see that her son was not interested in visiting her hometown. Meanwhile, Bobo was walking back and forth in the room. She knew that her son wanted to go back outside.

Mrs. Ryan knew that she had to use a different technique to persuade Bobo to go south with her. When Bobo came back into the house, which was late, Mrs. Ryan approached him with this suggestion: "Bobo, maybe we could go to my hometown during the Christmas holidays and you could ask Santa Claus to bring you a bicycle for Christmas. Then you could ride your bike in all that space that you would have around you at the old house."

Bobo came back to his mother where she was sitting. This gesture by Bobo showed her that Bobo was interested in this suggestion by his mother. He was interested in getting a new bike, since his old scooter that he used on the street was getting old and he needed a replacement. Mrs. Ryan told Bobo that they would discuss the trip later. Bobo returned outside.

This would be Bobo's first Christmas he spent with his grandmother. Bobo seemed to be excited as he told his father that Santa Claus was going to bring him a new bike for Christmas.

Mr. Ryan, asked Bobo, "Are you going to bring your new bike back home with you?"

"Yes," Bobo replied. "I want my friends to see my new bike."

"Are you going to let them ride your new bike?"

"No. Oh, well, I have to think about it, Dad."

"Just in case I am not able to visit your grandmother while you and your mother are there, will you let me ride your new bike, Bobo? . . .Ah . . . yes?"

"No," Bobo said, "because you are too big for my bike, you might break it, Dad."

"OK, Bobo, that means that I will have to buy my own bike for myself."

"Dad, you should have asked Santa Claus to bring you a new bike for Christmas."

"I don't think Santa Claus will bring me a bike, because he thinks that I am too big. . . . He only gives small boys like you new bikes for Christmas."

Bobo ran to his mother. "What is wrong with you, Bobo?"

"Dad wants to ride my new bike."

"Well," his mother said, "you don't want your father to ride your new bike?"

"No, because he might break it."

"OK, I won't let him ride your new bike. OK, Bobo?"

"Yes, Mom."

"Callie!"

"Yes, Bobby."

"I am going to get the tickets for you and Bobo, because I do not want to wait in line for a long time to get the tickets."

"Bobo is only five years old. Do you think that you have to get a ticket for him?"

"I will check to see if I have to get a ticket for him. I will be back soon, Callie."

"OK, Bobby."

"Callie!"

"Yes."

"Did you pack Bobo's snowsuit? It might be cold there during the Christmas holidays."

"Oh, Bobby, it doesn't get cold there as it does here. Anyway, Bobby, I *did* pack his snowsuit. It does not snow there. That is, I do not remember it snowing there when I was growing up.

"However, Bobby," Callie continued, "it used to get very cold in Avon, Georgia; I do not know how many degrees it would be, but you could see the icicles hanging from the pine needles and leaves of the trees or even see, if water developed on the roof, as it dripped down from the roof it would form icicles as well, hanging from the rooftop."

"In that case, Callie, Bobo can wear his snowsuit when it is cold there. I am leaving now, Callie. I will see if I can arrange for you to bring Bobo's bicycle back on the train when you and Bobo return to Brooklyn."

"OK, Bobby, and check on the time the train leaves Penn Station for the south."

* * *

Christmas Eve, Bobo's grandmother prepared a place for Santa Claus to put Bobo's bicycle and a few other gifts for him for the Christmas holidays. Bobo got in bed early, because he thought that if he got in bed early Santa Claus would come early to bring his new bike.

Miss Sally Ann got up early, and to her surprise, Bobo was getting up at the same time. "Bobo, I did not know that you were going to get up this early."

"Yes, Grandma, I wanted to see if Santa Claus brought my new bike."

Bobo walked into the living room. "Oh, Grandma! I have my new bike!"

"Yes? Let me see it." She walked into the living room to see Bobo's new bike.

Bobo wanted to take his new bike outside to ride it down the road in front of Grandma's house.

"It's too early, Bobo, for you to go outside. The sun is not up yet."

"I can see, Grandma."

"No, wait, put on your clothes and I will make breakfast for you and your mother. By that time, it will be lighter outside, and I will go out with you."

"Well, OK, Grandma."

It was not cold enough for Bobo to wear his snowsuit. Bobo simply put on his overalls, took his bike out, followed out by his grandma, and started riding down the road. Grandma stood outside watching Bobo ride his bike up and down the road in front of her house. Finally, Callie, Bobo's mother, came outside and was watching her son, Bobo ride his new bike.

Callie was so enthused over Bobo's enjoyment over his new bike that she rushed into her mother's house and wrote to Bobby to tell him of his son's enjoyment over his new bike. Riding it back and forth in front of his grandma's house, Bobo was the only boy outside at the time. Finally, two more boys came outside of their houses. Each of them had a bike. They joined Bobo as Bobo rode his bike in front of his grandmother's house. Soon some little girls came out. They didn't have any bikes; they simply ran alongside Bobo and the other boys as they rode back and forth in front of Miss Sally Ann's house.

At lunchtime, Bobo's mother called him for lunch. She waited and waited, but Bobo did not come in for his lunch.

Miss Sally Ann went out and spoke to the group of boys and girls. She asked, "Have any of you had breakfast or lunch yet?"

Their answers were "No."

"In that case," Miss Sally Ann said, "why don't all of you go and get your breakfast or lunch and return outside afterwards, for a long time to ride your bikes or whatever." They all agreed and this was how she was able to persuade Bobo to come in and get his lunch.

Bobo rode his bike for about ten hours Christmas Day. When he finally came in, he appeared to be exhausted. His mother or grandmother did not have to persuade Bobo to take his bath and go to bed. Bobo relented that the reason he did not want to come in to eat his lunch was because he thought that if he left his bike leaning against the steps someone might take it. But when they all left he felt safe in leaving his bike against the steps.

Miss Sally Ann told Bobo to leave his bike on the back porch, because it would be safe out there for the night. Now Bobo was tired and he felt that his bike was safe, so he got into bed and fell asleep.

The next day, Bobo, being used to his bike, let some of the other children ride his bike. Bobo slept so soundly the night before, maybe in his dream he remembered sharing his bike with the other children, and he did, just that. He appeared to be very cooperative in sharing his bike with others.

Callie wrote to Bobby to let him know that their vacation was over and that they would be leaving her mother's house after New Year's Day and would arrive at Penn Station on January 5, at twelve noon. Mr Ryan used one of his company's pickup trucks to pick up his wife and son as scheduled.

After the family greeted one another, Bobby did not hesitate to pick up the luggage and, of course, Bobo's bike. When Bobby brought the luggage and bike out to street-level, Bobo rode his bike on the street outside Penn Station to show his father that he could indeed ride. His father was convinced that he could ride his bike and suggested that at home he could or would have a lot of space to ride his bike.

When they arrived home, Bobo had to prove to his neighbors that he could ride his bike. Bobo demonstrated to the neighbors how he could ride his bike . . . even tried a few new tricks on his bike in front of his neighborhood audience.

Bobo was not willing to share his bike with his friends as yet, because he had to get used to his bike at home first. His neighbors were used to Bobo riding his old scooter up and down the street before he left to go to spend the Christmas holidays with his grandmother.

The Ryan family attended service at the Methodist church for the first time in the New Year. They were greeted by the congregation, as well as the pastor of the church. The chairman of the usher board did not hesitate to tell the Ryans that they were organizing young boys and girls to become ushers in the church, and they wanted Bobo to join the young usher board team. Mrs. Ryan submitted Bobo's name to be part of the new and young ushers. However, Mrs. Ryan wanted Bobo to continue as one of the acolytes until he reached six years old.

* * *

Bobo would be preparing himself for his sixth birthday in six months, and he was expecting to have a birthday party. Meanwhile, the members of the church were making their worship plans for the spring season, including Easter festivities at the church. The choir of the church had grown from twenty-six voices to thirty voices. Therefore, more space was needed to accommodate the choir.

The church was in the process of raising funds to enlarge the space for the choir, as well as renovate the whole church, before Easter. Meanwhile, the organist and director were planning on presenting Handel's masterpiece *The Messiah.* The director of the choir had already ordered new scores of the music for the large choir. The director of the choir realized that the arrangements of different parts of the musical composition remained the same. But it seemed that each year the choir members had to relearn the musical score all over again. That's because there were so many technicalities of singing each part as it should be sung, making one feel that the score itself was changing.

During the meeting with the organist and the director of the choir, Mrs. Ryan put in her request for her own copy of the score and said that she would pay for it herself.

After Mrs. Ryan put in her request for her own personal copy of the score, virtually every member of the choir made the same request. The choir director agreed and promised each member of the choir that he or she would get his or her personal copy of the score.

When Bobby came home to spend a few days with his family, Callie mentioned the plans made by the church for the Easter service days and that she had ordered a copy of *The Messiah* for herself.

Bobby jokingly said, "Maybe I should join the choir."

With a smile, Callie said, "They could use a few more good male voices in the choir."

Bobby said, "I have to support my family . . . you and Bobo, and I have to work in order to do just that. Maybe it's unfortunate that I have to spend so much time away from home.

"But it's the type of job that you have, and you have to listen to your boss in order to make a salary to support your family."

Callie informed Bobby that he had a good job and he should be proud of it. "There are some men who wish that they had your job. I have become adjusted to your being away, and it does not worry me at all. Even Bobo has gotten used to your being away from time to time."

"I will arrange my schedule so that I will be off during the Easter service days. I certainly want to hear your voice in the choir while you-all are singing Handel's masterpiece *The Messiah.*"

Callie added that she hoped that Bobby could separate her voice from the "thirty-member choir" voices that he would be hearing. Bobby informed Callie that he would be able to separate her voice from the others by listening very carefully, and watching her lips and listening for the sound of her voice.

"If you can do that, Bobby, I must say that you will be good."

"Callie, I know that your voice is good, because everything that you do is good."

Callie, with a blush on her face, as she took on a rosy tint, said, "Oh, Bobby, how can you give me all of that credit?"

Bobby's reply was: "Callie, that's because I know that you, whatever you do, always put all your gusto into what you are doing."

"Well, Bobby, I do try to do my best at what I am doing."

It was not only Bobby that enjoyed the performance of Handel's *Messiah.* It seemed that everyone sitting in the pews enjoyed the chorus rendition of the performance of the score as well. It was obvious by the emotional gestures of the members sitting in the pews that they were indeed enjoying that masterpiece. Bobby had noticed that his son, Bobo, was enjoying seeing his mother with the rest of the choir as they sang their parts from the score. Bobo, like the others sitting in the pew, was moving his hands, head, and body.

* * *

The next episode in the Ryan family was Bobo's upcoming birthday. He would be six years old. His mother was waiting for his sixth birthday before she could make her decision for him to become an usher in the church. The chairman of the usher board had already designated the type of clothing he wished them to wear . . . the boys: navy blue short pants with white shirts and a navy blue bow tie; the girls: navy blue skirts with white blouses. All of them would wear black shoes.

Before embarking on this new adventure for her son, Bobo, Mrs. Ryan discussed this assignment with her husband, Bobby. It was Callie's policy to see if her husband agreed with her decision outlining Bobo's future activities, whether at the church, at the school, or anyplace else; she liked to find out how he would accept these assignments for his young son.

Mrs. Ryan called her son, Bobo, in, sat him down, and explained the chairman's wishes about organizing a young boys' and girls' usher board in the church. She explained the responsibilities of an usher in the church. Bobo agreed to join the new usher board with the other children. Mrs. Ryan then purchased some navy blue material and proceeded to make Bobo's new outfits for the new usher . . . Bobo himself.

Miss Sally Ann, Callie's mother, a seamstress had taught her daughter Callie how to sew. Callie not only made Bobo's outfits; she made some for some of the other children as well.

The new young ushers were beautiful as they accepted their assignments and conducted themselves well in assisting the church members and friends in locating seats in the sanctuary, taking up the collection, and assisting anyone who needed help in locating the rest rooms, etc.

One of the dedicated members who paid special attention to the new young ushers was Miss Bowers. Miss Bowers was an old retired public school teacher from the neighborhood. Miss Bowers had retired about two years earlier. She was about five feet, six inches tall, and her hair was long and silvery gray in color. Miss Bowers was already a Sunday school teacher. But realizing her potential as a former public school teacher, felt, after seeing the young boys and girls perform as ushers she got the urge to form a class to teach them the fundamentals of early classroom work. She had realized that most of these kids would be entering school this fall for the first time.

How would she reach and be able to persuade those children to accept her suggestion? That was easy for Miss Bowers. She would simply start from the top. She attended a meeting after service with the pastor, laymen, and the superintendent of the Sunday school.

What was Miss Bowers's strategy? Just before the meeting was over, Miss Bowers let the group know that she had a suggestion, or a request, if you will, to make or put before the group before departing. Miss Bowers outlined her plans in organizing the class and added that it would be free. She indicated that the class for the first-timers attending school would not only admit the young members of the Methodist church but your neighbor children as well. Reverend Few spoke, saying that he thought that this was a good suggestion by Miss Bowers, and he assured her of his support in organizing the class for the first-timers to attend school. The others attending the meeting agreed with the pastor. Miss Bowers was at liberty to organize her class.

Bobo had advanced knowledge of classroom work, because his mother had already taught him what to expect when he entered school for the first time. As a matter of fact, Mrs. Ryan had already taught Bobo how to read little storybooks. Bobo learned his ABCs before he was taught to read. He could also count to 100, and he was able to sign his name.

Mrs. Ryan thought that Miss Bowers's suggestion for the kids was good. In spite of Bobo's advanced knowledge before entering school for the first time, she registered Bobo for the class. Mrs. Ryan felt that Bobo needed the experience of being in a class with other children.

Miss Bowers was so sure that the mothers and fathers would accept her suggestion, she proceeded to make out a few lesson plans for the class-to-be, and she showed these lesson plans to the pastor and the other concerned members of the church. The group had no problem with Miss Bowers's approach to reach the children. They all knew that Miss Bowers had been a dedicated teacher in the past, and they knew that she would put forward everything that she could offer to make the class a success.

When it came time for the young students to register in the public school, the young boys and girls in Miss Bowers's class did not want to leave their class at the church. The parents of the children had difficulty convincing the youngsters that Miss Bowers's class was only to prepare them for the public school classes.

Mrs. Ryan was able to convince Bobo that Miss Bowers's class was just to prepare him for class in the public school. Bobo appeared to understand, and his mother took him to school the first day, and she introduced herself to the new teacher, Miss Bess, and said, "This is my son, Bobo." Mrs. Ryan told Miss Bess that she would pick up Bobo after school.

When Mrs. Ryan went to pick up her son, Miss Bess, the new teacher, informed Mrs. Ryan that her son and a few other students were classified as "advanced" students. They were put in the advanced class, with Miss Macy as their teacher. Mrs. Ryan did not hesitate to introduce herself to Miss Macy, Bobo's other teacher, for the "bright students."

When Mr. Ryan came home on his break from his job, Callie brought him up-to-date on the progress of Bobo in school. Bobby assured his wife that she was doing a good job raising their son and gave her a big hug and kiss.

Bobby Sr. informed his son, Bobo, that he would be home for a few days and was going to take him to the zoo. Callie overheard the conversation and said, "What about me going with you-all?"

Bobby took his wife and his son, Bobo, to a small carnival located at the entrance of Prospect Park, and then took them to the zoo.

The few days that Bobby was at home, he took Bobo to school and picked him up after school. Callie was at work. During those few days, Bobby helped Callie monitor Bobo's grades for the entire year. Bobo was an honor student. His grades were good to excellent throughout the semester. For being a good student in school Dad gave Bobo a violin, not a Stradivarius violin, however. Dad informed his son that this new violin was an advanced gift for his sixth birthday, which was coming up soon.

Bobo's mother did not give her son an elaborate affair for his birthday, and later she was wondering if she did the right thing by not giving him a big birthday party. It seemed that Bobo did not enjoy his birthday affair and he did not show any interest in the new violin that his father had bought him, either.

Mrs. Ryan awakened one morning and began wondering about her son, Bobo, and what could she do to enhance his interest in something that would benefit him in his future life. She recalled how she had been interested in what her mother was doing and had pursued her mother's career. Today she was a seamstress, like her mother, and she had benefited from being a seamstress. But what about Bobo? What could she do for him?

Mrs. Ryan had raised Bobo from birth to his current age of six with only a little help from his father. She realized that her husband's job prevented him from being around too long at a time. But that was his job. He had to work for a living and to support his family.

Mr. Ryan's job was a long-distance truck driver. The job paid well, but it required him to be away, traveling to faraway places like California, Arizona, Ohio, etc., to mention some of the long-distance places that he had to go to deliver his cargo.

With a son as the only child in the family, a male image in the home is best for the boy. Usually the father is the role model for a son.

Since Mrs. Ryan had to make all of the decisions and selections of her son's activities, she had to rely on the male members of the church to help her in selecting what she should choose for her son's interest. Bobo was already attending Sunday school, he was one of the acolytes, and he was a member of the young usher board.

After serving as an usher for several weeks, Bobo showed signs that he was enjoying his position as an usher of the church. Mrs. Ryan then signed him up with the children's choir, but Bobo did not like singing with the other children his age. Mrs. Ryan believed in the concept of keeping a child busy in some meaningful activity, especially an activity that the child was interested in. If the child was interested in the activity, he would not become bored while participating in that activity. Mrs. Ryan did not force Bobo to sing in the children's choir.

Bobo was a chubby little boy. He liked to eat his mother's food. She observed his fondness for types of food and informed him that he could learn how to cook, especially the dishes that he liked most. Bobo was already the "clean-up boy." He washed the dishes and swept the floor, if it needed to be swept, after each meal. It seemed that Bobo enjoyed helping his mother in the kitchen. Maybe it was because his mother would cook the things that he liked most. After she cooked what Bobo liked, she would hand it to him saying, "This is what you like."

Mrs. Ryan purchased some red and white material made of cotton and made two small aprons for Bobo and one for herself. Since Bobo did not have his father in the household, he did not have that male image to imitate. Therefore, he was invariably taking on his mother's image in the kitchen, as it was the available image for him to follow.

Mrs. Ryan taught Bobo how to fry chicken, how to cook an egg, either scrambled or boiled, how to cook bacon for breakfast, and how to fry fish, etc. Soon Bobo wanted to learn how to make a cake or how to bake a cake, especially nut cake, the type that he liked best. Bobo's mother felt obligated to teach her son her skills, since her husband, Bobo's father, was away for long periods of time and when he was at home was usually tired and needed his time off from his job to rest. While at home, he spent most of his time resting for the next trip.

Mrs. Ryan decided to go a step further by teaching Bobo how to sew, first by using a needle and then by sewing on the sewing machine. Bobo was taught how to sew scrap material that was used later to make an old-fashioned quilt. Bobo was finally able to make a pair of short pants for himself. Bobo wore the first garments made by himself every day. His mother had to hide them at night, after he had gone to sleep, to wash them.

During the summer months, when Mr. Ryan was off from his job during his vacation, he would take his wife and son to the beach or on a picnic in the park. On one of his trips to the park an upsetting experience occurred for him to endure: While Mr. Ryan was relaxing, after his meal, in the park, he fell asleep. His son, Bobo, met some boys in his age group. They started playing by running and jumping, which is typical of young boys, or girls for that matter, and in doing so they drifted away from the picnic area.

The boys actually disappeared from the picnic area. Mrs. Ryan, after realizing that the boys had indeed disappeared from the area, silently got up, without awakening Mr. Ryan, and looked for the boys. Mrs. Ryan, mindful of the fact that her husband was enjoying this moment of relaxation, ventured out a little more but did not see the boys anywhere. Mrs. Ryan inquired of people, in the area, "Did you see several boys playing, and which way did they go?"

One lady pointed out the direction in which she had seen boys running and playing. But Mrs. Ryan was afraid to venture out farther. She returned to the picnic area, where she found Mr. Ryan still asleep. She knew that her husband was very tired; that's why he was sleeping so soundly.

Mrs. Ryan then ventured out again to a radius of about thirty feet from the picnic area. She looked, but Bobo and the other boys were nowhere to be seen. Mrs. Ryan recalled that the lady had pointed south from the picnic area. Mrs. Ryan thought of calling Bobo, but she felt that the echoes in the huge park would cause confusion. Therefore, she reluctantly returned to the picnic area, where she found that Mr. Ryan was waking up.

When Mr. Ryan did not see his son he asked, "Where is Bobo?"

Mrs. Ryan replied by saying "I am looking for him to return." She could see that her husband appeared to be upset.

He replied, "Why didn't you keep an eye on him?"

In a humble voice, she said, "I too, fell asleep for a short while . . . maybe for too long." At that point, she saw a group of boys coming toward the picnic area. She was praying to herself that Bobo was with that group of boys. They were approaching from a westerly direction from the picnic area. She kept looking. Finally, she saw Bobo coming with the group of boys. He was wearing a yellow-billed cap, and she recognized Bobo from the color of his cap, which she had bought for him.

The moment of frustration of both father and mother soon subsided, with the sight of their son returning to the picnic area. The Ryans chattered with the nearby neighbors in the park before departing for home.

For a long time Mr. Ryan did not own a car, because his job as a truck driver required most of his time be spent on the road, away from home with his family. Alternate side parking on the street was not an issue for car owners; they could park their cars on the street anywhere, at any time, and not worry about what would happen to their cars. This was in the 1930s. You could leave your car parked on the street for long periods of time and did not have to be worried about people stealing your car or your getting a ticket, for that matter; your car was safe. Your neighbors were very good neighbors at that time. If a neighbor at that time saw something happening to your car, they would, without hesitation, call the police and report it. In cases like someone having an accident that involved your car, the neighbor would report the whole incident to the police. You had good neighbors at that time.

Mr. Ryan discussed buying a car with his wife for a long time. Mrs. Ryan did not know how to drive a car. But Mr. Ryan had promised that he would teach her how to drive. He purchased a 1932 Chevrolet, a four-door sedan. The car salesman had demonstrated the car to Mr. and Mrs. Ryan, and the car appeared to be in very good condition. Mr. Ryan was driving, and ironically, they ended up at a picnic area not far from where they had been when Bobo wandered off. Bobo was in school at that time. They stayed for a while at the picnic area, and then Mr. Ryan continued to give his wife driving lessons.

Mr. Ryan's time at home was up, and he had to return to his job for several more days. Mr. Ryan parked the car on the street near their apartment.

Mr. and Mrs. Ryan did not own their own apartment; they were tenants, but they, like the rest of their neighbors, were good tenants, and they had a good landlord. At that time good tenants made good neighbors; good neighbors made good tenants. This was the type of people that lived near each other at that time.

When Mr. Ryan returned home from his trips, delivering goods and services to other parts of this country, he noticed that the car was parked exactly where he had parked it before he left. He jokingly said to his wife, "You mean that you did not drive the car at all?"

With a smile, Callie answered by saying, "I started to take Bobo to school one morning while it was raining but changed my mind, in fear of not getting to school at all that day."

Mr. Ryan invited his wife to come with him, as he was going to give her some more lessons in driving techniques. But the car would not start. After the car had remained on the street for several days, it would not start. Why? The battery was very weak. Mr. Ryan said, "I cannot tolerate a weak battery." Instead of having the battery charged, he purchased a new battery.

After he gave his wife a few more lessons in driving, she began to show signs of understanding the rigors of driving a car. She could park the car; she could back up the car; she knew how to give hand signals as well.

Mr. Ryan took her for her driving test; she passed the test and received her driving license, which was mailed to her a few days later. Mr. Ryan was away when her license was delivered to her. In spite of her having her driving license, she was afraid to move the car from the parked position. She, however, would start the car and let the motor run for a while on a daily basis. This procedure kept the battery well charged. Mr. Ryan on his return home found the car in good running condition.

When Mrs. Ryan gained her confidence in herself as a driver, she would drive the car to go shopping and to take Bobo to school and to her church, the Union Methodist Church. But this was not all that Mrs. Ryan had to learn about the car; what about the maintenance of the car? It took Mr. Ryan to discover that his wife did not know about the maintenance of the car. As she was driving, he noticed that the gasoline gauge was almost on "empty." He, simply asked her, "What makes the car run? What do you need to make the motor of the car run? What do you need to be able to cook the food that you cook?" His wife finally got the message that the car needed some type of fuel to make the motor run. "Then, how do you find out if it needs fuel?" He showed her the gasoline gauge, and she saw that the gasoline gauge was almost on empty. Without any more advice, he asked her to drive to a gasoline station, and he showed her how to put gas in the car. He also showed her how to check the oil, water, and the other fluids that the car needed to operate properly.

Mr. Ryan started taking his family on short trips while he was on his short breaks at home with his family. It seemed that when Mr. Ryan was driving he did not appear to be tired or sleepy. But when he reached home, he would end up in the living room and lying on the sofa, where he would soon fall asleep.

Mr. Ryan never developed the skills of a good role model for his son, Bobo. In the past, Mr. Ryan while at home on a break from his job spent most of his time resting from those long trips behind the steering wheel of a large truck.

Bobo had to depend on his mother for guidance. His mother became the role model for him. Her chores became Bobo's chores around the house. Bobo could prepare a meal for the family now. He could also prepare delicate dishes. His mother was planning on buying a typewriter so she could teach him how to type. As the supervisor of the typing section in her office, she felt that men would eventually join the ladies as typists.

During this stage of Bobo's life, his mother realized that she was the parent that would have to direct her son's way of life. Bobo's father, on the other hand, spent most of his time away from home. Truck drivers received about the same amount of time off their job as other workers who worked on other types of jobs. The difference was that truck drivers would sometimes be entitled to time off when they were in a different city, many miles away from home. Even between the truck routes there were what they called rest stops, where the long-distance truck drivers could stop for a few days to rest up. The truck drivers called these their rest-up stops.

At these rest-up stops, there were good restaurants with sections for entertainment. The truck drivers enjoyed these rest-up stops, where they could socialize with their comrades. Since Mr. Ryan was the president of the Truck Drivers' Association the other truck drivers looked up to him for guidance and suggestions.

The truck drivers had something in common, like their interest in one another as truck drivers. They were partners, to say the least.

The females would not let this opportunity pass them up. They frequently visited these rest stop areas purposely to meet the truck drivers. Some of the single truck drivers found girlfriends at these truck stops. In some cases, some of these love affairs ended up in marriage. Meanwhile, their trucks were being serviced, as well, at these rest areas.

Bobo's mother continued to plan for Bobo's future. She contacted the Boy Scout leader at the church to get information regarding the Boy Scouts, and she was told that Bobo would have to be eight years old to become a Cub Scout.

Bobo was only seven years old; however, his birthday was approaching soon.

Being head of household while Bobby was at work out of town was not an easy task for Bobo's mother to endure at this time. Now she was waiting for her son's next birthday so she could register him as a Cub Scout at the church, and it was obvious that she was planning on a big birthday party for him.

While Mrs. Ryan was trying to figure out what step to take next, the doorbell rang; it was her landlord, and he brought his wife, the landlady, with him. While the landlord was up on the roof, the landlady and Mrs. Ryan were talking. They realized that they had something in common. Mr. Ryan was away most of the time; the landlady complained that her husband invested in "rentable real estate" and it required a lot of his time to be spent away from home, working on his regular job and checking on his "rentable real estate."

Therefore, the landlady was trying to encourage her husband to sell some of his "rentable real estate," so he would have more time to spend at home.

That statement made by the landlady caused Mrs. Ryan to appear to be in shock when she realized what the landlady was saying. Mrs. Ryan said quickly, "You mean that you are going to sell this house?"

"Yes," responded the landlady.

Mrs. Ryan, with her hand up to her mouth, said, "Oh . . . oh, What now?"

The landlady in a low tone of voice said, "You can buy this house yourself."

The landlady and the landlord left to go food shopping, as the landlady had mentioned earlier. After the landlord and the landlady left, Mrs. Ryan went into deep thought . . . thinking that they would sell to somebody else and the Ryans would have to move, at a time like this, when Bobo is waiting for his eighth birthday so she could register him as a Cub Scout at the church and, no doubt, they would have to move.

Mrs. Ryan was thinking that if they had to move, their furniture might not fit in the new apartment, they would have to adjust to a new neighborhood and to new neighbors, the convenience might not be as good as it was here, etc.

At this point, Mrs. Ryan was wondering:

1. *How much do they want for this house? It seems to be in good condition.*
2. *How do you go about buying a house? We never had this experience before.*
3. *What is involved in buying a house? What do you have to look for?*

Back home, Mrs. Ryan reminisced, *my father and mother made those decisions when they bought land so they would own their own farm.* Mrs. Ryan's body virtually jumped up when she realized that back home it was very good to own your own land and to have your own farm. That gave you prestige in the neighborhood. *In that case,* she mused, *if it is good to own your own land and own farm, it is also good to own your own home. I need some help. Where can I get some advice at this time?*

Mrs. Ryan contacted Sarah and explained to her what she was faced with and said she needed some help in making her decision. Sarah had Callie recall having met Mrs. Zula, an elderly friend. Callie remembered that Mrs. Zula was about her mother's age and was very patient when she was talking to you.

Mrs. Ryan found out how much the landlord and landlady wanted for the house and the down payment for it as well. In explaining to Mrs. Zula, Mrs. Ryan pointed out that if they had to use their little savings account to make the down payment it would only leave them with about two hundred dollars left in the bank in case of an emergency.

Mrs. Zula pointed out to Mrs. Ryan that it was very good that they, in fact, did have the down payment for a house. She continued, "You do not have to worry about emergencies, because if you have a house, you can borrow money on the house, as a second mortgage." Mrs. Zula was an old homeowner, and she knew what was good about owning a house and the advantages of being your own landlord. She continued to explain to Mrs. Ryan that the money in the bank was a cash asset and the house was a fixed asset. She told Mrs. Ryan to make these comparisons: "The house is probably worth . . . say fifteen thousand dollars on today's market. That's the fixed asset. Now, compare your cash asset of . . . one thousand dollars with that value of the house. Which is better?"

That was enough advice that Mrs. Ryan needed to make her decision. She was determined to buy the house. She knew that her husband would leave that decision up to his wife, anyway. Mrs. Ryan wrote everything down, and when Mr. Ryan came home she explained everything to him. He agreed and they got the money out of the bank and bought the house.

Making this decision to buy the house resolved a lot of problems that would have occurred if they had not bought the house. Now Mrs. Ryan was relieved and could continue to pursue her goals for her son. Mrs. Ryan went to the library and asked for a book with information regarding Boy and Cub Scouts. She was given a book entitled *Boy Scouts of America.* Mrs. Ryan read the book. She was inspired by the motto, "Be prepared," the oath, and Scout law. She was also inspired when she read that the Boy Scouts of America was based on the concept of developing self-reliance and good citizenship through outdoor activities.

Mrs. Ryan read that each troop of, in Bobo's case the Cub Scouts, was sponsored by a civic organization, a school, or a church and received its charter from the local council, comprised of community leaders. Local councils sent representatives to the national council, which directed and administered the overall scout movement. She continued to read that these civic organizations would provide programs for the Boy Scouts as well. These civic organizations would also provide programs for the minority inner-city boys. Mrs. Ryan was satisfied with what she had read in this book, and she returned the book to the library. She knew that this was what she wanted for her son.

Now, when was Bobo's birthday? Mrs. Ryan knew exactly when it was to occur. Why? Because in order for Bobo to celebrate his eighth birthday as a Cub Scout, the party would have to be given after his actual birthday. Meanwhile, Mrs. Ryan had already planned his birthday party so he would celebrate it as a Cub Scout. The kids on the block knew when the birthday party was going to be, but they did not know that it would be after his actual birth date.

Mrs. Ryan had requested some of the mothers in the neighborhood to help her to control and serve the children that would be attending Bobo's birthday party.

Mr. Ryan was at home at the time of his son's big party and had four days to spend with his son. It was a great day for Mr. Ryan, since he missed so many celebrations with his family. Mrs. Ryan had her list of items that she had to purchase. Since Mr. Ryan was at home, he made the purchases like balloons, a few noisemakers, ice cream, a birthday cake, and a lot of junk food. It seems that all kids like junk food. Therefore, to assist the children, buy them some junk food.

Mr. Ryan, since he was at home for the weekend was able to attend service at the church, and he was able to meet some of Bobo's Scout leaders. Mr. Ryan was satisfied with how his wife was raising their son, Bobo.

Bobo attended the meetings given to teach the new Cub Scouts the fundamentals of the rigors of a life as a Cub Scout. As they were the first Cub Scout troop to be organized by the church, the Methodist church sponsored a trip to a camp in upstate New York for the new Scouts. Bobo's mother prepared his things to take with him on the three-week trip. Mrs. Ryan took Bobo to the church to join the other members of the troop.

Bobo's mother, not being accustomed to her son being away, was constantly worried about his safety. She eventually contacted the national council, which directed and administered the overall movement, to find out exactly where the Cub Scouts were located upstate. Mrs. Ryan boarded a bus that took her to a motel not far from the campsite. She at this point hired someone with a car to take her to the site where the troops were located. When she arrived, she saw Bobo, as well as the other Cub Scouts. Bobo was surprised to see his mother there and wondered why she came there to see him. The other boys were also surprised to see Bobo's mother coming to see him. She was the only mother there and the only female in the area at the time. As Bobo's mother was walking toward them, Bobo ran to his mother to greet her. This commotion stopped the troops from continuing to do their exercises.

The troop leaders heard Bobo saying, while he was running toward her, "Mama, why did you come here?" The leaders approached Mrs. Ryan to find out what had happened back home, etc. Mrs. Ryan answered them that it was only that she was not used to her son, Bobo, being away from her for long periods of time. "It was simply lonesome, being at home by myself."

The leaders assured Mrs. Ryan that her son would be in good hands for the rest of the period that they were scheduled to stay at the campsite. Mrs. Ryan sorta felt embarrassed after this happened, but she felt relieved knowing that her son was OK.

After finding out why his mother came to see him, Bobo insisted that everything there was nice: the food, the short trips, the lectures, and the sleeping facilities as well. "Don't worry, Mama," Bobo insisted. Bobo's mother left the campsite and was driven back to the motel where she was staying.

Sarah was also worried. Not about Bobo but about Callie herself. Callie had mentioned to Sarah that she was very lonesome, being by herself at home. Sarah had informed Callie that the boys would be all right, being away. They would get the best of care. It was their responsibility to take the boys to a safe place and for them to get the proper guidance, as well.

Sarah, however, was looking beyond Callie being lonesome. Sarah had noticed that Callie was acting strangely a few days before Bobo left to go on that trip. Sarah had called Callie, but there was no answer.

When Callie returned home, she called Sarah and told her that she had just returned from a trip upstate to see Bobo.

Sarah responded by saying, "I figured that you had gone upstate to see Bobo."

Callie said, "Yes, Sarah. I could not live with myself without knowing how Bobo was doing."

Sarah informed Callie that she was going to the grocery store and that she would stop by.

Callie said, "OK, Sarah."

With the keys to Callie's house Sarah opened the door and walked in. "Where are you?" Sarah asked.

"I am in the bathroom, Sarah."

They greeted each other and Sarah wanted to know how Callie was feeling. Callie told Sarah that she felt warm.

"You look like you are frustrated."

"I do not know," Callie said. "I just feel warm and weak."

"I would suggest that you go to the hospital, Callie . . . just for a checkup."

Callie said, "Maybe I should go to the hospital for a checkup."

"I will take you," Sarah insisted.

Callie said, "I will get dressed and take something with me."

"Take what?" Sarah asked. "You do not have to take anything with you. As a matter of fact, Callie, if they keep you, I will have to bring back what you are wearing now. Let the doctor make that decision, Callie."

"OK, Sarah."

Sarah took Callie to the hospital. Callie did not have an appointment, so Sarah took her to the emergency room. They had to wait thirty minutes before Callie was checked by the doctor. Callie's pressure was OK, but her temperature was high. It was above normal. The doctor gave Callie some medicine and told her to relax for a few minutes. When the doctor returned, he checked Callie's temperature again and found that it was still high. The doctor suggested that Callie remain in the hospital for a few days. The doctor tried to get Callie's temperature down, but her temperature appeared to be stubborn. Sarah folded Callie's clothes and told Callie that she would return the next day to see how she was doing.

The next day, Sarah returned to the hospital. She saw the doctor as she entered the hospital and asked about Callie's condition. The doctor told Sarah that Callie's condition was not good. Sarah visited Callie's room, talked to her, and told her that the doctor was going to keep her another day or two.

Callie seemed to be relaxing but was still feeling warm. Callie stayed in the hospital for three days before the doctor discharged her. Sarah picked her up, stopped by the grocery store, bought a few things for Callie, and then took her home. Sarah made sure that Callie was OK before she left.

* * *

Callie heard someone opening the door. She thought it was Sarah returning. But to her surprise, it was her husband, Bobby. Callie appeared to be surprised to see her husband coming in at this time.

Bobby entered the room where his wife was resting; he kissed her on the cheek and felt her pulse and asked her how she was feeling.

She said, "Better, better than I was a few days ago. Did Sarah call you, Bobby? Did Sarah call your office to let you know that I was sick?"

Bobby said, "No."

Callie said, "Oh."

"For how long were you sick, Callie?"

"For three days that I was in the hospital with a fever, the doctor told me."

"How do you feel now?"

"I feel good at this time. I was not expecting you at this time, Bobby. Is this your regular time off from your job? I guess that I forgot your working schedule. I remember now," Callie said.

"How is Bobo?"

"He is fine and he is enjoying being with the other boys. I went to see him at camp a few days ago. He told me that he is enjoying the outing with the other Cub Scouts."

"You mean that you went to the area where the Cub Scouts were camping out?"

"Yes," Bobby. I only stayed one night in the nearby motel."

"Was that because you were worrying about Bobo?"

"Yes, I was worrying about Bobo. You see, Bobby, this is the first time that Bobo has been away from me."

"How was the campsite where the Cub Scouts were located?"

"I observed that there was a lot of space in and around the area where they were located. . . . trees, lakes, and a very big field, which appears to have been a farming area many years ago. I even saw a few small animals running about the area. That's how it should be in a camping area. I know that Bobo is enjoying that trip."

"What you have to remember, Callie, is that Bobo is getting older and he will be going places with the Cub Scouts and when he gets older he will become a regular Boy Scout."

"Yes, Bobby, I know, but that's what I have to get used to, as time goes by. This means that when he is away I will be at home by myself. Sarah has her own responsibilities to take care of. She cannot be with me on a daily basis."

"When did you get back from the hospital, Callie?"

"Just a few hours ago. Sarah picked me up and brought me home after picking up some groceries at the store."

"Oh, I almost got here before you . . . ah?"

"Yes, Bobby. I was not expecting you so early, Bobby. If you had been a few hours earlier, Bobby, you would have arrived before me."

"Well, you don't know when something is going to happen. You just have to take care of yourself and don't worry about Bobo."

"You are right, Bobby, but it seems that I just cannot help worrying sometimes."

"Just try and then try harder to control your emotions, Callie."

"I will try to do that. I will get up and cook dinner."

"While you are cooking, I will speak to our neighbors."

"All right, Bobby."

Since Bobby had returned home, he checked Bobo's bicycle. He found that one tire was flat. He repaired and inflated the bicycle tire and left the bicycle leaning up against the wall in the hallway. "What time will the bus arrive, Callie?"

"About three-thirty P.M."

At 3:00 P.M., Bobby walked to the Methodist church, where he found a few more parents waiting for their sons.

The bus arrived on time. The kids got off the bus and ran to their parents. Bobby greeted his son and asked him where his suitcase was.

"On the bus," Bobo replied.

Bobby picked-up his son's suitcase, and they walked home.

When Bobby and his son reached home, Callie had the table set and waiting for them to eat. Callie informed Bobby that it was time to get school supplies for Bobo, who would be entering school in a few weeks.

"What grade will you be in this semester, Bobo?"

"I will be in the fourth grade, Dad."

"Very good, then you will have to study hard so you will pass all of your subjects with good grades so you will be promoted to the fifth grade. . . . You are getting smarter and smarter."

Bobo saw his bicycle leaning up against the wall in the hallway when they came in, and after his dinner he slipped out with his bicycle and rode it down the street to the section where his friend lived. His friend's little sister saw Bobo outside and told her brother that Bobo was there on his bicycle. They rode their bikes to another of their friends' house, and all three of them rode their bikes to the area of the church.

Meanwhile, Bobo's father came out of the bathroom and was looking for his son. "Where is Bobo?" he asked his wife, Callie.

"He and his friends are riding their bikes on the street."

"My goodness, I only was talking with him a few minutes ago, and now he is already outside, riding his bike. I do not get too much time to spend and talk with him when I am at home."

"Well, Bobby, you are not here too often, and he is used to playing with his friends when he is not with me. This is what he is used to doing, Bobby."

During Callie and Bobby's discussion about their son, Bobo, Bobby said, "He is growing up; therefore, we should get a little larger size when we purchase his new clothes." Callie agreed, and she set their schedule to go shopping the next day while Bobo was at church, rehearsing his role in the church as an usher.

Bobo's father was at home when the school opened after Bobo became a Cub Scout. Bobo's father, as he prepared to take his son to school for the first day of the semester, asked his son, "As a Cub Scout, what are you supposed to do when you enter your first class of this semester?"

Bobo stood up in an erect position, as if to salute and said, "Be prepared."

"That's the right attitude, Son; be prepared."

Mr. Ryan met the new teachers that would be in charge of Bobo's classes and he warned Bobo to be a good boy in school and obey his teachers.

Bobby left the school building after assuring himself that his son was in good hands with his new teachers. Bobo was used to his father leaving home to go to work and was used to his father being away on his job, as a truck driver, for several days at a time before he would be able to return home to be with his family.

Bobo did have someone to rely on when he returned home from school each day. Bobo expected to have his mother's shoulder to lean on when he was at home. Bobo was having a few math problems. He asked his mother to show him how to work some of his math problems. She did, and she checked out his homework assignments with him as well. Callie was accustomed to drilling Bobo over his homework assignments, and Bobo was also accustomed to his mother's concern about his achievements in school. It was his mother's interest in him that kept his average up on a daily basis, not down.

Mrs. Ryan realized that that the Christmas holiday season was nearing and as a planner she would have to start her plans early. It was Mrs. Ryan's duty, it seemed, to get an early start, not just for Christmas but for any adventure that she embarked on as a head of household. Therefore, she knew that she had to start her shopping spree several weeks before the "holiday rush." This way, she would have a head start and she would not be so late as to get leftovers. What she got would be fresh and not picked-over items. This year was no exception; she had made out her list and she had checked it twice, maybe more.

She realized that Bobo's bicycle was in good shape, his scooter was also in good condition, and he had a few game sets. Therefore, she was going to buy him some new clothes. He was a fast-growing boy; therefore, his clothes got too small for him before they wore out.

Bobo, the only child, seemed to be imitating his mother in many ways. He seemed to move about the kitchen in the same manner as his mother. "Like father, like son." But in this case, it was "like mother, like son." Bobo thought that his mother was the only one that he could look up to for guidance. Bobo's mother helped her son, Bobo, make his decisions, what he should do now, and what he should do next, etc., etc.

Bobo's father's time was mostly spent on the road, driving a long, cumbersome truck. Bobo's father was not around the household long enough for Bobo to develop in his father's image or his skills. Therefore, he, Bobo, developed his mother's skills and ways of life. His mother raised him from a child to the age of eight. He, however, spent some time staying with some of his little friends all night and sometimes on weekends. He, Bobo, loved to play with his friends on the block.

Bobo was no exception but at this time of year, like all the kids in the block and other areas, was looking forward to the Christmas holidays. I can recall when I was a child it seemed that Christmas was forever coming, and I think that Bobo, as well as the other kids on the block, felt the same way. Bobo's mother would let her son have all of the freedom when his friends were visiting him. He did not have to wash the dishes after the meals when his friends were visiting him. Other times, Callie would have Bobo washing the dishes after the meals and sweeping the floor as well. Bobo was a good cook already. One thing that Bobo did not learn from his mother was how to drive a nail with a hammer. That was because his mother did not know how to drive a nail with a hammer herself. Bobo did, however, learn how to replace the washers in the kitchen faucets. He learned how to do this from the plumber who often took care of these minor repairs in the Ryan household. Callie taught her son the skills that she herself was able to master.

Bobo's mother had a workable holiday season schedule, and now that Christmas and the New Year holidays had been enjoyed by all, it was time to plan for the spring: Easter and Bobo's ninth birthday party, all both coming up in the very near future. Bobo was expecting to pass on to the fifth grade right after his ninth birthday party, in June of this year, 1943. Bobo had been one step ahead of his classmates because his mother taught him the early fundamentals of the ABCs, as well as how to read a little.

After Bobo's mother spent some time in the hospital a few months ago, she did not appear to be in good health at this time. She had to visit her doctor last week, and it seemed that she needed to go back to the hospital. Sarah was over to see her twice this week already and it was just Wednesday. Callie told Sarah that she felt "hot" most of the time. It was last year when Callie spent almost a week in the hospital with a very high temperature.

On Sarah's next visit to see Callie, she suggested to Callie that maybe she should send for her mother to come and spend some time with her. Sarah had to go to work herself, and Callie usually obeyed Sarah's suggestions. Callie gave Sarah the money to buy her mother's ticket to come to Brooklyn as soon as possible. Callie sent more than enough money for her mother's ticket, because she thought that her mother might need to buy something for herself for the trip to Brooklyn from Avon, Georgia.

Callie's mother, Miss Sally Ann Watts, notified Sarah that she would arrive at Penn Station in February 1943. Callie did not feel well enough to meet her mother at the station, so she asked Sarah to meet her when she arrived.

When Sarah and Bobo's grandmother returned from Penn Station, Callie greeted her mother and informed them that her husband would be coming home tomorrow. He was breaking in a new long-distance truck driver.

Bobby greeted his mother-in-law upon arriving at home. As Bobo was in school but would be home soon, Bobby, in his own way, examined his wife, Callie to see how she was feeling. He told her that she looked a little anemic. Callie assured him that her appetite was good and seemed to be in good shape and that she was hungry now. She asked Bobby to bring her some food to eat. Bobby, with a smile, said, "Yes, of course I'll bring you some food to eat. . . . You can ask for your choice of menu. . . . If it's not here, I will get it for you."

Callie, smiling said, "You have to get sick to get such good service."

"You do not have to get sick to get good service, Callie. You deserve good service any time you want something for yourself when I am at home."

"You are right, Bobby. I was just teasing."

"Hi! Dad!" Bobo said when he entered the room where his mother was lying in bed.

"How was school today, Bobo?"

"Fine. I got eighty-four on my math test yesterday."

"Very good, Son. . . . Keep it up and you will not have any trouble passing on to the next grade."

"I know; I know," Bobo replied.

"Ah, you are very optimistic that you will be promoted. That's OK; it's good to be optimistic when you are sure of yourself and what you are capable of doing in school. . . . I have no problem with that type of feeling about yourself."

* * *

While Sarah, Callie, Bobby, and Miss Sally Ann were sitting in the living room, talking, Miss Sally Ann informed the others that she had been here about a month now, looking after her daughter. It was March 15, 1943, and Callie seemed to be feeling much better now, and Miss Sally Ann was thinking that she could return home.

Sarah responded by saying, "Aunt Sally Ann, why do you have to leave now?"

Bobby responded by saying, "Mama, you do not have to leave us now; we enjoy having you here with us."

Miss Sally Ann was surprised that Bobby called her Mama. This was the first time that he had called her Mama. That, of course, made her feel closer to him as her son-in-law.

"Certainly Bobo enjoys having you here with us. He likes the way you make those flapjacks for him to eat. It seems that we are not able to duplicate how you make those flapjacks."

Sarah responded by saying that Bobo was not the only one that enjoyed those flapjacks. "Aunt Sally Ann, I know someone else who enjoys them as well as Bobo."

Everybody was smiling, because it was obvious whom Sarah was referring to, Bobby, of course.

Miss Sally Ann told them that the recipe for making those flapjacks was her secret. She, however, said, "The recipe is simple, but I guess you have to know how to mix the different parts to make them fluffy," smiling as she said that. Anyway, Miss Sally Ann said that she did not have to go back home to Avon, Georgia, now. "I can stay a little longer with you all. I do not have anything that is so important, except my church. . . . I think that the members miss me, like I miss them and the church."

Callie returned to the living room from the bathroom saying "I heard the conversation. They are right, Mama; you do not have to leave us now. You can make our home your home as well."

Miss Sally Ann responded quickly, "No I have to go back home where I can serve God in my church."

"Mama, you do not have to go back home to serve God. We have a good church here, the Methodist church where I brought you when you were here last time, remember? Reverend Few would like to assist you in any way that he possibly can to make you happy."

"Is he married, Callie?"

"Yes, Mama, but there are others at the church that are not married."

Miss Sally Ann with a big smile said, "In that case, I will stay a little while longer."

Miss Sally Ann told her daughter and Sarah that at the church back home, God knew her.

Callie, her daughter responded, saying, "Mama, God knows you at any church; all you have to do is pray and ask him for guidance, and he will help you."

"Yes, I guess that you are right, Callie. It's just that he remembers me at my church because I have been there for so long."

The next morning when Miss Sally Ann got up, she approached her daughter with a demanding request that she should go home before Easter.

Callie gave in and said, "OK, Mama, if that pleases you, I will ask Bobby to pick up your ticket."

Sarah came over, and when her aunt gave her the news that she was going home so she would be there to worship in her church for Easter, Sarah said, "In that case, why don't you get a round-trip ticket? After all, Callie is not as well as you might think she is."

"That is OK by me, if my son-in-law can afford to get me a round-trip ticket."

Sarah said, "If he cannot afford to buy you a round-trip ticket, I will pay it myself."

Miss Sally Ann said, "I can see that you all are serious about my returning after Easter."

Sarah said, "Yes, Aunt Sally Ann."

When Bobby was given the news, he purchased a round-trip ticket for his mother-in-law. Bobby then put his mother-in-law's suitcase in the car and took her to Penn Station.

After Easter, Miss Sally Ann notified Sarah that she was returning to Brooklyn. She knew that whatever she told Sarah, it was just like telling her daughter, Callie, anyway.

When Sarah left work, she stopped by to see Callie and to tell her that her mother was returning to Brooklyn. She was scheduled to arrive next week . . . Wednesday at 4:00 P.M.

Callie relayed the information to her son, Bobo, and her husband, Bobby.

Bobby was happy that his grandmother was returning to Brooklyn to live with them, because he felt that when his grandmother was present in the household she was obligated to look out for him, and especially to cook those flapjacks for him. He, Bobo, told his Aunt Sarah that he would come straight home from school, meaning that he wouldn't stop to play on his way home.

Sarah said, "OK, Bobo, I will be waiting for you."

When Bobo's grandmother arrived, she gave Bobo a little toy that she had bought for him in Avon, Georgia. The toy was like a little fan that rotated when air was forced upon the blades. Bobo took out his bike and attached his toy to the handlebars of his bicycle. The toy fan rotated when he rode his bike. Miss Sally Ann, as usual, cooked and set the table for the family to eat. She looked out the window but did not see Bobo anywhere near. She said, "Sarah, will you please go out and get that boy? It's time to eat."

When Sarah went outside, she saw Bobo riding his bike back and forth . . . watching his little rotating fan spinning on its axle. Sarah knew that Bobo was enjoying his little toy. She, too, became entranced just watching Bobo enjoy himself. She forgot her mission and found herself just standing there watching Bobo.

Soon Miss Sally Ann said, "My goodness, I sent Sarah outside to bring Bobo in to eat his food, and she is staying outside as well. I guess I'll have to go outside myself and bring both of them inside. . . . The food is getting cold." With a "huff and a buff," she said, "I will catch Bobo by his nose or his ear and I will catch Sarah by a strand of her hair, and I will bring both of them inside to eat." She rushed outside and saw Sarah watching Bobo and found herself watching Bobo as he enjoyed himself riding his bike and watching the little fan spin around its axle.

Finally, Miss Sally Ann recalled her mission and brought them inside for dinner. At the dinner table, Miss Sally Ann told them that her intention had been to go outside and catch Bobo by his nose or ear and Sarah by a strand of her hair and bring both of them in for dinner.

Miss Sally Ann continued, saying, "If your food is cold, you will have to eat it anyway."

Callie simply sat at the table and smiled. She remembered how her mother used to get upset when something did not meet her approval.

Sarah cleared herself by saying that she was enjoying seeing Bobo enjoy himself. Sarah continued, saying, "Aunt Sally Ann, remember that you bought that toy for Bobo to enjoy himself, right?"

Miss Sally Ann said, "I guess I should not get upset because I bought the spinning fan so he would enjoy playing with it. I will have to ask for forgiveness, but there is a time for a person to forgive and to forget. Now the doorbell is ringing; I wonder who that could be." Miss Sally Ann went to the door. She said, "You-all eat while I answer the door. . . . Do not let the food get colder."

"Hello!" The neighbor said. "Tell Bobo that he better move his bike, because the boys are looking at the toy that he has on his bicycle. . . . They might steal it."

Bobo brought the bike inside, and he returned to the table to finish eating. Miss Sally Ann scolded Bobo saying, "Take your time and eat properly; tomorrow is another day. You do not have to rush to go back outside to ride your bike. Take your time and eat like you're supposed to."

"OK, Grandma," Bobo answered.

"Anyway," Miss Sally Ann said, "it's too late for you to go back outside. I was going to wash the dishes for you so you could go back outside to ride your bike, but it's too late now. You can wash the dishes yourself."

"OK, Grandma," Bobo answered.

"Callie!"

"Yes, Mama."

"You have to go shopping to buy some groceries; we need a few items in the kitchen."

Callie told her mother that Bobby would be home the day after tomorrow and he would take them shopping.

"Very well," Miss Sally Ann said.

The conversation went on among the ladies. Sarah got up to leave and told them to have a good evening as she walked out of the house.

"Mama! Mama!"

"Yes, Callie? . . ."

"I have to prepare for Bobo's ninth birthday party."

"When is that, Callie?"

"It's the last of this month . . . the last of June."

"I know how you feel, Callie, but if you are not up to it . . . just let him miss one of his birthdays. . . . I do not think that you are well enough to give a birthday party for your son this year."

"Well, Mama, I have been giving birthday parties for eight years already, and I wish that I could give him a birthday party this year . . . for his ninth birthday party."

"May I make a suggestion, Callie? I realize that the boy is getting larger and older."

"Aren't we all getting older?"

"We are not growing anymore, but certainly we are getting older."

"Yes, Mama."

"Then why don't you ask someone at the church to check to see if there are any more children at the church that might be having a birthday party on the same date as your son, Bobo? And maybe you all could have, uh, a birthday party together."

"Mama, I think that would be great, to have a huge birthday party for several kids at one time . . . good suggestion, Mama."

"Certainly, that would relieve you of some of those responsibilities, at a time like this . . . since you are not well enough to sponsor the birthday party all by yourself."

'You are right, Mama. I will ask Sarah to speak to some of the ladies at the church when she goes to the usher board meeting Wednesday night."

"The doctor told you not to exert yourself too much, remember?"

"Yes, Mama."

Sarah was able to locate three mothers whose children were having birthday parties the last of June. Sarah suggested to them, "Why not have a joint birthday party for, in this case, three boys and one girl?"

The ladies agreed and they started making their plans for the joint birthday party. Callie was told not to worry, because Bobo would enjoy himself better this way, because he enjoyed being with his peers.

* * *

"Don't worry about this being the first year that you were not able to give your son a birthday party. Let me tell you, he enjoyed himself immensely. You should have seen him when they played a game . . . boys against the girls. I do not think Bobo wanted to stop playing when the game was over."

This made Callie smile when her mother told her that about Bobo. "Anyway, he is nine years old now and he is in the fifth grade. . . . His peers are a year older than him."

"Well, Callie, that's because you taught him before he was old enough to go to school. He got a head start on the other children."

"Mama?"

"Yes, Callie."

"Who was that calling when I was in the bathroom?"

"That was Bobby. I told him that you were feeling sick earlier. How do you feel now?"

"Not very good. . . . I am going to lie down for a while."

"OK, Callie. Bobby said that he will be a little late coming, because he has to stop by the dry cleaners to pick up his suit."

"All right, Mama."

Bobby reached home about forty-five minutes before Bobo got home from school. Meanwhile, Bobby checked Callie as he greeted his mother-in-law. Callie was still in bed. Callie told him that she was not feeling well. Bobby suggested that she go to the hospital. Callie did not want to go to the hospital and agreed to go to the hospital tomorrow or the next day, if she was not feeling better by then.

Miss Sally Ann asked her son-in-law to take her to the grocery store, because, as she stated, they were short on a few items that they needed for dinner, today, tomorrow and for the rest of the week.

Bobby told his mother-in-law, "OK, but let's wait for Bobo before we leave."

When Bobo arrived, he went with them to the grocery store. Bobo wanted to stock up on junk food. His father told him, "Junk food is not as nutritious as the food that your grandmother cooks."

When they returned from the grocery store, Bobby checked on his wife as she lay in bed. He could tell, right away, that her condition was not good at all. She was a little incoherent when she spoke to him. He called Sarah and asked her to come over, so he could get Sarah's opinion about his wife, Callie. When Sarah arrived, she checked Callie and found her to be the same as Bobby had described her to be . . . incoherent in her speech pattern.

By this time, Miss Sally Ann came into the room where Callie was lying in bed. The decision was obvious. "Take Callie to the hospital, right away." They did not call an ambulance, because Bobby was able to carry her to the car. They waited for the doctor to give them the diagnosis of Callie's condition. The doctor suggested that they leave her in the hospital for a few days, so the other doctors could make their own diagnosis on Callie's condition, as well. Since Callie was in the hospital, they were able to check on her periodically during the day and night.

After Callie was in the hospital for several days, her condition improved somewhat. This was good news for the family, because Bobo wanted to see his mother. Bobo's father was away at this time, instructing the new long-distance truck driver who was scheduled to take over Bobby's route while Bobby was spending several days with his family and sick wife.

Bobby asked the doctor if it was possible for him to bring his son to the hospital to see his mother. Bobby did not want his son to see his mother with all of those tubes sticking out of her body. The doctor told Bobby that he would give Callie medication so he could take the tubes out of her body for at least one hour while Bobo was visiting his mother. Sarah was at the hospital earlier, and she made up her face so she would look natural while her son was visiting her.

During Bobo's visit, his mother told him that she was very sick and if anything happened to her, she wanted him to be a good boy and to remember all of the things that she taught him, how to live a good life, how to treat his neighbors, his friends, and most of all, obey his father, his grandmother, and Sarah and to study hard so he would always pass to the next grade . . . which meant that he would be getting higher and higher . . . smarter and smarter.

Bobo was standing . . . leaning against the side of the bed and holding his mother's hand said, "I will do all of the things that you are asking me to do and I will obey my father, my aunt, and my grandmother."

Bobby came and took Bobo by his hand as Bobo was saying, "Get well, Mama, so you can come home," and took him home.

The doctor came in and replaced the tubes in Callie . . . but Callie soon *died.* The doctor had known that there was no hope of Callie living any longer. He had revealed this information to Bobby, Miss Sally Ann, and Sarah, earlier, and they were expecting this would come to pass.

Later that night, not knowing that the family of Callie was in the hospital when she died, the nurse called and informed Miss Sally Ann that Callie had died. Time of death: 9:50 P.M.

The next day, Sarah came over to visit the family. Miss Sally Ann asked Sarah if she would notify the Department of Welfare of Callie's death. It was known at the office where Callie was one of the supervisors that she (Callie) was very sick, and they sorta expected that she would not live too long when she checked out to go to the hospital. Therefore, Callie's passing did not come as a surprise at her office. They all made plans to attend her funeral.

Sarah had to call her job to let them know why she was not going to report to work. Sarah's boss knew Callie and asked Sarah for the time of her funeral.

Sarah, while she was on her way to visit Bobby and Miss Sally Ann, met Bobo on his way to school as she approached the house. She noticed that Bobo appeared to be jolly. She spoke to Bobo, saying, "Have a good day at school."

Bobo said, "Thanks, Aunt Sarah," and continued on his way to school.

When she arrived, she opened the door with her keys. She found Bobby and Miss Sally Ann sitting in the living room. She, immediately blasted Bobby and Miss Sally Ann for not telling Bobo of his mother's death.

Bobby admitted that he could not find the words to use to tell his son of his mother's death, because Bobo was so fond of his mother. "We have to find a way to tell him. Otherwise, he might go into shock when they tell him of his mother's death."

Sarah responded by saying that they had to be very cautious in telling him of his mother's death.

Bobby said maybe he should go to school to pick Bobo up. This way, he would feel that something had happened and that would prevent him from becoming too surprised and maybe he would not go into shock.

Sarah and Miss Sally Ann agreed, saying, "Tell him that his mother left us and she is not coming back home anymore."

As they sat in the living room, they simply cried together for a while. When they were able to compose themselves, they made the funeral arrangements.

Sarah called the church and was able to speak directly to Reverend Few as he sat in his study. Reverend Few prepared the eulogy and made the other arrangements.

Miss Sally Ann suggested taking Callie's body back to Avon, Georgia, for burial. Bobby did not agree to taking her body back to Avon, Georgia, because he felt that Bobo might want to visit her grave and it should be convenient for him to do so.

Bobby continued, saying taking his wife's body back to her hometown of Avon, Georgia, would not be a good idea because of his son's love for his mother. Sarah agreed with Bobby. Miss Sally Ann was outnumbered; the burial would be in a cemetery there in Brooklyn.

Now what about Bobo? The question was how to reach Bobo to tell him that his mother had died. They would take Sarah's suggestion by using caution in doing so, yet how? Sarah seemed to be the one who should tell Bobo of his mother's death, because she had worked with children at the child care center for several years now and she seemed to understand children from her experience working with children. She understood their behavior. You have to figure them out . . . to see how they accept life and death.

They waited for Bobo to arrive from school. Sarah saw him coming, and she went outside to greet him.

After she greeted Bobo, Bobo asked "Aunt Sarah, were you here all day?" Because Bobo met his aunt early that morning when he was on his way to school, and seeing her here, almost at the end of the day, he wanted to know if she was here all day.

This was a cue for Sarah to break the news to Bobo of his mother's death. She said, "You see, Bobo, the reason that I am still here is because something happened to your mother in the hospital. You could see that she was not feeling well when you were there to see her . . . right?"

Bobo said, "Yes."

Sarah suggested, as she put her arms around him, "Be calm, because something happened to your mother."

Bobo knew then why his aunt had been at the house all day. He, quickly, asked, "Did Mama die?"

This is what Sarah wanted Bobo to ask; she did not want to say, "Your mother died."

"Last night, your mother left us, and she won't be coming back home to be with us anymore." At this point, Sarah could not hold back the tears filling her eyes.

Bobo's eyes quickly filled up with tears. When Bobo entered the house, he found his father and grandmother also crying.

Bobo seemed to be taking the news of his mother's death in a calm manner until his grandmother walked over to him, put her arms around him, and said, "Your mother has gone home to Jesus to rest."

It was this statement about his mother's passing by his grandmother that shook him up; Bobo got up and walked out of the room and out of the house.

When Miss Sally Ann finished cooking, she went outside and called Bobo, "Bobo, where are you?" Bobo did not answer her call. She looked around but did not see any sign of Bobo. She called again and again. A neighbor heard her calling Bobo and told Miss Sally Ann that she had seen Bobo, pointing in the direction where she had seen Bobo running quickly down the street. Miss Sally Ann went back into the house and told his father. Sarah heard Miss Sally Ann telling Bobby of Bobo's plight and said, "That's a normal reaction of a child under these circumstances, to act in this manner."

Bobby told his mother-in-law that he would look for Bobo later. Meanwhile, Bobo's playmate's mother called and said that Bobo was there and he seemed to be in shock and was crying. Sarah explained to her why Bobo was upset and that his father would be by to pick him up. Sarah also told the lady that it was an expected reaction by Bobo to act that way. She continued, saying, "Bobo was very fond of his mother, and maybe he feels that she cannot be replaced."

The lady on the phone said, "I understand."

Bobby went to pick up his son. His playmate's mother said that she had offered Bobo dinner, but he said that he was not hungry. She continued, saying that Sarah had told her the reason for Bobo's actions and that she could understand his reactions. She also advised Bobby to let Bobo get over his mother's passing gradually. "Do not rush him. He can adjust himself if you just leave it up to him. Meanwhile, take him places of interest; this will help him get over his grief."

On their way home, Bobo asked his father if he could stay home tomorrow from school. His father agreed that he could stay home from school and that they would go to the circus early tomorrow morning. Bobo felt a little uplifted when his father said that they would go to the circus. When they reached home, Bobo ate some of his food and went into his room. It was about 7:30 P.M. when Bobo went into his room, and for several minutes his father did not hear any more noise. He went into Bobo's room and found Bobo in bed. Bobby did not arouse him . . . just let him relax in his own way.

Sarah, Bobby, and Miss Sally Ann were still sitting in the living room finalizing the funeral arrangements for Callie. Sarah, realizing how Callie's voice had stood out as she sang with the choir at the Methodist church, felt that some of the songs that she sang with the choir should be played at her funeral as well. Bobby and Miss Sally Ann agreed and asked which ones would be appropriate to play at her funeral. Sarah responded saying, "Certainly Handel's masterpiece *The Messiah,* because all the members of the church as well as friends who attended service, especially Easter Sunday, would feel the same way. A lot of the members of the church, as well as friends of Callie, had always complimented Callie on her soprano voice to me when service was over."

Sarah continued, saying that *The Messiah* should be played at the wake and "The Hallelujah Chorus" should be played at the end of the funeral service at the church. She told Bobby and Miss Sally Ann that she had albums of this masterpiece at home and would furnish the records to be played for this purpose.

Bobby and Miss Sally Ann both had faith in Sarah, and they felt that they should agree with Sarah and give her credit for staying abreast with these events at the church. Bobby and Miss Sally Ann would be approached by people after service offering any comments about Callie or anybody else, for that matter, at their gratitude in enjoying what they were participating in at the church or elsewhere.

Sarah informed Bobby and Miss Sally Ann that she would ask her friend who played the recordings of "The Bridal Chorus" by Richard Wagner and "The Wedding March" by Felix Mendelssohn at her wedding to play Handel's *Messiah* at the wake and "The Hallelujah Chorus" at the end of the funeral service at the church.

The pastor of the church, Reverend Few, would deliver the eulogy. Among the praises Reverend Few mentioned about Callie's life on

Earth and in the church, in eulogizing Mrs. Callie Mae Ryan, was that her soprano voice would continue always to be heard in the choir, as an echo bouncing off the walls of this Methodist church.

At the cemetery, Bobby and Sarah held Bobo by his hands and his father told him that he could visit his mother's grave in the cemetery at any time that he wanted to and he could also put a flower on her grave, in memory of her good deeds for him. His father emphasized to "Just remember your mother as she was in real life." Bobo's gestures were to agree with his father's request in remembering his mother in real life and not in her grave.

After the burial, all members of the church and all of their friends were invited back to the church, where they would be served a meal. Here the church members and friends were constantly stopping by to offer their sympathy and their condolences to the bereaved family.

Realizing the loss of the mother of a child in the Ryan family, the members of the church and their friends offered their aid in any way that they could help them to recover from the loss of the faithful servant of the household, the late Mrs. Callie Mae Ryan. Mr. Ryan was very grateful for their concern in offering their help to restore a peaceful household.

When the meal was about over, Reverend Few told Sarah that he wanted to speak to her about Bobo. Sarah informed Reverend Few that Bobo's reaction after his mother's death could be very devastating to Bobo. "You see," she continued, "Bobo depended on his mother for everything, for guidance, and grieved and appeared to be very distressed or upset when she was not around. Usually, she was there when he went to bed, when he got up, when he ate, when he went to school, when he returned from school, and even when he went out to play and returned home his mother was there to greet him. She was his source of advice. His mother was his close companion, his faithful companion, and his source of the proper guidance."

"Without his mother Bobo is in a world of his own. His father, his grandmother, and even his aunt, Sarah, as faithful as she was to the Ryan family, could not replace Bobo's mother, the late Mrs. Callie Mae Ryan.

"Bobo's scholastic ability was a little above average, and I hope that he does not give up his ability to excel in his classes in school. I will, however, talk to him. He might confide in me, as an adviser for him, and maybe not. I will also ask my supervisor, who specialized in early childhood guidance, to talk to him. Maybe we can convince him that you have to go on with your life and to continue to do the same things that you were accustomed to doing before a great loss in the composition of the household of a 'parental guidance council,' if you will. And you should even try to do better to enhance your life for the better, not the worst side of your life."

Reverend Few cornered Bobo just before he was about to join some of his little friends and asked him to take a walk with him. He explained to Bobo that life should and must go on . . . regardless of the circumstances that might get in the way from time to time. "You do not give up. Your life is different and you should set an example for others to follow. Life is beautiful. Do not let it be any other way."

Bobo promised the pastor that he would try to follow his advice.

Sarah, as a peacemaker, spent the night at the Ryan house. After breakfast the next morning, they all agreed to take Bobo back to the cemetery so he would visit his mother's grave again. They all felt that in some way this might help him to get over his mother's passing.

After Bobo left his mother's grave site, his father, his grandmother, and Aunt Sarah walked back to the side of the grave site and, almost in unison, said, "Good-bye, Callie. . . . You were only thirty-five years old. Why did you leave us so soon? We loved you . . . but I guess it was GOD who loved you best."

Bobo returned to his mother's grave site. With his hands clasped and holding his arms up and looking up, his arms were in an inverted V, he said, "Mama, I will always miss you." And Bobo, with tears in his eyes, walked away. "Mama! . . . Mama!"

10

Bobo and His Grandmother

Bobo's readjustment to family life after the death of his mother was an uphill battle for his grandmother, Miss Sally Ann, to say the least. How should she approach this inevitable task? To help Miss Sally Ann make that decision, she contacted, first the pastor of the Methodist church, second, the Youth Council, and third, willing neighbors who were willing to share their concern with Bobo and his grandmother.

Miss Sally Ann realized that it would be very difficult to try to raise Bobo from the age of nine, especially here in the same house where his mother had spent so much time with him in raising him from birth to the age of nine. Miss Sally Ann suggested getting a small apartment in a different location, but not too far from their original home.

Miss Sally Ann consulted her son-in-law Bobby and Sarah about helping her to locate such an apartment. Both of them agreed to help her to find another apartment nearby.

The next day, Bobby was lucky to find an apartment about four blocks away from his house. Sarah also found an apartment, but it was almost seven blocks away. Miss Sally Ann chose the apartment that her son-in-law found. Then Sarah and Bobby helped Miss Sally Ann to furnish the apartment.

Bobo was introduced to the new apartment, but he did not want to leave his old address. Bobo was still nine years old. His next birthday would be right after the closing of the school year. He would be ten years old, but that was too young for a boy to go for long distances with his father in a large truck. Bobby realized that his son was too young to go with him on trips. Miss Sally Ann realized that he was too young to go with his father on those long trips, so it was up to his grandmother to try to raise Bobo in her own way.

For the next several days, plus when Bobo left school, instead of going to his grandmother's apartment, he would go by the old address.

When Bobo's father was at work, the house was vacant. Bobo did not have a key to the house, so he would sit on the steps in front of the house for a few hours. Miss Sally Ann knew when school was out and if Bobo did not show up at her apartment she knew where to go to find him. Miss Sally Ann would lock her apartment and walk back to the old address. Usually, she would find him sitting on the front steps, looking in one of his books.

His grandmother could understand what Bobo was going through, so she would handle him gently. She would talk to him, first, and then she was able to persuade him to come with her to her apartment.

With Miss Sally Ann's past experience in raising and understanding children, she knew exactly how to deal with his problem. She knew that she would have to go through the process of weaning Bobo from his once-customary address, where he was born and where he grew up from birth to the age of nine.

Bobo's father also knew that he had a problem with his son. When Bobo's father was at home on his break from work, he had to rest up for his next trip with a load of cargo to carry to faraway places before he would be able to get another chance to rest up for the next trip. This was a recurring type of behavior for Mr. Ryan to deal with on a daily basis. Mr. Ryan did not want his son to be in the house when he was there to rest up, for two reasons:

1. His son's presence in the house while he was there to rest up would prevent him from getting the proper amount of rest to prepare him for the next trip on his job.
2. Bobo's being in the house where he was born and where he grew up would not be good for him to endure, after his mother's death. This, Mr. Ryan felt, would create a bigger problem with his son.

When Bobo's father was at home to rest up, Grandma would bring him up-to-date . . . revealing her complaints in trying to continue raising little Bobo. Realizing that school would be closing soon for the summer, Miss Sally Ann suggested to her son-in-law that it would be good for Bobo to spend the summer months in Avon, Georgia. Bobby agreed, but Bobo did not want any part of that suggestion. He wanted to be near his playmates. His grandmother informed him that he could meet new playmates to play with, but little Bobo did not change his mind.

Miss Sally Ann was left with only one suggestion, that is, to do the best that she could with Bobo.

Miss Sally Ann did not give up on Bobo; she took him to the church and asked the Cub Scout leader to include Bobo in the summer activities for the Cub Scouts. Miss Sally Ann was successful in encouraging several other mothers to send their sons to join up with the Cub Scout leader, who arranged to take take the boys to different parks where there were facilities for different sports like softball, baseball, and basketball.

In midsummer, they would go on hikes, usually in the upstate area. The church furnished the bus to take the boys to these different places of interest.

Since Bobo was away for the summer, Bobby purchased a ticket for his mother-in-law to go back to her hometown for the summer months while Bobo was away. This period of the summer worked out for both Bobo and his grandmother, Bobo being with his playmates and Grandma spending some time in her own hometown.

What about Bobo's father? Well, he was happy, too, because as long as he felt that his son was happy he was also happy, and he could relax better knowing that everybody of concern was happy.

All good things will and must eventually come to an end. The enjoyment of the summer months must return to a more somber time to settle down and face reality again . . . back to the time when you would be faced with the next several months. Bobo was no exception, because he had to return to school . . . whether he liked it or not. It was Grandma who has to deal with Bobo's problems, not his father.

Miss Sally Ann was a little optimistic about Bobo's behavior being better when he returned to school after he spent the summer months at play with his playmates. She thought that all different activities with his peers would, in some way, cause him to forget about his mother's death . . . at least partially, but this was not the case with Bobo.

When Bobo returned to school for the fall semester, after a month had passed his grandmother noticed that his grades began to drop lower and lower. Bobo's grandmother tried very hard to replace his mother, but that was impossible as far as Bobo was concerned. Miss Sally Ann dressed herself up one day, and she went by Bobo's school and spoke to his teacher, Miss Slack. Miss Slack informed Miss Sally Ann that Bobo's behavior in school and in class was very good, but he seemed to be thinking about something foreign and not about what she was trying to teach him in class. Miss Slack told Miss Sally Ann that she had already sent a note to Bobo's father inviting him to come to see her about his son.

When Mr. Ryan stopped by the school, Miss Slack informed Mr. Ryan that his son did not seem to be interested in his grades. He liked to draw objects that had nothing to do with his classwork. His mind seemed to drift from time to time. "I am not able to reach him. . . . I thought that I was an effective teacher. I have received several commendations in the past few years. But with Bobo, no matter what method I use, I am still unable to reach him."

Mr. Ryan informed Miss Slack that Bobo had been raised by his devoted mother from birth up to the age of nine, "I am a long-distance truck driver. Most of my time is spent on the road . . . with breaks at truck stops situated at regular intervals along the route.

"I am usually away from home for several days at a time. When I am in town and at home, I have to spend part of my time with Bobo and the other part of my time resting up for my next long trip. It is for this reason that I am unable to spend a lot of time with my son. I know that it's hard for my son, but I have to work. When I was looking for a job, I was recommended to the truck drivers' association by a friend of mine. I needed a job and it was unfortunate that I had to settle with or accept a job as a truck driver and it turned out to be a long-distance truck driver's job.

"I was single at that time, and it did not occur to me, at that time, that I would eventually get married and start to raise a family. . . . I know that it is better, in a family, when there are two parents available to raise the children. The way it is now, my son does not have that fatherly image for him to imitate. . . . He does not have a male pattern to follow. Therefore, he had to depend on his mother for just about everything. He knows how to keep house, and he knows how to cook. He even walks like his mother at times. He learned what his mother was capable of teaching him. . . . He can sew on his mother's sewing machine.

"He has a problem . . . a big problem. After his mother died, I guess that he feels that nobody can replace his mother. He doesn't want to listen to anybody else for advice. He feels that nobody else can direct him on a different path from the one that he is currently following. He probably feels lost in a world all by himself.

"I will, however, try to reach him, as a father, and I will inform him that he soon will be approaching his high school graduation and he should not stop until he gets his high school diploma, because that high school diploma will be a certificate conferring an honor on his behalf . . . something that he has accomplished in his education. Nobody can take that knowledge away from him. If I cannot convince him to change his attitude and try to make good grades, then I will ask the pastor of the Methodist church to talk to him again.

"His grandmother tries to reach him every day. I will also ask his Scout leader to talk to him. If none of these persuasions fail to reach him, then, Miss Slack, I will have to leave it up to you as his teacher. . . . I know that you have tried to reach him, but for my sake, please try again. . . . Thank you."

Bobo was going through some type of change in his life, after his mother died, so his father was going to take some time off his job to stay with his son for a week or two . . . hoping to bring about a better change in his son's life.

Mr. Ryan informed his mother-in-law that he was going to take time off from his job, hoping that would help his son to face reality and change his way of living in a different world of his own. Mr. Ryan told Miss Sally Ann that he would not let Bobo live with him in his house, because being in the same house where he grew up in with his mother would be a no-no. That would bring back memories of his mother and make it worse for him.

Mr. Ryan started spending a lot of time at his mother-in-law's apartment with Bobo, so he would not have to take him home with him. Mr. Ryan would take Bobo to school and pick him up after school. He helped Bobo with his homework and would take him on trips to the zoo and other places of interest.

Bobo's grades improved after his father took time off from his job to help his son with his school assignments. Bobo finished the fifth grade and was promoted to the sixth grade, with fairly good grades. It seemed that his father's image of being with him for a period of time gave Bobo encouragement by assuring him of the parental guidance that he needed to encourage him to do better. At this point, his father thought that his son would continue to do better while he was away on his job . . . left with his grandmother to guide him. . . .

What would happen to Bobo and his grandmother from this point on? Mr. Ryan was interested in his son finishing high school, not dropping out of school. It seemed that Bobo had a long way yet to go before he finished high school. Would he make it that far? Certainly, his father would say, "Yes."

Bobo returned to school this fall in the sixth grade. He had a new teacher and new classmates to deal with. Bobo was ten years old. He was one year younger than his classmates. Remember that Bobo's mother was able to teach him the early fundamentals and he was promoted one grade when he entered school for the first time, although his classmates would not be able to tell that Bobo was one year younger than they were because Bobo was virtually the same size as the other children in his class. At this point in life, children do not think of age; they only think of the individual's presence and not how old the individual is, etc. They are concerned only with having a playmate.

Bobo's new teacher was small in stature and with a fine voice free from imperfection. Bobo took advantage of her ineptness right away when he reported to class. He would not obey her, and he would report to class late. The new teacher could not tolerate Bobo's behavior and reported him to the school principal. The principal invited Bobo to his office. The principal laid down the rules and regulations of the school to Bobo and told him that the school would not tolerate his type of behavior.

Mrs. Daily, although small in stature, was considered to be one of the most effective teachers in the public school system. She was small in stature, but she was a "giant" in her perfection as a public school teacher.

Mrs. Daily had won an award for being one of the most effective teachers of this decade. Mrs. Daily's secret weapon was getting the whole class's undivided attention before presenting her attack. What was her "attack"? She simply presented her lesson plan at this point. That was her secret weapon. She succeeded in doing that or succeeded in using that technique until Bobo came to her class. Bobo changed all of that.

At this point, Mrs. Daily had no choice but to go back to the principal of the school with her second complaint against Bobo.

The principal of the school informed Bobo that he would either obey the teachers in this school or would be suspended from the school, not tomorrow or next week, but today. The principal, on second thought, decided to transfer Bobo to another class in the school.

Mrs. Daily and the other teachers on her floor agreed with the principal's decision to transfer Bobo to another class. They agreed that

Bobo should remain in school so he would be promoted to the next-highest grade at the end of the school year.

When Bobo reported to his new class, he carefully sized up the new teacher, who was a heavy, robust black male teacher. Bobo decided within himself that he had better obey this teacher or he could be thrown out of class by this teacher himself, without the principal's advice.

Bobo changed his ways in class; he became a good student for the entire school semester, and his grades were average. Bobo participated in the athletic activities at the school and the activities at the methodist church as well.

Bobo was very anxious to get out of Mr. Dodd's class. Bobo knew that he could not have his own way in Mr. Dodd's class. It was "straighten up and fly right" in Mr. Dodd's class or be thrown out of class.

* * *

It was at this point in Bobo's visits to my living room, that he told me of preparing himself for his eleventh birthday with his grandmother. He told me that he was not getting along very well with his grandmother. As he described to me in giving me his story of growing up in Brooklyn without his mother's guidance, he told me that his grandmother was too "hard" on him. He said that she was too strict with him. She did not want him to stay out at night after eight o'clock P.M. At age eleven, he felt that he could look out for himself. He felt that he did not have to be reprimanded by his grandmother so often.

When his eleventh birthday came, nothing was done about it. No birthday party was given for him, nor did anybody even mention his birthday to him. His mother used to give him a birthday party each time he had a birthday. In my opinion, Bobo felt that nobody cared anything about him anymore. Maybe it was because he felt that nobody cared about him that he ended up on the street at age eleven.

Bobo's grandmother wanted him to be in the house by eight o'clock at night. There were many nights that Bobo did not show up at all. His grandmother visited a lot of her neighbors while she was looking for him, but no one could help her, because they had not seen Bobo themselves.

On one of Bobo's visits to my living room, he told me that he would go with his father to Penn Station to pick up his grandmother when she was coming to stay with them. When his father was at work and his grandmother was coming to stay with them, his Aunt Sarah would go to meet her at the station. He said that he would also go with his Aunt Sarah to pick up his grandmother when she was coming to stay with them.

Bobo said that he noticed that some men were lying on the seats at times when they went to the station to pick up his grandmother. He asked his aunt, "Why are these men always lying around on the seats here in the station when we go to pick up Grandma?"

His aunt told Bobo, "They are homeless men. They come here, especially in the wintertime, to keep warm during the night and daytime to sleep. They do not have a place to live, so they come here. Here they are warm and if it is raining they are dry. They do not get wet in the rain. Sometimes they beg for money to buy food to eat. They do not have a place to live, nor do they have a job. You should not grow up to be like these men here in the station."

Bobo's Aunt Sarah did not tell him that these men were classified as "bums." She did, however, tell Bobo not to grow up to be a bum on the street.

Did Bobo remember those men at the station when he did not come home for three nights? Subway fare was only a nickel in the forties, and Bobo simply went to Penn Station for the night. He had his allowance money, so he did not have a problem buying some food to eat. Since he was there where somebody would bother him, that is, in order for the cops not to ask him questions, he stayed close to one of the men that he felt could pass for his father. Then the cops would think, *There is a father and his son,* and would not ask any questions of either of them.

When Bobo finally came home, he not only found out that his grandmother was looking for him; he found out that his grandmother and his Aunt Sarah had notified or reported him missing to the police department and they, the policemen, were looking for him as well. No one at that time would even think that an eleven-year-old boy would seek refuge or cover at a train station like the men who were staying there as "bums."

When Bobo left home, as he told me on one of his visits to my living room, he was planning to stay with one of his old friends for a few nights like he had when his mother was alive. She gave him permission to stay with one of his friends at that time for a few nights, and no questions were asked. But Bobo failed to locate his old friend. Bobo stood on the street wondering what to do next.

Bobo was peeved, because no one had thought of him when his eleventh birthday came. As he stood on the street, he recalled that no one had given him a birthday party when he was ten years old, either. But he felt that the reason for not giving him a birthday party when he reached ten years old was because his mother had died only one year earlier. But now it was two years ago his mother had died, and no one even thought of him when he reached age eleven.

Bobo was accustomed to being given a birthday party each year when his mother was alive. Now he felt that nobody thought about him anymore. As Bobo stood on the street, he thought of what his Aunt Sarah had told him about why those men were staying at Penn Station. He then boarded the subway and ended up at Penn Station. After he stayed one night, he decided to stay another night, then another night.

Bobo was dirty . . . not only, his clothes, but his body as well. He did not tell his grandmother or his Aunt Sarah where he stayed. He simply said, "I stayed with a friend."

Later, however, Bobo told his grandmother and his Aunt Sarah that he stayed at Penn Station.

His grandmother said, "Why at Penn Station?"

Bobo replied that his Aunt Sarah had told him that those men that they saw lying around on the benches were men who did not have a place to stay, so they came to Penn Station for a place to stay. "That's why I went to Penn Station to stay."

His Aunt Sarah was upset when Bobo said that his aunt had told him the reason that those men were staying there was because they did not have a place to stay. His aunt had thought that she was discouraging Bobo, not encouraging him that Penn Station was a place for him to go to seek refuge for the night.

His grandmother asked him, 'Why did you go there? You have a place to stay . . . a nice place to stay."

Bobo said that he felt that no one thought about him anymore, since his mother was dead.

His grandmother replied, "That is not true. We do care for you."

Grandma outlined a few things that she did for him, and his aunt mentioned the things that she has done for him, since his mother died. Bobo simply nodded his head, saying in a low voice, "Yes."

Grandma had a big job to do in order to get Bobo cleaned up again. Bobo was not reprimanded or scolded. His grandmother and aunt simply at the same time told him and pointed out to him that if he continued to do things like that, he would eventually end up as a "bum," like those men on the street and staying at Penn Station. "Your life will be worthless. . . . You will not own anything. . . . You will not be looked up to as a man of value. . . . You will not be able to be a role model for a male child." They continued, saying, "You will be just a bum on the street. Is that what you want? Bobo? You will not have any self-esteem. Nobody will respect you as a man. . . . Think about it, Bobo."

Bobo did think about his future and returned to school, and his grades were better for the whole semester.

Sarah called Bobo's father at his office and brought him up-to-date on Bobo's behavior for the last month or so. Mr. Ryan took time off from his job to spend some time with his son, Bobo. He, Mr. Ryan, tried to rehabilitate his son before he checked him out, to see how he was doing in school. He did, however, notice that his son's behavior had changed somewhat. His grades, he noticed, had improved somewhat, and his overall character had improved.

Mr. Ryan contacted Sarah and told her that his son was showing signs of improvement before he had a chance to offer his demands of what he should or should not do. Sarah responded by telling Mr. Ryan that she and Miss Sally Ann had talked to him at length, advising him of the danger that he might face if he did not change his way of life now. Sarah continued telling Mr. Ryan that this was the reason Bobo had changed his way of life.

At this point, Mr. Ryan felt that he could return to his job, leaving the full responsibility up to Bobo's grandmother. Miss Sally Ann realized that Bobo was eleven years old. He could join the Boy Scouts. She pursued that possibility and was able to sign Bobo up to join the Boy Scout troop. Miss Sally Ann did not hesitate; she told the Boy Scout leader of Bobo's behavior in the past and that he should not take for granted that Bobo would be a good Boy Scout. "You have to keep checking on him, make him follow the rules and the regulations of the responsibilities of a Boy Scout." The pastor of the Methodist church would also be mindful of the fact that Bobo had a problem since his mother's death, and he would keep an eye on Bobo as well.

When Miss Sally Ann returned home, she called Bobo in so she could talk to him. Bobo was hesitant to come inside. His grandmother insisted that he come in now, so she could talk to him. Reluctantly Bobo came inside to listen to his grandmother.

Bobo walked in the room, looked at his grandmother, then sat down, in a slouchy way or manner, with his legs and feet stretched out. His grandmother told him that she had signed him up with the Boy Scout leader at the Methodist church to include him on the roster as a Boy Scout of America.

Bobo said, "Uh, why did you do that, Grandma?"

"I thought that you wanted to become a Boy Scout at the church," Miss Sally Ann said.

Bobo did not show any enthusiasm or any interest in what his grandmother had done for him. Miss Sally Ann, observing her grandson's lack of interest in what she had done for him, said, "I thought that you wanted to become a Boy Scout of America? Being a Boy Scout is higher than a Cub Scout. . . . Don't you want to be a Boy Scout, Bobo?" Meanwhile, she silently said to herself, *What can I do for this boy?*

Finally, Bobo said, "I did not make up my mind yet on what I want to do, Grandma."

Bobo continued to go out and stay out late at nights. Ten o'clock at night is late for an eleven-year-old boy to be coming home by himself at night.

Bobo's grandmother was getting old, but she was still active and she would do things in a cunning manner; she slipped out one night after Bobo had left the house to see if she could find out what Bobo was up to when he went out and why he stayed out until ten o'clock at night. Miss Sally Ann did not want her grandson to recognize her while she was spying on him as he walked along the streets. She had to disguise herself in such a way that Bobo would not recognize her. She dressed in one of her son-in-laws' overall suits, with one of his old hats. "My," she said when she looked in a mirror at herself, "I do not recognize myself; I know Bobo will not recognize me."

Miss Sally Ann found out where Bobo was going with the help of some of the neighbors in the area. To her surprise, she found out that Bobo was spending a lot of his time watching the horses as they roamed around the lot provided for horses. Miss Sally Ann did not know how to classify Bobo's behavior with his association of "the boy and the beast." Miss Sally Ann returned home, sat in the living room, and tried to figure out why Bobo selected the beast (horses, in this case) to help him overcome his loneliness.

On one of Bobo's visits to my living room, he told me that there used to be horse stables located on Buffalo Avenue between Atlantic Avenue and Herkimer Street. Bobo indicated that there were about five or six horses kept in those stables at night, and they would roam about the lot in the daytime. He said that in the lot or large yard where the horses walked around and sometimes just stood in one spot for long periods of time, he observed that there were receptacles shaped like elongated boxes that they kept full of water for the horses to drink and the lot was also equipped with racks where hay was placed for the horses to eat.

Since Bobo had been raised by his mother alone, because his father was always on the job, which required him to be on the road for long periods of time, going from one place or city to another delivering cargo from one city to the next city, as a long-distance truck driver, he did not have much time to spend at home and with his wife and son, Bobo. Bobo did not have a brother or sister to share his mother's love and did not have anybody to play with; he would get to feel just like being alone. He found solace in just watching the horses as they roamed about the large lot where they would be found . . . just standing, switching their tails, moving their heads, or shaking their heads and looking around, for long periods of time.

* * *

In spite of Bobo's horrible behavior toward me at times, when he discovered that I was alone and sitting in my living room he would knock on my door and ask if he could come in. I could tell that he wanted some kind of advice or something else had prompted him to be eager to come into my living room to talk to me.

I never refused to let him in my living room. During his visit, he seemed to be in his better mood. It was from these visits to my living room that I found out all of Bobo's past while he was growing up from birth to the time, at age nine, when his mother died, and now at age eleven, when he ended up on the streets. Many times, he would repeat some of the things that he had already told me on previous visits to my living room.

Now that he had found himself on the streets, like all male children, he looked for that fatherly image to use as a role model and imitated his father's ways and tried to repeat the same movements as his father in doing things for himself and for others. If he does not have a father who is available, the male child will invariably imitate his mother's ways of doing things. This will lead to a void in a male child's reaction to what he will do in the future.

It appeared that Bobo could not find or did not get this fatherly guidance at home; therefore, he was seeking to fill this void in his life with someone on the outside. If, however, he found this guidance from some of his peers on the outside, good or bad, whatever patterns of behavior practiced by the boys on the street would be followed or practiced by the boy Bobo, on the street looking for some type of guidance to follow. The lonely child will follow these rules and regulations from anyone he puts trust in or confidence in, at home, on the streets, or elsewhere. This will be a void in his life that he will always be seeking to fulfill in his life cycle.

At this point, it seemed that Bobo could not find himself. Bobo would spend a lot of his time in the parks during this particular summer. A lot of children would spend time in the park, and Bobo did not find it difficult finding other children to play with. Some of the children would be playing baseball, some would be playing basketball, some would be playing tennis, and some would be playing volleyball.

Bobo did not participate in any of these sports. Instead, he would harass the girls who would be jumping rope, playing hopscotch, or just playing hide and seek.

Bobo would wait until the girls would be jumping rope, then would suddenly jump in with the girl that was jumping rope. This would cause the rope to get tangled in their feet. The girls would yell at him and ask him to leave them alone.

Then Bobo would go to the girls who were engaged in hopscotch. When a girl would be going through the routine of hopscotch, Bobo would start at the opposite end of the game jumping in the opposite direction of the girl who would be jumping in the right direction of the game. The girls would yell at him and ask him to leave them alone.

One of the girls took off one of her shoes and threw it at Bobo. Bobo picked up the shoe and started to walk away with the girl's shoe. A group of girls took off after Bobo. Several of the girls started pounding on him with their fists. Bobo threw the girl's shoe back to her, then walked away. The girls yelled, "Do not come back here!"

While Bobo was walking through the park, he came upon a group of girls; two of the girls were fighting. Bobo intervened, breaking up the fight between the two girls. Here Bobo was a hero. The girls applauded him for his courage in breaking up the fight between the two girls. This gesture of Bobo in breaking up the fight gained him some new friends.

The new girls laughed with Bobo, and some of them shared their lunch with Bobo. Bobo introduced himself to the girls, and he learned some of the girls' names as well. He even learned where each of them lived. Bobo told them that he was in the sixth grade in school. The group of girls sorta inspired Bobo. Some of these girls were in the sixth grade, some were in the fifth grade, and some were in the seventh grade. The girls in the seventh grade inspired Bobo the most. When Bobo returned to school after the summer break, he was a good student. It seems that Bobo wanted to compete with the girls in the seventh grade.

Bobo's father and his grandmother knew that Bobo had improved his grades in school but did not know what had inspired him to study his lessons and do his homework on time during these times that he was hard to reach.

* * *

Bobo was not a good tenant. Maybe it was because he had a missing link in his life as he was growing up, with his father absent most of the time. I accepted him when he would visit me in my living room, in spite of his harsh attitude toward me. Maybe it was because I could see that there was something missing in his life . . . and it seemed that he was trying to correct that void in his life. . . . I simply accepted him whenever he asked me if he could come into my living room to talk to me.

On one of his visits to my living room one day, I asked him if he ever had any good connections or moments with his father at any time while he was growing up.

Bobo simply said there was only one time that he could recall having a good relationship with his dad. He said there was only one occasion that he could recall having a good time with his father . . . that he could remember . . . that he enjoyed being with his father. . . . It was one of the Christmas holidays . . . after Christmas. "He bought me a large rubber ball . . . about five inches in diameter. I went with my dad to the grocery store to get something for my mother. . . . I carried my rubber ball with me. . . . My father suggested that I run in front of him for several feet. . . . I had given him, my father, the ball. . . . After I ran several feet in front of him, he said, 'Stop.' As I stopped and looked back, he threw the ball to me. . . . I caught the ball . . . like football players catch footballs . . . during a game of football. I enjoyed playing with my father very much in this manner and thought that I could only enjoy playing with my father like this and nobody else could give me that type of enjoyment . . . like my father could give me.

"My father and I played in this manner several times when we were going to the grocery store." Bobo said, "I really enjoyed that little episode with my dad . . . immensely." But that was the only time that his father played with him. After his father returned to work, Bobo had to rely on his peers on the street to fill that void in his life.

I asked Bobo about how old he was when he enjoyed playing ball with his father. Bobo said that he was about five years old at that time. Not having his father around for long periods of time and with nobody else in the household to play with him caused him to become a loner. His mother was unable to fulfill those wishes for him. Sometimes he would feel like just being alone.

When he would go to watch the horses, he would be by himself. It seems that the horses would fascinate him, and he would spend a lot of time at the stables, just watching the horses as they stood about the lot swishing their tails and just looking around, possibly looking at Bobo.

Bobo was not always on his best behavior. The evil side of Bobo would persuade him to do mischievous things at times. Sometimes when Bobo would be on his way to visit the horses stables, he would fill his pockets with rocks. After watching the horses for a while, Bobo would pelt the horses with rocks. This type of behavior would cause the horses to run around the lot, sometimes bumping into each other. When the horses would become very annoyed they would start making noises. This type of behavior by the horses would be repeated over and over, again and again.

When the caretaker would hear the horses making so much noise and seeming to be very upset, he would come out to check to see what was causing the horses to become upset. At this point, Bobo would cunningly slip away from the scene . . . leaving the caretaker wondering what was causing the horses to become so upset or aroused. Bobo would return home and would, often, end up playing with some of his games, especially when his playmates were not around at that time of day.

On Bobo's next trip to the horse stables, he met three boys who said that they lived in the area and they were in the process of organizing a "street gang." They asked Bobo to join them in organizing this street gang. They told Bobo that they wanted about eight or ten boys to start the gang. Later they said that they could increase the number of gang members . . . if needed in the future. Bobo asked the boys what they would have to do. The three boys said that they would have to protect their area or territory from other boys from a different area or territory. Bobo could not understand what the boys were trying to tell him. One of the boys told Bobo that the leader of the gang could tell him about their responsibility to protect their territory better. Bobo could not interpret what the boys were trying to tell him. Bobo left the boys and instead of going to the horse stables went back home.

Usually, Miss Sally Ann was not too strict with her grandson, especially in the late spring and summer months of the year. Then again, she would find it necessary to check on Bobo and find out why he insisted on staying out late at night. Bobo was very frank with his answers to his grandmother. He said that sometimes he was with his friends and sometimes he just went to see the horses.

"Horses!?" his grandmother asked.

"Yes, the horses," Bobo replied. "Sometimes, in the daytime, I go by the horse stables, just to see the horses."

"For goodness' sake Bobo, where are these horses that you are talking about?"

"Not far from here, Grandma, at Herkimer Street and Buffalo Avenue . . . and Atlantic Avenue . . . in that area, Grandma."

When Bobby was not around to give Bobo his allowance, he would run errands for some of the elderly neighbors. Some of the elderly neighbors knew Bobo and his grandmother. They also knew and understood the plight that Bobo was experiencing at this stage of life. They knew his father, Mr. Ryan. They knew that Mr. Ryan was a long-distance truck driver and was not home for long periods of time. Realizing that Bobo's father was away for most of the time, they would give Miss Sally Ann a hand in supervising Bobo . . . trying to help keep Bobo in line and out of mischief . . . as often as they could help. They would pay

Bobo for running errands for them and often recommended other neighbors hire him to run their errands. Bobo was never broke. Bobo always had money in his pockets.

The elderly neighbors knew that if Bobo could not get money when he needed it, he would eventually be encouraged to develop the skills of stealing, robbing, and snatching ladies' pocketbooks to get his spending money.

Bobo, being intrigued by the horses, decided to return to the stables to watch them. On his way, he saw two of the three boys that he had seen on one of his previous trips to the horse stables. They recognized one another, and the boys told Bobo that the leader of the gang was across the street, visiting one of the other boys. They asked Bobo if he could wait for a few minutes to see the leader.

Bobo waited to see the leader. He came out with the other boy and was introduced to Bobo. The leader explained to Bobo the purpose of the gang and the responsibilities involved in being a member of the Blue Jacks. This was the name of the gang, Bobo was told by the leader of the gang. The leader was able to persuade Bobo to join the Blue Jacks gang. The leader invited Bobo to the next meeting of the gang. Then he left to go meet some of the other boys in the area.

After Bobo joined the gang, the Blue Jacks, he was not obligated to spend a lot of time with the members of the gang. Therefore, Bobo had a lot of time to run his errands for the elder neighbors, and he had time to visit the horse stables. At this point, Bobo had gotten used to the horses and their reactions toward him. . . . He would get closer to the horses . . . close enough to rub his hands down in front of the horses' heads . . . would those be called the horses' faces? Anyway, the horses seem to be enjoying what Bobo was doing to them, and Bobo got a thrill out of what he was doing to the horses. He continued to pet the horses when he would go to see them.

Bobo was now getting closer and closer to becoming a full-fledged member. However, Bobo continued to be by himself at times. He seemed to enjoy himself when he was alone. Maybe that was because he was raised as the only child in the family. In spite of these extra things that he was doing, he did, however, continue going to school . . . thanks to his grandmother's encouragement on a daily basis . . . also thanks to the girls that helped to encourage him also on a daily basis. He was simply inspired to see the girls each day that he was in class.

One day, Bobo was feeling kinda blue . . . sorta depressed in his feelings. He gathered up a few rocks, put them into his pockets, and went to the horse stables. When Bobo arrived to the lot where the horses were, he just stood there watching the horses as they came toward him. The horses were used to Bobo petting them from the last few times that he was there watching them. Bobo noticed that there were only three horses left in the lot. They had gotten rid of some of the horses. On Bobo's last visit to the horse stables, he had aroused them to the extent that they were upset and running about the lot. The caretaker remembered that the horses had gotten upset a few weeks ago, and he wondered what made them become so upset. Since that time, he was on the "lookout" to see if he could find the "culprit" who upset the horses before.

The caretaker had figured that it could have been a pack of stray dogs passing the lot that disturbed the horses. The caretaker was mindful of this possibility, and he did not give up hope. He wanted to be sure that it was, in fact, a pack of dogs that caused this uproar among the horses. Bobo, however, did not know that the caretaker was on the lookout for this unidentified culprit to appear on the scene.

Bobo did not realize that the caretaker was on the watch to find out who was upsetting the horses. Being alert, the caretaker had invited some of his friends to help him to find out who was upsetting the horses. These friends of the caretaker were standing by his side when Bobo arrived on the scene.

The caretaker, as well as his friends, were spread out on the outside, out of sight of Bobo. Bobo pelted one of the horses with a big rock. This horse ran around the other horse. By this time, Bobo had pelted the other horse. Both horses were running around each other and they started making noises. Bobo hesitated for a while. Meanwhile, the caretaker and his friends were getting in position behind Bobo.

Suddenly Bobo started pelting the horses in rapid succession. The horses became unruly in their emotions as they ran about the lot. The caretaker and his friends closed in on Bobo. Bobo had used up all of his rocks, and he was just standing there watching the horses running around each other and making noises as the caretaker and his friends closed in on Bobo. Bobo was surprised and was unable to run away from them. The caretaker asked Bobo why he pelted the horses with the rocks. Bobo did not have an answer on the spur of the moment. Then he answered, saying, "Just for fun."

The caretaker said, "Just for fun?"

By this time, the friends of the caretaker started pounding on Bobo with their fists . . . and saying, "Just for fun, eh?"

When they had finished beating Bobo, he left with aches and pains and a bloody nose. The caretaker warned Bobo that if he returned, the beating process would be greater. "We hope that you understand that. If not, we will remind you with greater force in our fists."

The carekater did not have any more trouble with Bobo. The horses, no doubt, missed the petting from Bobo, because they enjoyed being petted by Bobo's hands.

Bobo, being on the street, found himself without any money in his pockets. He visited some of the elderly neighbors to see if they wanted him to run any more errands for them. A few of the elderly neighbors needed a few supplies from the store. Bobo soon had some money to put in his pockets to tide him over until his father returned home from his job.

Bobo, not having the opportunity to visit the horse stables anymore, found himself with nothing to do to amuse himself and started spending more time with the gang members on the streets . . . the Blue Jacks.

On one of Bobo's visits to my living room, I was curious to find out why they, the gang members, called themselves the Blue Jacks? Bobo pointed out to me that the members were supposed to wear blue jackets. Instead of calling themselves the Blue Jackets, they decided to just say the "Blue Jacks" instead.

Bobo continued, saying that the members now totaled twenty-five in number. The area that the Blue Jacks were supposed to protect, as they stated, would be the area of Saratoga Avenue to Troy Avenue, east to west, Bergen Street to Chauncey Street, north to south. This area was to be protected from rival gangs. The Blue Jacks would not allow other gang members to invade their territory. They, the Blue Jacks, would always be on the lookout for rival gangs to enter their territory without permission.

Since there were rival gang members in their respective areas, they were vulnerable to one another, as they had to protect their designated areas from the rival gangs, as they were obligated to do as their policy, adopted to save their territory from other gang members. This was considered a "just claim" that all rival gang members followed . . . religiously.

This type of domination would result in gang fights because they felt that they were obligated to protect their territory. At this stage of domination, they did not use guns or knives to defend themselves and their territory. They would, however, use sticks and rocks. They did not kill any of the rival gang members. If, however, one gang member's head count outnumbered the rival gang head count. Usually this would happen to the invading gang members; then the home-based gang members would outnumber the rival gang members. Therefore, the home-based gang members were considered the winners. This same type of domination behavior would result if the Blue Jacks would invade another gang's territory.

I was able to get Bobo's age on one of his visits to my living room. I then counted back from 1992 to 1948, as Bobo's age was about fourteen or fifteen in 1948.

It was in 1948 that I purchased a dry-cleaning store, which was called a tailor shop at that time. I had just gotten my discharge from the U.S. Army at that time and needed a job. This was one way to become self-employed. I had an income. I operated my store on the corner of Albany and St. Mark's Avenue. I recalled that there was a small number of boys in the area just beginning to form a gang. It was obvious that it would be called a street gang. I was not familiar with the type of tactics used by the boys in the area. One lady in the area, I recall, had seven children . . . four boys and three girls. Ironically, this lady had a different father for each of her children. . . . This is true.

Anyway, since I was a schoolteacher prior to my army career, it seemed that I had the knack of advising or just lecturing someone on what should or not should be done in different situations. The boys in the area soon found out that they could talk to me and I would listen to them. They told me that they had formed a gang in the area and they called themselves the Bats. Like Bobo's colleagues, the Bats were responsible for their territory. Now I am curious to know why they were called or had selected the name Bats. Not baseball bats. These gang members were referring to themselves as Bats. I looked up the meaning of *bats* in the dictionary and I came up with: "Bats are night-flying, insect-eating mammals with arms and legs connected by a membrane and used as wings."

I noticed that these gang members, the Bats, would walk with their arms down and slightly out from their body and extending back from their hand area. They would walk with a rocking motion . . . maybe to indicate that they were ready to take off in flight on a moment's notice.

I recall one day three or four of the Bat members came into my store with what they called a zip gun. I noticed that the object called the trigger was propelled by an ordinary rubber band. One of the members pointed out to me how it was supposed to be fired. There was a vacant lot in the rear of the building where my store was located. This gang member invited me to go with them to the rear of the building where they were going to demonstrate to me how the zip gun should be fired. I went with them to the lot to witness the firing of his newly made zip gun.

Joe was the name of the gang member who made the zip gun. Joe pointed the zip gun down toward the ground, but he was afraid to pull the trigger. He thought that his zip gun might backfire and he would end up with the bullet in him instead of the ground. That demonstration was not to be because of fear.

I saw Joe several days later, and he told me that he had destroyed his zip gun. Maybe it was out of fear in its type of operation that caused Joe to discard his zip gun forever.

From my tenant Bobo's visits to my living room I learned about how the Blue Jacks gang operated during Bobo's tenure as a gang member. Now I am going back several years to the time when I learned about the Bats gang and how they operated. The territory they, the Bats, operated in was from Troy Avenue to Nostrand Avenue, east to west, and from MacDonough Street to Bergen Street, north to south. Now I can say that the gang Bobo belonged to was a rival gang to the Bats gang.

I recall that there was an incident that happened several feet from my store. According to my recollections, a member of another gang strayed into the Bats territory and was beaten up by the members of the Bats gang. There was another incident that happened, apparently with another gang member in the Bats territory. Several Bat members rushed into my store and closed the door behind them. I asked what happened. One of the members pointed to a guy standing across the street holding a gun in his hand The guy with the gun soon left the area. There was no confrontation by any of the members of the Bats gang. They were happy that he left on his own.

I guess that you can say that this was about the time when the gang members started to become violent toward one another. Then it became dangerous for any young man to walk the street by himself. Rival gang members would think that he was from another gang and attack him. You should wear your colors, like blue jackets for the Blue Jacks. I do not recall the Bats' having any type of colors that they identified themselves with. They, however, would walk in a switching motion with their arms extending back and their hands opened, as if to fly.

The girls in the area where the members of the Bats had organized their gang were not members of the gang, per se. They were loyal to the members of the gang and socialized with them as well. One day, a group of girls came into my store. They did not have to ask me if they could come into my store. Like the members of the Bats gang, they would simply walk into my store, because they knew that they were accepted from previous visits in my store. They did not, however, consider me their equal, but a friend and I would give them good advice if they needed to be advised. These girls knew that I would accept them in my store. Therefore, they would without hesitation walk into my store. After they entered my store, I talked to them for a while; then I continued to do my work.

There was a section in my store, next to the plate-glass window, where you could sit down on what resembled a bench. Some of the girls would simply stand up while they were talking. My sense of hearing was very good, and I could hear everything that they were saying. They had no fear of saying anything in my presence; therefore, I could hear everything that they were discussing. They did not at any time whisper during their conversation.

It seems at that time there was a new girl in the area. She had just moved into the neighborhood with her parents. She was attending the same school where she met these girls who had formed a group of girls who were loyal to the members of the Bats gang. It seems that the new girl in the area had to fit into the same class as the loyal girls, if you will. The new girl had to become a member of the same clan in order to be accepted in the same activities as the loyal girls, to be counted as one with the same qualities . . . same decorum . . . to become whatever was suitable or proper . . . to show good taste in behavior, speech patterns, the proper dress, etc.

The new girl was dominated by peer pressure, and she felt that she had to conform with the loyal girls or be left out of the clan. At this point, the new girl did not know what type of initiation ritual she would have to participate in in order to fit in the same class, if you will, as these loyal girls.

The leader of the loyal girls arranged a meeting with the new girl in order to introduce the new girl to the type of initiation that she had to conform with in order to become a member of their clan. When the leader of the group reached this point, she looked at me . . . and I pretended that I did not hear anything that they were saying or discussing.

The leader continued saying that the new girl, in order to become a full-fledged member, had to have sex with one of the members of the Bats gang. When the leader said that, the girls in the store laughed . . . and they laughed. I also laughed, but I still pretended that I did know what they were talking about. The leader continued, saying that the new girl realized what the leader was saying. She cringed and backed off. The girls in the store laughed and laughed again and again at those remarks. The leader paused to let the new girl think about what she had to do in order to become a member of the clan.

At this point, the new girl had walked away, but she returned to the group . . . and just stood there, motionless. Finally, the new girl spoke up. She said, "I did not, at any time in my life, have sex with anybody. It will be a difficult task for me to conform with your request at this time." The girls laughed again.

One girl asked, "What did she do?"

The leader of the group said, "We gave her a name, the Virgin Girl." They continued to call the new girl the Virgin Girl for several weeks hence.

The Virgin Girl assured them that she would conform with their request in about three or four weeks.

The number of weeks that the Virgin Girl had requested passed. She returned to the group of girls who were on her case and informed the girls that she was ready for her first experience of a "sexual act."

The girls in my store were explaining how they introduced the Virgin Girl to the member of the Blue Jacks gang. The leader of the girls said that they were very concerned about the Virgin Girl, because she was the first girl to join their group that had never had sex before.

The leader of the group invited the virgin over and offered her a seat and told her to relax. The leader explained very simply and carefully, step-by-step, to the Virgin Girl how the member of the street gang had agreed to be very careful with his approach to her. The male prodigy also agreed to adhere to her emotions under all circumstances. The leader informed the male prodigy that if he followed his version as he had explained it, she would be accepted by the group of girls involved in this case.

The Virgin Girl did not say no or reject what was planned for her to experience. These girls proceeded with their plans by selecting the same vacant lot that Joe had selected to demonstrate the firing of his zip gun. It was in the late spring and the grass was very tall in one section of the lot. It was near the corner of the lot and offered a shade of privacy. The girls in my store said that they carried the Virgin Girl to this spot in the lot. As the Virgin Girl stood there, motionless, the girls matted down an area with their feet by walking around in the tall grass. It was like a rug when they finished and simulated a small mattress. The flattened area was soft enough to cushion their movements.

The girls informed the Virgin Girl how she should prepare herself for this first sexual act.

The boy selected for this sexual act came over to this prepared area, and right away he told the girls to move back. The girls laughed but complied with his request. The selected member of the street gang prepared himself as an old pro . . . in this type of assignment. Soon he proceeded with the act, but he seemed to be having a problem in the beginning. For one thing, she did not know how to lie for the act in question. After he positioned her, he proceeded with the act. He still had a problem. This time, it was when he was trying to insert his penis in her. He, however, proceeded with his persistent motion.

After a few minutes had passed, the leader of the girls walked over silently. She asked the Virgin Girl, "Is it in yet?" A few seconds passed, and there was no answer from the Virgin Girl. Very soon after the leader inquired about the Virgin Girl's experience thus far, one of the other girls walked over and asked the Virgin Girl the same question, but she did not get an answer, either. Finally, all of a sudden, the Virgin Girl said, "Aw! . . . Aw! . . ."

Then "a-a-w!" Then it seemed that she had relaxed somewhat. The girls were laughing continuously for a while. The Virgin Girl had lost her identity. They could not continue calling her the Virgin Girl. She was now a full-fledged member of the loyal girls.

Why did the Virgin Girl go through with this ordeal? A good question. . . . After the Virgin Girl moved into the neighborhood, she met these girls who were friendly with the members of the Bats gang. Being a neighbor, the Virgin Girl felt that she would be left alone . . . would not be accepted in the clique of the other girls. If the popular girls act a certain way, then other girls feel they should act the same way, too. If girls feel that they have to fit into a particular image to be accepted and if that image is very constraining (to force or compel) that you can only say or do certain things or have certain feelings, then they may find themselves left out.

When the Virgin Girl's parents moved into this new neighborhood, the Virgin Girl found herself in a new environment and she thought that it would be very painful to be left all alone . . . to have no friends and no relationships. She felt that it would be unbearable. That's why she agreed to give up her virginity. The peer pressure was unbearable for her to endure. Now she, the Virgin Girl, was just one of the girls.

According to Bobo, there were several street gangs in the city. They were located in different parts of the city. They basically created the same type of disturbance wherever they were located. Bobo visited my living room, and he did not, at any time, mention having loyal girls patronizing their gang members, like the loyal girls that patronized the members of the Bats gang. Bobo did, however, tell me that he used to get into a lot of trouble with the law. Bobo used to be the youngest student in his class . . . but Bobo got into trouble with the law and he had to spend one year in jail. Now he was the same age and in the class as the other students.

Bobo was now fifteen years old, and he was in tenth grade. Bobo continued to go to school, but he was constantly getting into trouble with the law. He cut a boy with a small knife one day, and the principal called the police department to have Bobo arrested. Bobo's father was at home at the time, and he bailed him out. Bobo's father gave Bobo a warning not to get into trouble anymore.

Bobo got into trouble again. The police department held Bobo, since he was a minor, until they were able to contact his parents. Mr. Ryan, Bobo's father, was away on his job, somewhere on the road, driving his truck. The police captain asked Bobo who they could contact in his family. Bobo gave the police captain his grandmother's telephone number.

The police captain called Bobo's grandmother and informed her that they were holding her grandson there in the precinct for a crime that he had committed at school. The captain did not tell Bobo's grandmother the nature of the crime; they simply said that they were holding Bobo until they could contact one of his parents.

When Miss Sally Ann reached the precinct, she, not being familiar with precincts, was surprised to see so many policemen, a lot of boys, and a lot of girls milling around in the precinct station. Miss Sally Ann asked one of the cops nearby, "Why on earth are these boys and girls here, just walking around in this place?"

The cop answered by saying that "these boys and girls were creating a disturbance near the church on Fulton Street, and we picked them up and brought them here. They were disturbing the peace. It's our duty to try to prevent this type of behavior from happening, especially near a church."

Miss Sally Ann told the policemen that she knew where that church was located. She continued, saying that boys and girls were always in that area, but they did not hurt anybody. They just played and played all the time. They seemed not to have anything else to do with themselves. They just annoyed people who tried to serve God in that Church. They should try to save themselves from sin.

Miss Sally Ann turned toward one boy who was near her at the time, and asked him, "Why do you all act like you do? You know that it's wrong to annoy people all the time, like you do. I bet that your mother don't know where you are now." The other kids were near and heard what Miss Sally Ann was telling this boy.

Not only did the other boys and girls hear what Miss Sally Ann was saying, the police captain, who was sitting nearby, also, heard what Miss Sally Ann was saying. The captain turned to her and said, "Miss, what is your name?"

"My name is Sally Ann." She was a small lady, about five feet, three inches tall, weighing about 115 pounds, and her hair was silver gray, and she let the captain know that she was Bobo's grandmother. "Where is my grandson?" Miss Sally Ann did not see her grandson with the group of boys and girls there milling around in the precinct.

Miss Sally Ann continued telling the captain that she lived near that church where he picked up those boys and girls. "That's not my church. I have to take a trolley car to get to my church. I know that these children always hang out near that church on Fulton Street. I don't know why these children do that. I know that their parents and the school taught them that doing bad things can get you into trouble. They should know better by now."

Miss Sally Ann turned toward the boys and girls and said, "Why don't you-all just stop annoying people at that church? They are serving

God. You should be serving God yourselves; maybe you would find better things to do with yourselves."

The captain said, "Miss Sally Ann, I was going to give these kids a lecture, and then I was going to let them go home. But, you just gave them a good lecture, and you know what? I am going to let them go home to their parents."

"Thank you, Captain. Maybe these kids learned a lesson this time, and maybe they won't annoy people anymore."

"Let us hope so . . . miss."

"But where is my grandson? I do not see him, anywhere."

"What is your grandson's name, miss?"

"His name is Bobo."

"Oh," said the captain. "Why didn't you report to me when you came here . . . to the precinct? I did not know what that you are the person that I called to report here to check on your grandson."

"Well, when I came here I saw so many policemen, boys, and girls, I guess I forgot why I came here. Where is my grandson?"

"He is locked up."

"Why is he locked up, Captain? I thought he was with these other children."

"No," said the captain, "You see, your grandson was reported to me by the principal of the school, who told me that your grandson cut a boy on his finger with a knife. That's a crime. That's why he is locked up."

"Oh, where did my grandson get a knife?"

"That's what we would like to know, Miss Sally Ann."

"Can I take him home with me, Captain?"

"No, I am afraid you cannot, miss. He has to appear in court tomorrow morning at ten. You may come to court tomorrow morning, and you will see your grandson at that time, Miss Sally Ann. For goodness' sake, what is that boy going to do next?"

The next day, Miss Sally Ann was in court to see if she could bail her grandson out, like his father did, the last time that he was picked up by the cops. Then maybe she could take him home.

When the judge called for Bobo's case, he found out that the boy cut, L.J., was not present in court. He was told that the boy L.J. was not cut seriously; that's why he was not coming to court today.

The judge asked Bobo, "Did you or did you not cut the boy L.J. on his finger?"

"It was an accident, sir."

At this point, one of the lawyers asked permission to speak to Bobo. Permission was granted. The lawyer told Bobo, "When you are talking to the judge, you are supposed to refer to him as Your Honor before you speak to him."

"Counsel," asked the Judge, "are you representing this boy in court?"

"No, Your Honor, I was just telling him how to address you before he speaks to you."

"Very well," said the judge. "Then why did you talk to him? Do you know him, counsel?"

"Yes, Your Honor, I represented him in court at previous hearings before."

"Do you know about this case, counsel? Then what happened in this case? If you know, counsel, exactly what happened to bring this case before the court?"

"A group of boys, Your Honor, were gathering pecans from under the pecan trees before they were ready to be gathered, when they were almost ready to be gathered. Bobo was using his little knife to open the pecans. All children play, sometimes at the wrong time. This boy L.J. ran up to Bobo, as if to hit him with something. Bobo threw up his hands at the same time. L.J.'s hand was near, and the little knife blade cut L.J.'s little finger superficially. It was not a deep cut. L.J. ran home. The principal of the school did not see the cut on L.J.'s finger. He could, only, assume that it was a deep cut on L.J.'s finger, and he called the police department to report the incident. The policeman responded, picked Bobo up, and carried him to the precinct house without any knowledge of how serious the cut was. That's the extent of my knowledge of the incident, Your Honor."

"Very well, counsel.

"Why do you carry a knife, in the first place, Bobo?"

"Your Honor, I use the knife to sharpen pencils."

"Don't you, or rather, is there a pencil sharpener in the classroom?"

"Yes, Your Honor, but it does not work very good . . . at times."

"A knife, son, can get you into trouble. I am going to turn you over to your parents."

This case was dismissed on the grounds that two boys were engaged in horseplay and the boy L.J. threw up his hand in the process. He was not cut purposely by Bobo. Either boy could have been responsible for the accident. Miss Sally Ann took her grandson home.

Being frightened by this incident, Bobo stayed home for several days before venturing out on the street with the other members of the gang. Miss Sally Ann, no matter what kind of trouble he got into, wanted him to stay in school until he graduated from high school. Usually, when something like this incident happened, Bobo was a good boy for a while and then he seemed to forget about the past and his image changed for his future on the street.

After this knife incident at the school when he was reported to the principal of the school for his misconduct as a student, Bobo was arrested. His grandmother, Miss Sally Ann, started doubting her ability to control her grandson Bobo. She without any doubt wanted Bobo to finish high school, in keeping with the wishes of her daughter, Callie, who was now deceased. Miss Sally Ann suggested to Bobo that maybe he should resign from the street gang called the Blue Jacks.

When Bobo was in a good mood, he would, no doubt, agree with his grandmother. But when Bobo was in a bad mood, he would resent his grandmother's request and his grandmother would not be able to persuade her grandson to change his ways and then concentrate on his homework so he would graduate from high school with high marks.

Bobo's grandmother remembered that when her daughter was alive she wanted, without a doubt, her son, Bobo, to be one of the best boys in the Methodist church. She did try to accomplish that goal by having him appointed as one of the acolytes in the Methodist church; then she included his name when they were organizing the children's usher board and, finally, the Cub Scouts. Bobo's grandmother tried to carry on those advancements by having him join the Boy Scouts when he reached the age qualified to do so. In spite of Miss Sally Ann's way of encouraging Bobo to follow her plans by joining the Boy Scouts, she failed, because at this point Bobo was not interested in joining anything else at the Methodist church. This request to Bobo apparently came when he was in one of his bad moods, and nothing could change his mind except what he wanted to do for himself. Therefore, Bobo did not show any interest in joining the Boy Scouts of America. Maybe it was because his mother was not there to make that decision as she did when she was alive and controlled her son's behavior.

It seemed that Bobo thought that his mother was the only one that could make decisions for him. This did not discourage his grandmother, however, because it was she who encouraged Bobo to continue in school. That was his grandmother's goal, for Bobo to finish high school. That was her ultimate goal in raising her grandson. Bobo's grandmother emphasized to him that after he finished the eleventh grade, then he had only one more year to finish high school.

Miss Sally Ann had already contacted the Boy Scout leader at the Methodist church to see if he would be able to persuade her grandson to join the Boy Scout troop on their hiking trip this summer. Keeping Bobo busy during the summer would help him to stay out of trouble.

After the Boy Scout leader approached Bobo, at the request of his grandmother, who was a faithful member of the Methodist church, Bobo told his grandmother that he had been asked by the Boy Scout leader to join the troop on their hiking trip at summer somewhere in upstate New York. Bobo told Grandma that he would let the Scout leader know his decision by next Sunday.

The leader of the Boy Scout troop was one person who felt that if anybody could be persuaded to do something, he was that person. What approach did the leader take to reach Bobo? The Boy Scout leader knew one of the boys who was a member of the same street gang as Bobo. He therefore spoke to that boy and was able to persuade him to join the Boy Scout troop on this hiking trip this summer. It was this technique used by the scout leader that persuaded Bobo to join the troop on that hiking trip for the summer.

The Boy Scout troop departed from the Methodist church's grounds and was in the upstate area by 3:00 P.M. Time enough to pitch tents before sunset. Miss Sally Ann was free to visit her hometown, Avon, Georgia, for those months that Bobo was away.

* * *

Time was up. It was time for Bobo and his grandmother to return to the streets of Brooklyn. Bobo as well as his grandmother had enjoyed the summer away from the streets of the city of New York. It seemed that Bobo was very anxious to return to school this semester. Why, Bobo? Bobo was very anxious to return to school and to meet his old classmates, as well as or especially the new girls from out-of-town. There were a few new neighbors who had moved from the South to live in Brooklyn. Bobo was lucky to meet a new girlfriend, who was in eleventh grade. Bobo was in twelfth grade.

When Bobo entered school this semester, it seemed that he was in a different rank. He became very prestigious among his peers. Why Bobo? Well, it seemed that Bobo had to change his ways in order to compete with the other boys, especially the new boys who had moved from the South with their parents and become part of the neighborhood. They knew nothing about street gangs, and they acted in a very prestigious way; that's why Bobo changed his ways. There is an old saying: "When in Rome, you act as the Romans do." This is the reverse of that old saying. In this case with Bobo, it seemed that he had to act like the newcomers who invaded his territory or he might not measure up to a class that the new girls would like to be associated with. Bobo thought that he might lose his new girlfriend.

Miss Sally Ann couldn't believe her grandson had changed his ways all of a sudden. Grandma had no problems with her grandson going to school, and she did not have any problems with him studying his lessons. He was a changed boy. How could new peers cause Bobo to change? An answer this question in Bobo's life cycle is based on the fact that boys and girls born in the South, at this time, were living below the economic standards . . . or just above the poverty level, and they were striving to reach the higher goals in their lives. They felt that the only way to reach this goal was through education.

From Bobo's visits to my living room and the stories that he told me about his family background, I do not think that his grandmother ever found out why Bobo changed his ways of living on the streets of Brooklyn prior to this last semester in school for Bobo. Nevertheless, she welcomed the change in his life cycle.

Miss Sally Ann did not have any trouble with her grandson until it was time for him to prepare himself for graduation from high school. Miss Sally Ann was lucky, because Bobo's father took time off from his job to help his son prepare for his graduation. There were certain rules and regulations to follow in their dress in preparation for graduation. Mr. Ryan, Bobo's father, helped him to select the things that he needed for his graduation from high school and made the necessary purchases in plenty of time for him to adjust and practice how to march down the aisle to receive his diploma.

Bobo told me that he took his new girlfriend to the junior-senior prom. He continued, saying that this was one of the most enjoyable times in his life. She was a junior and he was a senior. The only problem was that good times do not last too long . . . then it's back to the old grind of life. Bobo did not give going to college a thought. It was over for Bobo. His father was grateful that Bobo did finish high school. His father had in mind breaking his son in on a long-distance truck driving job.

When Bobo visited my living room to continue talking about his graduation from high school, he told me that sometimes he felt very joyful and sometimes felt very sad and did not want to be with anybody. He felt that he wanted to be alone. Bobo did, in fact, become a loner again. Most of his old classmates were going to college, but going to college never was considered by Bobo. This was when I discovered that Bobo had two different personalities . . . one good and one bad. Sometimes he felt like how he used to feel when he would go to the horse stable just to pelt them with rocks.

Since Bobo had finished high school, he felt that he was capable of being a leader . . . leader of what? Bobo thought that he could become a leader of the Blue Jacks gang. In order to become a leader of a street gang, you have to prove yourself brave, tough, and strong. What could Bobo do to prove himself capable of being a leader of the street gang? Bobo realized that he had to do something that would classify him as capable of being a leader.

As Bobo indicated to me as we talked in my living room, he did not go out looking for trouble, but as he was lonely and went out, just walking on the street, he apparently walked into another gang's territory. He was confronted by two boys in a section of Bed Stuy. These boys appeared to be bullies. These two bull-headed boys Bobo believed to be members of a gang in that area confronted Bobo somewhere near Broadway. These two boys were smaller than Bobo in stature. They apparently thought that the two of them could beat up Bobo without a problem.

One of the two boys ran by Bobo . . . hitting him in the process. The other boy charged Bobo as the first boy was ready to return with another blow to Bobo's head. By this time, Bobo had his knife out and was ready to cut the first boy that ran by him, hitting him on the head. In a fast motion, Bobo was able to cut both boys. They were bleeding as they ran away from the area.

Both boys had to go to the hospital. This time, Bobo had a larger knife that measured eight inches with the blade opened.

The parents of the two boys contacted the police precinct and reported the incident. The boys did not know where to find Bobo. They did not know which area Bob was from. Therefore, they could not tell the policemen where to look for Bobo. Meanwhile, Bobo had proven himself to himself but not the members of the gang that he was capable of being a leader of the gang.

One day, one of the boys spotted Bobo on the street and notified the policeman that he saw on his beat nearby. Bobo was arrested and carried to the precinct house. During the search of Bobo, they found Bobo's knife on him. Due to the size of Bobo's knife they classified the knife as a weapon. Bobo told me that he recalled them saying, "This boy is armed and dangerous." They figured that Bobo had been out on the street for the purpose of wounding someone.

Bobo was notified that he had to appear in court to testify against these boys. The court hearing was set for a given time and date. Bobo and his lawyer appeared in court to testify before the judge. In Bobo's testimony, he told the judge that he had to defend himself against these two boys, since he was alone.

Bobo did not have any witnesses to testify on his behalf. The judge, based on Bobo's history of being arrested several times before, found Bobo guilty of the crime and gave him a few years in jail.

Bobo's father and grandmother appeared with him in court, Bobo's grandmother tried to defend him, but to no avail. Bobo's father, who had bailed his son out several times before, refused to bail him out this time. Bobo's father figured that if he let his son serve time in jail, this experience would help him to change his ways while on the streets in the future.

Miss Sally Ann, after hearing the sentence imposed on her grandson in this case, told her son-in-law on their way back home that she was going back to her hometown, Avon, Georgia. Bobby, her son-in-law, agreed, and he purchased her ticket for her trip back home. Bobo's grandmother returned to jail to talk to her grandson . . . telling him that if he had listened to her, he would not be in jail today. But he did not listen to her, or anybody else, for that matter.

Bobo emphasized to his grandmother that he had been defending himself from those two boys. Bobo's grandmother told him that she believed his testimony to be true, but the judge based his decision on Bobo's past and figured that since Bobo had such a large knife he was not just carrying that knife around to sharpen pencils. "Remember, Bobo, you did not have a witness to substantiate what you said in your testimony as true.

"I am leaving Bobo. . . . Take care of yourself. . . . I am going back home to live a peaceful life for the rest of my days here on Earth."

Miss Sally Ann walked out of the jailhouse with her hands extended upward, her ticket in her hand. She said, "I am free," and she recited the psalm of David . . . the Twenty-third Psalm: "The Lord is my Shepherd; I shall not want. He maketh me to lie down in green pastures: he leadeth me beside the still waters. He restoreth my soul: He leadeth me in the paths of righteousness for his name's sake. Yea, though I walk through the valley of the shadow of death, I will fear no evil; for thou art with me; thy rod and thy staff they comfort me. Thou preparest a table before me in the presence of mine enemies; thou anointest my head with oil; my cup runneth over. Surely goodness and mercy shall follow me all the days of my life; and I will dwell in the house of the Lord for ever."

* * *

Bobo was eighteen years old when he became eligible for parole. His father started breaking him in as a long-distance truck driver.

After a few years as a long-distance truck driver, Bobo got married and went into isolation . . . until he reached the ripe old age of fifty-five or fifty-six, when he appeared at my address, while I was sitting on my stoop. He said that he was looking for a room to rent, and did I have one that he could rent?

11

Bobo as a Member of the Gang

Bobo's father had informed his son that he was on parole and that he was not a free man. Mr. Ryan stressed to his son that he was liberated from prison because of his good behavior as a prisoner and that he could not escape from his captors. If, however, Bobo tried to escape from the custody of his captors by moving to another city, he would be caught and his time as a prisoner would be increased to the maximum amount of time that he would have to serve in prison.

Bobo told his father that he understood the requirements of the prison system and that he would not try to break the rules of the prison system.

At this point, Bobo asked his father if he could visit some of his friends before leaving on his first truck-driving trip.

Bobo's record as a member of the Blue Jacks gang extended back to the age of eleven, when he found himself on the streets of Brooklyn, looking for companionship.

As I mentioned before, Bobo's father was not able to share in raising him because of his job as a long-distance truck driver. Bobo's grandmother had a difficult time trying to raise him properly after the death of his mother at or when Bobo was only nine years old. Bobo did not join the street gang until he was eleven years old.

Being members of a gang, the boys thought that they had to prove themselves as tough, capable of defending themselves against members of a different gang and tough guys on the street who were looking for trouble. Members of these gangs used knives and weapons that they made themselves. One of Bobo's weapons that he made was an old sock with a rock in the toe. This was similar to a blackjack.

Bobo was constantly getting into trouble. He was arrested many times for fighting boys on the street. Mr. Ryan, Bobo's father, had to get a lawyer to represent his son in court. Mr. Ryan was mindful of the fact that his absence no doubt contributed toward Bobo's uncontrollable behavior. Mrs. Ryan did a good job in raising Bobo, but it was unfortunate that she died when Bobo was only nine years old.

Mr. Ryan would talk to his son and warn him against creating problems for him and Bobo's maternal grandmother. Bobo continued on his rampage. When Bobo almost killed a boy on the street was when Mr. Ryan had to make his decision. He, Mr. Ryan, realized that paying a lawyer to represent his son in jail and paying his fine simply put Bobo back out on the street.

When Bobo was put in jail to serve several years in prison, before he would be eligible for parole, Mr. Ryan felt that having his son serve time in prison would be a better solution to get Bobo to realize his type of behavior would not be tolerated anymore. Serving time in jail gave Bobo second thoughts about getting into trouble in the future. Certainly he did not want to spend a lot of time in jail, off the street.

At this time, Bobo was in his late teens. Mr. Ryan put Bobo in a truck-driving class.

I learned about Bobo's past from Bobo himself, during his visits to my living room. When I needed a lawyer to represent me in court, I selected Mr. Jasper to represent me in court against Bobo not knowing that Mr. Jasper was Bobo's lawyer when he, Bobo, got into trouble while he was a member of the street gang.

Bobo visited the old site where the members of the street gang used to hang out during their rampage on the streets of Brooklyn in their, as they referred to it, territory. Here they discussed how they were responsible for taking care of the area that they called their own. Other street gangs were not allowed to invade their territory without permission.

Bobo was surprised to find out that most of the old gang members were in jail or had changed their way of life and moved away.

The remaining members of the old street gang were surprised to see Bobo and wondered what had happened to him in the last several years. Bobo informed his old friends that his father has sent him to the truck-driving school after he was on parole. Bobo did not hesitate to tell them that he was embarking on a new career as a truck driver.

Bobo found out that their old leader of the street gang, the Blue

Jacks, was still in prison and had several years yet to go before he would be eligible for parole.

Bobo bade the few remaining members good-bye and told them that he would not be returning anytime soon.

12

Bobo as a Long-Distance Truck Driver

Since Bobo was giving his father such a hard time while he was a member of the street gang, his father decided to break him in as a long-distance truck driver. Bobo revealed to me the whole story of how he was broken in on his first job. On this particular visit to my living room, I could tell that Bobo had something on his mind that he wanted to tell me. He sat down and exhaled, and then he relaxed.

He related to me how he entered the truck-driving field as a permanent long-distance truck driver. Bobo said that his father was fed up with his street gang activity, the money that he was spending to get Bobo out of trouble, and his uncontrollable behavior.

Bobo said that his father registered him in a truck driver's school, paid his tuition, checked out his living quarters at the school, and only gave him enough money for current needs. Bobo said that he attended the truck driver's school, but it seemed that he learned more about driving a truck by just watching his father drive his truck.

Bobo said that he followed the same procedure that his father did in handling the truck. Bobo not only drove his truck like his father; he ended up traveling the same route that his father traveled for so many years.

Bobo stated that there was a certain amount of enjoyment in driving a truck. He stated that it is better when you can drive at a fast rate of speed. This way, he said, you did not get tired as you did when you were driving at a slow rate of speed. For truck drivers, there are areas where you can stop to rest up. These areas are called truck stops.

At these truck stops, you not only get your truck serviced; they also have a certain amount of entertainment. There are restaurants, places where you can get drinks, places to dance or just socialize with members of the opposite sex.

Bobo made a comparison between baseball players and truck drivers. He said, "When baseball players report for spring training, a number of young females also report at the dugout, clad only in short dresses, short skirts, and low-cut covering at the neck area."

Here I can quote from the *Daily News*, dated March 22, 1992: "Mets Mating Game. After-hours bullpen has crowded field." Some of these girls wear high heels, and some wear low heels. Nevertheless, their dresses or skirts reach only about halfway down their thigh area.

At the truck stop area, you will find that some of the girls dress similarly. Bobo said at the truck drivers' retreat you would find fewer girls, but if you ended up without one all you had to do was call a certain number, and pronto, you would get one.

After driving a truck for several years, Bobo said, he had learned to adjust his rest stops so he would not get too sleepy in between the rest stops. If, however, there was a time when he would get sleepy in between the rest stops, he would pull over on the side of the highway, plant his flares on the side of truck and sleep for about forty-five minutes; then he was ready to go again.

In elaborating on driving a truck, Bobo said that it was a good job and it paid well. Any job, he said, depended on what you liked or disliked. If you did not like a job, then you should prepare yourself for a job that you liked. Then you try to be a good worker . . . do your job like it is supposed to be done, abide by all rules and regulations, be on time, do not loaf on your job, and produce all that you can for your boss or employer. Being a good worker puts you in line for a raise or promotion, salary increases, or a citation or an award.

Bobo said that his father was a good worker and was promoted several times.

Bobo continued, saying that his father was given the positions of, first supervisor of the truck drivers, and, second, president of the truck drivers' association.

Again Bobo continued, saying that his father set a good example for him to follow in his footsteps. Bobo said that when he was twenty-one years old he had a lot of energy. After driving his truck for about ten hours, he would stop at one of the rest areas to rest. He would turn his truck over for service, then he would take a shower, dress, and go to the restaurant for dinner.

Bobo continued to tell me about his experiences as a truck driver. After driving a truck for a number of years, you begin to enjoy the frills around what you come in contact with. You are going from one state to another, and you are meeting different people. You learn about different cultures, different ideals, and different lifestyles from the different people that you come in contact with. Yet they are all human beings.

This particular night, Bobo said he felt that he could party all night, and it seemed that he tried to do just that. He said that he partied for a few hours, drinking and talking with different females in the nightclub. For one thing, with so many girls that were available, Bobo said, he lost control of himself and began to get very high. Bobo said that he left the club and went to his room. Before he could undress and get into bed, a knock on the door was heard. When he opened the door, he saw a nice-looking girl standing outside. She said, "May I come in?" He let her come into his room. As they were talking, another knock on his door was heard. Again he opened the door, and again he saw a nice-looking girl standing on the outside. This time, this young lady did not ask to come in; she simply walked in without any hesitation whatsoever and sat down. Bobo was puzzled. He could not remember inviting this girl to his room.

Yet, the first girl that came to his room could have been the intruder, and the last girl could have been the girl that he, in fact, did invite to his room. Bobo told the last girl that he did not invite her to his room. She said, "Yes, you did."

Bobo then turned to the first girl that came to his room and said, "Then it was you that I did not invite to my room."

The first girl insisted that he did invite her to his room and pointed out the area where they were talking when he invited her to this room. Bobo could not dispute it, because he remembered being in that area when they were talking to each other.

There were two chairs in the room. The girls occupied the chairs, while Bobo sat on the side of the bed. Bobo pondered in his mind, *What to do next? What course of action should I take at this time?* Bobo offered the girls drinks at the bar. The girls did not want to go back to the nightclub.

Bobo, at this point, asked the girls what he should do. Should he flip a coin to select one of them to remain in his room? The girls did not agree to this procedure to select one of them. Bobo then suggested that he could invite one of the other truck drivers to join them in his room. The girls did not agree to this type of selection, either.

Bobo decided to let the girls sleep in the bed while he cuddled himself on a blanket on the floor beside the bed. In about thirty minutes, Bobo heard one of the girls snoring. She, too, had appeared to be very high when she came into his room. Bobo cunningly got up and sneaked to the side of the bed where the other girl appeared to be sober. The sober girl took advantage of this opportunity, and she eased herself off the bed and onto the blanket on the floor beside Bobo. The snoring girl continued to snore while Bobo and the sober girl prepared themselves for a lovemaking scene. They whispered to each other, because they did not want to wake the snoring girl.

After the sober girl and Bobo washed up, the sober girl returned to bed while Bobo returned to his pallet on the floor. Bobo had problems going to sleep because of the hard floor. The blanket did not offer enough cushioning to be comfortable to Bobo. The sober girl had had an enjoyable interlude with Bobo, and now she was ready to go to sleep for the night. Bobo could only squirm on the blanket on the floor, in pain from the hard floor. In addition to the blanket, the floor was covered with a rug, but the floor was still hard to Bobo. Bobo was only able to sleep about two or three hours.

After Bobo had slept about four hours, the drunken girl got up and ran to the bathroom. On her way back, she stopped by Bobo's pallet on the floor. She woke up Bobo. Bobo said, "Be quiet." The other girl was still asleep. They then spoke in whispers. The drunken girl, who was now sober, thought that if she made love to Bobo, she would be putting something over the first sober girl. She did not hesitate to embrace Bobo as he lay on the blanket on the floor.

This first drunken girl, who was now sober, thought that she had put something over the first sober girl by making love to Bobo while she was asleep. The second girl washed up and returned to bed. At this point, Bobo was very tired, and he slept an hour past the time that he was scheduled to get up. After they got dressed, Bobo took the girls to breakfast. It was Bobo who had a secret, not the last girl that he made love to. Yet each girl thought that she had a secret from the other, having made love to Bobo while the other was sleeping.

While Bobo was paying the bills for breakfast, he was wondering if the girls would ever find out about their ordeal the night before. Bobo felt that he would never see these girls again, because each time he would stop at these rest stops he would meet new girls. While Bobo was waiting for his coworkers to pick up their trucks, these girls were standing a little ways from the departure area. Bobo bade the girls good-bye, and he left the area.

Finally, the truck drivers assembled and got their instructions for the next trip to the other state where cargo was to be delivered. Bobo left wondering if the girls found out what actually happened the night before. Bobo never found out, nor did he see the girls again. This was a common practice for truck drivers, to meet new girls for the first time and not see them anymore.

After several years of experience driving a truck, Bobo met new truck-driving friends. Through these friendships, Bobo and the other truck drivers would form convoys on the highways. They would talk to one another by way of the CB system. This contact helped the truck drivers to stay alert and abreast of any change taking place during their journey.

All of the truck drivers would look forward to meeting new girls when they stopped at the truck stops to rest. After Bobo experienced sharing his room with two different girls in the same night, Bobo had something to talk about over his CB system to the other truck drivers. Most of the other truck drivers did not believe Bobo's story about making love to two different girls in his room in one night. When the truck drivers stopped at the next rest area, Bobo explained, in detail, to the other drivers actually how this happened.

Bobo delivered his story to the other truck drivers, in timely fashion. Some of them did not believe Bobo's story. They would laugh, laugh, and laugh as Bobo related his story to them. One of the guys asked Bobo, "Who do you think you are? Superman?"

One of the older truck drivers, who had driven a truck on this route for more than ten years, came to Bobo's rescue. After he heard Bobo's story about ending up with two different girls in his room and what transpired during that night, the older truck driver said, "Wait, you guys. A few years ago, I spent the night in a room at one of the truck stops with two different girls myself."

The other drivers looked at one another and the older driver and said, "Did you have a dual love affair with two different girls like Bobo did?"

The older truck driver said, "It appeared that this extra girl was stranded and needed a place to stay for the night. I let her stay with us. There was no hanky-panky with the stranded girl. The stranded girl was the one to sleep on the pallet on the floor. This was an accommodation for the stranded girl. The girls at these truck stops outnumbered the truck drivers, and some ended up not having a place to stay for the night.

Bobo, with the help of the older truck driver, was able to convince the other truck drivers that his story was true. From that day, Bobo was very careful when he stopped to rest at the other truck stops. He, however, continued forming convoys with the other truck drivers. It was "Bon voyage," for them and they continued keeping in touch through the CB system.

Bobo continued building his truck-driving experience, delivering cargo from the North to the Southwest area. He did not believe that he would end up as the president of the truck drivers' association, like his father had ended up.

Bobo was living alone, and he had to spend his time off from his job alone. He did not that type of lifestyle. One of the girls that Bobo picked up at one of the rest areas appeared to be a lovable person, and Bobo succeeded in persuading her to spend some time at his apartment while he was on one of his breaks. When Bobo's time was up, the girl that he had staying with him was very anxious to leave his living quarters. Bobo knew that she would not make him a good companion to live with . . . forever.

At this point, Bobo realized that these girls found at the truck stops were more like hustlers and would not make good wives. Some of the truck drivers did, however, marry some of these girls.

Bobo, with the advice of some of his superiors, started attending church services on his breaks, here in New York and in California. After a few years looking for a good female companion, Bobo found one at one of the churches in California.

Bobo courted his new female friend until he felt that she would, in fact, make him a good wife. Bobo and his new friend discussed getting married and where they would like to live. Bobo's female friend was the recipient of an inheritance of a parcel of land, which included a house. Bobo did not have enough money to buy a house; therefore, he felt that he had no other choice but to accept what his new female friend had to get started off in life.

Bobo did not want to live in California. He wanted to live in New York City, where he grew up in the Methodist church and on the streets of Brooklyn where he was a gang member. This, however, might not have been a good choice, because Bobo used to get into such trouble with the law.

Bobo got married and he went into isolation after he was able to transfer his base from New York to California. Here they had one child, a daughter. When the daughter reached age three, Bobo could not take it anymore, and Bobo had to have his way. Bobo got homesick, and he insisted that they move to the state of New York. Bobo's wife did not want to leave her house and go to the state of New York, where Bobo did not own anything of value. When Bobo made up his mind to move back to New York, that's what Bobo was going to do, with or without his family.

Bobo's wife did the right thing when she suggested that he could move back to New York and see what he could prepare for his family in the state of New York. Bobo did not hesitate; he moved back to New York. Bobo was unable to get a transfer from California back to New York. Bobo was able to get a long-distance truck-driving job in the state of New Jersey.

Bobo was planning on sending for his family before he met with an accident, which involved a lady (white) and her car and the truck that Bobo was driving. According to the accident report, Bobo was in the right and the lady was at fault. She cut him off in the lane where he was driving. Yet she claimed that she was in the right.

The reporting officer, in his version of the accident, put Bobo in the right. Bobo was satisfied with the officer's report of the accident. Yet they wanted a report from Bobo himself. The lady involved had already given her report, which she tried to put herself in the right.

Bobo reported that on this day he went and picked up his truck and was headed to the New Jersey Turnpike with his cargo, a trip that would have lasted about one week. As he arrived at about Exit 4, a lady driving her car ran into his truck at the right door of the cab of the truck. It appeared that she was trying to cut him off from the right of his truck. They had to wait about one hour before the patrol car arrived on the scene.

When the patrolman arrived, the lady rushed over to him with her story of the accident. Bobo indicated that the visible marks on the truck indicated that the lady was at fault. The two patrolmen also appeared to be in favor of the lady involved, saying that she had the right-of-way at that point. Bobo had made up his report of the accident, which clearly showed that the lady was at fault and caused the accident to happen. A witness who was parked on the side of the road indicated that the lady had cut across the side of the lane where the truck was traveling and run into the side of the truck.

Bobo and the officers had a short argument about who had the right-of-way. Bobo pointed to his truck, showing the officers the section where the lady's car hit his truck.

Because of the short fracas of the officers and Bobo, the officers manhandled Bobo and ended up putting Bobo in handcuffs. They took him to jail. During the fracas, the officers were using their nightsticks on Bobo. Bobo was slightly injured and was given the opportunity to take his medicine. At the precinct house, Bobo was able to make contact with his lawyer. A case was brought against the officers, for their form of brutality, which ended up as not being necessary.

Bobo was in his early fifties at this time. Over the years Bobo had a mild case of diabetes. He did not have to use insulin shots. He had some type of tablets that he was taking. After Bobo was taken to the precinct house, and was locked up, he had a relapse and was seen by someone lying on the floor of the jail cell. Paramedics were sent to the jail cell to check on Bobo's condition. Bobo requested an attorney from his jail cell. After the attorney arrived at the jail cell, Bobo relayed his account of the accident and the way that the patrolmen had treated him.

Bobo filed a suit against the lady who cut him off when he was entering the New Jersey Turnpike at Exit 4, plus her insurance company. Bobo then filed a suit against the patrolmen who had arrested him and filed a suit against the entire police department for not letting him take his medication. Bobo indicated that this was the reason that he had a relapse when he became dizzy and fell in the jail cell.

On one of Bobo's visits to my living room, he asked me to read the brief that his attorney had given him. According to Bobo's attorney's brief, Bobo had a relapse because of the police's type of behavior, manhandling him and not letting him take his medication when it was needed.

Bobo's first attorney soon dropped Bobo's case against the police department and the lady that cut him off as he attempted to enter the New Jersey Turnpike.

Bobo was soon released from the police department and left to fend for himself. This episode ended Bobo's career as a long-distance truck driver. Bobo sought a new attorney for his case.

Bon voyage to my tenant Bobo.

13

The Third Phase of Bobo's Tenancy

While reviewing Bobo's early life as a child to adulthood, I can clearly see that he had a serious problem in his early life; the most serious problem was that his mother died when he was nine years old. By the time of her death, she had molded her son into her own image . . . an image that no one else could change to remold him into another image.

Bobo's father was not available to guide him in that fatherly image, like most male children follow. Like father, like son, etc. Since that fatherly image was nonexistent, that was a big void in Bobo's life. Bobo's grandmother was the next of kin to try to raise Bobo like her daughter had been raising him. But she was unable to change Bobo's way of life. She was, however, able to persuade him to finish high school, in spite of his ties with the street gang members.

Bobo, like most children, looked elsewhere to fill that void in his life. Bobo found different patterns of behavior in the members of the street gang. These gang members had a behavioral problem, maybe more serious than Bobo's problem, but who could tell Bobo that he was looking in the wrong direction for guidance? This behavioral problem of Bobo led him to develop a dual personality . . . one that would never be changed during his lifetime here on this Earth.

It was Bobo's dual personality that helped him to persuade me to rent a room in my house to him. He was on his best behavior when he asked me to rent him a room, he even linked himself with a deacon in the church as one of his best friends, and he only could be a good guy . . . in my eyesight, at that time. I could not realize that Bobo was a walking "time bomb," waiting to "explode" in my face. We, however, continued our relationship in court when we were scheduled to appear on a given date.

When we were scheduled to appear in court, Bobo had a good alibi: Bobo would get his walking cane to assist him while was walking.

He would hobble along with his walking cane, as if he could not walk without his walking cane. It did help, however, because the judge would call the disabled first to appear for their hearing before the able respondents would be called to testify.

In view of Bobo's alibi, I did not have to wait in line to hear my case against Bobo.

Annie, one of Bobo's girls, had been trained to assist Bobo with his walking cane. It did appear for real that Bobo could not walk without his walking-cane. But I knew better, because when we were not scheduled to appear in court, Bobo could walk as well as I could walk.

When Annie was not around, Bobo had Sally to assist him. One day, it appeared that Bobo was on his way to maybe the Department of Social Services. He went downstairs with his walking cane. When Bobo reached the stoop, he was met by two fellows. I thought that these guys were two of Bobo's friends. But as Bobo attempted to go down the front steps, an argument started between Bobo and these two guys.

After I heard the argument, I went up and stood inside the fence of the yard leading up from the basement room. As I stood there, listening to them argue, it appeared that Bobo had failed to keep a promise that he had made to these guys.

A fracas started between Bobo and these two guys. One of them grabbed Bobo's walking cane as Bobo was using his cane to ward them off.

This guy that grabbed Bobo's walking cane held it up as if he were going to hit Bobo with Bobo's own walking cane. He did not hit Bobo with the walking cane. It appeared that they were leaving with Bobo's walking cane. Bobo started after them. The guy with Bobo's walking cane threw the walking cane in an open lot near the scene of the fracas. Bobo was frustrated as they started after Bobo.

At this point, Sally heard the noise, looked out of the window, saw that Bobo was in trouble, and ran downstairs clad only in her panties. When she reached the scene, these guys were no longer interested in Bobo; their eyes were focused on Sally. It seems that Sally did not dress, on purpose, before she came running downstairs. Anyway, these guys, it seems, forgot what they wanted to do with Bobo. Meanwhile, Bobo was telling Sally to go back upstairs. Bobo was virtually pushing Sally back upstairs.

This scene almost caused a traffic jam in front of my house. The people in their cars and the people who were walking by at that time stopped to watch Sally and these guys and Bobo, of course. Bobo was able to persuade Sally to go back upstairs. These guys simply walked away. The area became calm again.

Bobo was able to get his walking cane from the vacant lot, and by that time Sally had dressed and come back down stairs. She assisted Bobo as he left to go to the Department of Social Services. Meanwhile, as I stood inside the fence of my yard, the people who were passing seeing all of those people standing around asked me what was going on here in this area.

There was a gate leading to my yard, and I kept this gate locked with a padlock and chain to keep Bobo's friends who might want to come into the yard out. Otherwise, they would be all over the place.

In this general area, there were three large buildings. Across the street in front of my house was the rear of the post office building. To my right, there was another large building, which had been used as a storage building for furniture several years ago. Today this building was converted to a church. To my extreme left, there was a five-story building that had recently been renovated into a housing complex. This section of Brooklyn was known as Bedford Stuyvesant.

It seemed that after I rented a room to my tenant Bobo, there was not a dull moment around this area. Something was always going on around here, like, for instance, when Sally came running downstairs to help Bobo with those guys. She was mumbling something, as if she was saying, "Leave Bobo alone." These guys were not interested in what Sally was saying; their interest was in how Sally was dressed or not dressed. Her being dressed only in her panties attracted the interest of people passing in their cars as well as the people who had left the subway station and passed this area on their way home.

One lady, who looked to be about sixty years old, was near me at the time; she asked me, "Do you know this lady? Or this young lady?"

I simply, pointed to Bobo, telling this lady that Sally was his (Bobo's) friend.

One guy that came by after he found out what had happened said, "You mean that I missed all of that?" I smiled at the manner of how this guy was reacting, when he was saying that he missed all of that.

Low and behold, a squad car drove up on the opposite side of the street. A few minutes later, another squad car drove up and parked behind the first squad car. One of the officers asked a man on the other side of the street what was happening in the area. This man pointed me out to the officer. The officer came over to me, and I told him what had happened.

The officer asked, "Where is she now?"

"She left," I said.

He made out his report and left the area.

As the squad cars were leaving, there were several people still standing around the area. Plus the people who were leaving the subway station saw the squad cars leaving. They also were curious and were asking questions as to why so many people were standing in this area.

I was wondering what might have happened to Bobo if Sally had not attracted the attention of those guys who were after Bobo. Well, Sally, being clad only in her panties, certainly changed the picture of what was going on before she came downstairs. Maybe her doing so saved Bobo's life or saved him from getting beaten up by those guys. Anyway, the whole episode of Sally's intervening, in the manner that she did appear, could have been a "blessing in disguise" for Bobo.

A large number of young girls would flock around Bobo. It was like Bobo was a "healer" or something. And these girls, it seemed, would come to see him for his "blessings." My neighbor who was living next-door had problems with some of Bobo's female friends coming into the neighborhood and calling Bobo from the street level. At one point, I clocked the numerous times that these girls would come into this area and call Bobo from the outside . . . to let him know that they were here and wanted to see him. This type of behavior would occur day or night. The neighbor accused Bobo of harboring a prostitute. Bobo denied this accusation, however. I do know that some of these girls were seen by me as they hustled on the street, usually at night.

You would think that this was enough excitement to happen in this area over a short space of time. But not so in this area. Why? Because Bobo was here. One day, two of Bobo's friends arrived in front of my house. I was in the basement at that time. They called Bobo several times, but Bobo did not answer right away. I thought that he was out.

Suddenly I heard two girls arguing. I came upstairs and saw that one girl was wearing slacks and the smaller girl was wearing a miniskirt. It seemed that this argument had gotten out of hand. I noticed that the girl who was dressed in slacks was very dominant over the girl that was dressed in the miniskirt. The girl dressed in slacks was fighting the smaller girl like a young man would fight a lady. Bobo came downstairs at this point. He attempted to break up the fight between these two girls.

Bobo was able to break up the fight between these two girls. Bobo told me later that the girl dressed in slacks was a lesbian. The lesbian told Bobo that she had given the smaller girl some money; the smaller girl had accepted the money from her, but failed to keep her promise to the girl dressed in slacks. What was her promise? It seemed that the smaller girl had promised to perform a sexual act with the girl dressed in slacks.

Bobo instructed the smaller girl that if she made a promise to the girl dressed in slacks, she should keep her promise or return the money to the girl dressed in slacks. Bobo was able to settle that dispute between these two girls.

At this point, I began seeing one of Bobo's male friends hanging around him. For what reason I did not know. For several days I saw this guy that Bobo referred to as Bob. It seemed that Bob moved in with Bobo. In Bobo's room, there was one double bed, one single bed, and one chair-bed. Why all of these beds in one room? I did not get the answer for that question from Bobo. Certainly these beds were to accommodate Bobo's many friends.

One of the many girls that visited Bobo was this girl that Bobo called Timid. I noticed that Timid would act very strange at times. She appeared to be shy. She also appeared to act like a dope addict at times.

It seemed that the girl, Timid, did not have control over her emotions. It also appeared that she thought that something was going to happen to her . . . and that she would not be able to prevent it from happening. Certainly, Timid had a complex of some kind. Maybe she felt that she was inferior to the other girls that she wanted to compete with.

Anyway, it seemed that Bobo's best male friend, Bob, had the right solution to Timid's problem. I saw Bob and Timid together many times. It appeared that Timid felt secure being with Bob. Maybe she wanted protection from someone . . . like Bob. This relationship between Bob and Timid went on for several weeks.

One night, I heard voices coming from Bobo, Bob, Timid, and Annie, one of Bobo's girlfriends. Finally, I heard loud music being played upstairs. Bobo was always complaining about his health not being good; therefore, I did not think that he would indulge in any kind of drinking of alcoholic beverages. But from the sound of laughter, it seemed that they were using something to stimulate them to bring on this type of reaction or that type of behavior. I finally concluded that they were having a party.

Bobo had a way to make you think that he was unable to do certain things, yet Bobo seemed to have everything under control. The girls would listen to him. He appeared to be their consoler, and the number of girls seemed to increase from time to time. Bobo was never never alone.

The noise upstairs subsided and I was able to sleep in peace throughout the night. The next morning, I heard someone leaving. I had formed the habit of looking to see who it was leaving the building. It was Timid. I said, "My goodness, it's Timid." She had spent the night upstairs with Bobo, Bob, and Annie.

The older you get, the more you learn about human behavior . . . good traits or bad traits . . . depending on the individuals involved . . . as an individual, you have your desires and your feelings. If you are a male, then it is understood that your desires would be to be with a female, or vice-versa.

I did not know that lesbians looked for street women, or women hustlers who hustled for a living . . . like some men who have their desires to satisfy and feel that it is easier and more likely to happen when you get someone who is readily available for that purpose. However, having your own companion to fulfill these desires would be a better solution.

I recall being in the presence of three people; one man and two ladies. One lady was telling the other lady about her husband. This lady said, "You know, my husband is an alcoholic and sometimes he comes home too drunk to take care of his homework, but you know something? It's better to have a piece of a man than not to have a man at all." This lady continued, saying that in spite of his coming home many nights too drunk to undress himself for bed, she helped him undress and she put him to bed. "I am not going to put him out of the house, nor am I going to ask him for a divorce, because when he is sober he can perform his duty in the bed like any other man. I am satisfied and I can live with him in peace."

It seemed that privacy with Bobo did not mean anything to him. Timid left Bob upstairs, where he continued to live with Bobo and Annie. Annie replaced Sally, whom Bobo had put out of his room some time ago. But how could Bobo live with Annie as his friend while Bobo continued to live with them in one room, with no privacy? Did Bobo leave Bob upstairs with Annie while he went out of the room? It seemed that Bobo should feel uncomfortable having Bob living with him while his lady friend was present in the one room.

Bob was not only invading Bobo's privacy; he was a menace to society, or at least he was a menace to the landlord. One day I was up on the parlor floor in the room that used to be my bedroom. I had to move downstairs in the basement room, since there was a constant flow of traffic by the large number of girls that were coming and going upstairs to see Bobo. This day, I heard water leaking from the ceiling area. It was leaking on the head of the bed, in the pillow area. Luckily, I had the bed covered with a plastic sheet.

I rushed upstairs, calling Bobo in the process, and I was telling him that water was leaking on my bed downstairs. Bobo went into the bathroom, and I heard him telling Bob, "You're supposed to put the shower curtain on the inside of the tub while taking a shower and not on the outside of the bathtub."

It was not unusual for Bobo to complain to me if the plumbing was not working properly or something was wrong with the fixtures. I returned downstairs . . . disgusted with Bobo and Bob. As I was returning downstairs, I heard Bobo telling Bob again that the shower curtain should be on the inside, not on the outside, of the tub while he was taking a shower.

Bobo had explained to me on an earlier date that he did not take showers, because he liked to soak himself in a tub of hot water.

One day while Bobo was away, I went upstairs with my wrenches and disconnected the shower pipes and put a plug in the shower water line, so nobody could take a shower anymore.

I was expecting Bobo to complain about not having the use of the shower line, but he did not complain. Maybe it was because he took baths and not showers.

I was expecting Bobo to complain to the judge at the next court hearing. I thought that this was Bobo's complaint, since he usually had a complaint to present to the judge. But Bobo did complain about the kitchen sink being clogged in the drain line. Bobo would cause these problems when he needed a complaint against the landlord and would present them to the judge at the next hearing. These complaints against the landlord would prolong the hearings, landlord against tenant.

How did Bobo create these complaints? Bobo had a lot of surplus food in the kitchen. In these items of surplus food, there were a few bags of cornmeal, rice, and other articles of surplus food. Bobo would simply pour cornmeal down the drain pipe, and when it reached the "trap" in the drain line it would settle at the bottom of the trap. When it got wet, it swelled. This wet cornmeal would expand in the trap, causing the drain line to become clogged. This was a good complaint for Bobo. The judge did not listen to my complaints against Bobo. Bobo would always win over in court.

From these complaints against the landlord Bobo knew that the judge would give him more time to live in his room and not pay any rent to the landlord.

Our next court hearing was postponed for another month or so. Therefore, I prepared myself to go on a vacation and return before the next court hearing. Just being away helps me to calm my nerves a little, although I could not forget the hassle that I was having with my tenant Bobo.

I extended my vacation from two weeks to three weeks, yet I hated to have to return to the same problems that I had been having with my tenant Bobo. It had been more than a year since our court hearings had been on the court calendar.

Since the judge did not give my lawyer a chance to speak up on my behalf, I feel that was the reason that my lawyer did not have a reason to delve into my case thoroughly. I felt strongly that the judge was going to put me in jail. It seemed that this was what he wanted to do. The judge did not check my valid receipts, which would have proven that I had, in fact, removed those violations. Since the judge did not give my lawyer a chance to testify on my behalf, I felt that he would eventually put me in jail. For what, may I ask? I am unable to explain the bad points against my tenant Bobo; that case could go on for another year.

At this point, it seemed that I would have to get another lawyer to represent me in court against my tenant Bobo. Since my present lawyer was black, maybe if I got a white lawyer the judge would listen to him . . . and maybe he would delve into my case with all of his might, and maybe I would win my case and collect my rent.

I had no other choice but to believe that after I changed lawyers I could feel optimistic that I would, in fact, win my case and collect all of my rent so I could maintain my house like it should be maintained.

It is a good feeling when you think that you are going to win your case in court, especially when you are in court with a case against a tenant like my tenant Bobo. I was now returning from my three weeks' vacation, and I could only ask myself, *What am I going to be confronted with when I reach my house, where I hope that I can rest up from my long drive from the South to the North?*

As I drove up to park in front of my house, I could not fail to see one of Bobo's girlfriends, Sally, sitting on the stoop. I said to myself, *My goodness, Sally is back.* Bobo put Sally out of his room about three weeks before I left to go on my vacation. Sally spoke to me and offered her help unloading my car.

I refused Sally's request to help me to unload my car by telling her that I had everything under control. I only unloaded the things that I had on the front seat, things that were visible from the outside. I figured that after Sally left, I would unload the things from the trunk of the car.

I noticed when Sally was leaving that she was pregnant. She was beginning to show. She could have been three or four months pregnant.

As I was taking the last bags out of the trunk of the car, I saw Bobo coming from down the street. By the time that I reached the gate to the yard, Bobo was close enough to speak to me. He spoke in a grumbling manner of voice. This was not unusual to me, for Bobo to speak to me in this manner. He never spoke to me like he was willing to speak to me. It seemed that he had a grudge against me. I guess he did have a grudge against me, for one reason or another. Have you ever heard the words *haves* and *haves-not*? Well, it seemed that Bobo was jealous of me, because he felt that I had more than what he had or owned.

I noticed that when he came down to talk to me while I was sitting in my living room if he saw that I had something of value, he would say, "I do not have one of those." I recall that I upholstered an old studio couch with new material, and the studio couch looked like new. Bobo saw the studio couch and said, "I do not have a couch like that."

I felt that Bobo should have been glad to see his landlord returning from his vacation. After all, Bobo cannot fight me when I am away . . . I mean fight me with words, not with fists.

Bobo was an evil man. I had the chance to learn about his background, from the day he was born to the day at the age of nine when he lost his mother.

From Bobo's visits to my living room I learned a lot about his past. He related to me, many times, that his mother used to tell him about her past, so many times it would seem like her past was like a bedtime story. If you make comparisons with how Bobo was raised by his mother and how he is today, you can clearly see why he is so evil. I guess that's why he has to take it out on somebody . . . and that somebody happened to be his landlord. Very unfortunate indeed.

* * *

A few months had passed since my vacation, and I noticed that Sally did not go up and down the stairs anymore. It did not take me long to find out about the condition of Sally. One day, Bobo yelled from upstairs saying, "Mr. B., please call nine-nine-one! I think that Sally is going into labor." I called 911, and soon an ambulance came. After the ambulance approached, Bobo met the paramedics at the sidewalk area. He pointed out to the paramedics the reaction of Sally and that she appeared to be in pain.

The paramedics went upstairs to check on Sally. Soon the paramedics were leaving without Sally. It seems that it was a false alarm, because Sally was not in labor.

Two more months passed, and the same episode occurred. Bobo started yelling from upstairs, asking me to call 911, again, because Sally was going into labor. This time, Sally was screaming as if her pain was unbearable. The paramedics did not come soon, and Bobo started yelling and asking me to call 911 again. "Call the ambulance, Mr. B." Sally was continuing to scream out with pain.

The paramedics finally arrived. Bobo was again downstairs to meet them as they arrived. After a few minutes, the paramedics left, this time with Sally aboard.

A few days passed since Sally was in the hospital. One day, Bobo approached me saying that Sally had given birth to a baby girl.

Several more days passed. Finally, I saw Sally. But she did not have a baby with her as she approached the house. For a few days after her arrival back at Bobo's room I noticed that she would leave about 11:00 A.M. every day. One day, she finally told me that she was going to the hospital to feed the baby. She continued to leave every day to go to the hospital to feed the baby.

Finally, one day Bob accompanied Sally to the hospital to feed the baby. Several more days passed, and I heard that Sally had put her baby up for adoption. Meanwhile, I wondered how Sally could raise a baby girl upstairs in one room with Bobo and all of the young girls that I saw going up and down the stairs during the day or night. But I guess when Bobo went with Sally to the hospital it was to help her with the plans to put the baby up for adoption She did not have any space for a crib, anyway.

I think that Bobo and Sally made the right decision by not bringing her baby here to raise her in a one-room, sharing-with-others situation. Raising a child in this type of environment would create a child without the proper morals. The child raised in this type of environment would be inadequately supervised, and the child would grow up like a monster child. A child raised under these conditions might create a child who, when he or she grew up, might not be able to reason between what is good and what is bad.

A child that grows up under these conditions might, in a way, be like Bobo himself. However, Bobo's mother was doing a good job raising him, but it was unfortunate that she died when he was nine years old. The manner in which Bobo's mother was raising him, he thought, could not be duplicated. Bobo did not have that fatherly image for him to imitate, so he followed the patterns that he saw in his peers on the street. This was why he used to get into so much trouble with the law. And, finally, he was put away for a long period of time.

14

The Fourth Phase of Bobo's Tenancy

One morning I went upstairs, on my way to my living room, and I noticed a bicycle parked in the hallway, leaning against the staircase. I said, "What's next? It's good that you cannot park a car in the hallway. With the bicycle, it takes up space, with the handlebars and the pedals sticking out in the area where you have to walk." I was not surprised at what Bobo might do.

Later, when I saw Bobo, he told me that the bicycle belonged to his cousin, JoJo. Bobo's cousin was a young male about six feet tall; he weighed about 165 pounds and had a light brown complexion, and he was eighteen years old. Bobo said that his cousin, JoJo, came by to see him sometimes, and he asked him to spend the night. His cousin lived about eleven miles away from here.

This was not the only time that Bobo's cousin came by to see Bobo. The bicycle took up a lot of space in the hallway, and I had problems getting by the bicycle in the hallway.

I knew that complaining to Bobo about the bicycle using up so much space in the hallway, how it was very inconvenient to pass the bicycle while it was there, would only get an argument from Bobo. I just did not complain about my inconvenience. Each time that JoJo would come by, he would spend the night upstairs.

I do not remember which young girl was staying with Bobo one time that JoJo spent the night with Bobo. It could have been one of these girls: Sally, Annie, Jessie, Mary, Julia, Christine, or Debbie. It did not seem to matter who was staying upstairs at that time. I could only wonder what was going on upstairs while JoJo spent the night with Bobo. Bobo could have been introducing his cousin, JoJo, to his (Bobo's) type of behavior . . . like spending the night in bed with a young lady.

A neighbor who became suspicious of Bobo told me that he believed that Bobo and his many friends were engaged in some type of drug use. If my neighbor was correct in his assumption, they certainly knew how to conceal their activities, upstairs or elsewhere.

I could not accuse anybody of using drugs, because I had absolutely no proof of such type of behavior going on upstairs. However, I was suspicious myself, sometime ago, but I was not able to pinpoint any such activity going on in my house. I recall that once I smelled smoke coming from upstairs and I rushed upstairs complaining that I smelled smoke and it was an unpleasant type of odor. Bobo told me that he was using Ben-Gay on himself.

For now, Sally was back and seemed to be in control of who stayed with Bobo in his room upstairs. Sally was back and she was back on the streets, soliciting or advertising her favors, same as before.

I was on my way home, one night, and I saw Sally on the street about one block away from where I lived. Sally apparently recognized my car, and she virtually tried to disappear by hiding behind the cars parked on the street. I pretended that I did not see her or recognize her in that area. I proceeded to go home. The next day, I saw Sally and spoke to her, as always, but did not mention that I saw her a few blocks away the night before.

Occasionally I would hear Sally calling Bobo Daddy. I could not, for the life of me, figure out what was going on in that one room upstairs. Yet I knew that there was what you might call incest between father and daughter. One night, Sally was late coming home. Sally called Bobo from the street, since Bobo kept his doorbell jammed. Bobo I heard going downstairs to open the door for Sally.

Shortly after Sally was upstairs, she apparently undressed and had gotten into bed when I heard her yelling, "Get off me! Get off me!" Then I heard footsteps running out into the hall in the upstairs area. Then everything appeared to be normal again. Apparently, Sally had returned to bed, and either she had agreed to accept Bobo or Bobo himself had given up the idea of sexual contact at that time.

How could you not hear all of these commotions if they were occurring over your head, in the upstairs area? This type of behavior among Bobo and Sally and the other girls seemed to be a common practice in the upstairs area. This was not the first time that Sally came home late and I heard the same type of struggle between Bobo and Sally. She (Sally) would always yell out, "Get off me!"

I could only assume that it was when Sally undressed and got into bed that Bobo would make his attack on her.

One day, Bobo called me upstairs to fix something in the kitchen sink. When I was going upstairs, Bobo yelled, "Mr. B., do not come upstairs now, because the girls, Jessie and Mary, are asleep. They worked late last night, and they are still sleeping. I will call you later, Mr. B., when they are awake."

I had gotten up far enough to see one of the girls on the single bed and the other girl lying on the double bed. Out, they were motionless as they slept. My eyes were fixed on the girl lying on the single bed, and I was just standing there looking at her as she slept. She must have felt my presence, because she moved and raised her head and she looked at me for a while; then I returned downstairs. She did look like she was very sleepy. The girl on the double bed was not aroused when Bobo was telling me that the girls had worked very late and they were tired.

I think that Bobo realized that I must have heard Sally yelling, "Get off me!" several times. Bobo, with his head hanging down, confessed to me that Sally was, as he put it, his "old lady." Last year, he said that she was twenty-three years old; now, one year later, she could only be twenty-four years old. How could she be an old lady? That's just an expression; "she is my old lady."

I did not offer any comments about Bobo telling me once that she was his daughter and now telling me that she was his old lady. I think that Bobo wanted me to offer some comments about his change in Sally's relationship to him. Bobo's confession to me about Sally's relationship to him did not matter to me in the least. Bobo further confessed to me that Sally's baby was his baby. "I am the father of Sally's baby," he said. Here, again, it did not matter to me. So Bobo was the father of Sally's baby girl . . . what else was new? Nothing surprised me anymore when Bobo was involved.

One Sunday morning, I saw Bobo and Sally all dressed up and on their way to the morning service at a nearby church. This was unusual, for me to see Bobo dressed and on his way to church. Bobo did look like a handsome guy, but this was the first time that I saw him going to church. Bobo used that technique to persuade me to rent him the room upstairs. Due to his saying that he was a religious man and was active in church, along with Deacon Jack, thinking that he would make a good tenant, I rented the room upstairs to him. That was one of my greatest mistakes.

Bobo was a medium-brown-complected guy, slightly stout. He was about five feet, eight inches tall. Sally was about five feet, two inches, tall . . . a little darker in complexion. She had short hair, while Bobo had curly hair. They strolled along the street. Bobo had a slight switch in his walking movements. He was walking without his walking cane. Not unusual, I would say.

I had always noticed that Sally also walked with a little switch in her movements . . . similar to the way that Bobo walked. I was not going to form any conclusions from my observation of this couple. I would simply say that they seemed to be an odd couple.

One day, Bobo rushed upstairs, in haste he broke off his key in the cylinder lock. He asked me if I had an extra key that he could use to open the door. I said, "Yes." I went upstairs and attempted to put my key in the slot for the key and found that Bobo had broken off part of his key in the door cylinder. I could not put my key into the slot. I could not take the part of the key that was in the cylinder out. It was a slam lock. I got a screwdriver and wedged the screwdriver between the slam lock and the part that the slam lock fit into. I was able to open the door.

Bobo wanted me to replace the door cylinder at my own expense, which I refused to do. Instead of replacing the door cylinder, he simply got himself a screwdriver, and that's how he opened the door for the rest of his tenancy. He did not, however, use the broken-off key in the door cylinder as a complaint against the landlord in court. Bobo did not assume any responsibility for replacing anything in the house, even when he was responsible for doing the damage to the property. What a guy Bobo was.

Since Sally gave her baby up for adoption, she had been receiving letters from the supervisor at the hospital. One day, the supervisor came by the house, looking for Sally. The supervisor did not tell me why she insisted that Sally report to the hospital. She simply left a message requesting Sally to report to the hospital as soon as possible.

Sally, without my permission, gave my telephone number to the supervisor at the hospital.

It was Bobo who used some of his schemes to get my telephone number, and he gave it to Sally, probably telling her to use it while she was in the hospital and give it to the supervisor in case they might want to contact her when she was discharged from the hospital.

My house was a building with two stories. I occupied the lower floors, the parlor and basement floors. My bedroom used to be on the parlor floor, in the back room. But now my bedroom was on the basement floor, the front room. My kitchen was in the back room on the basement floor. I was forced to move my bedroom downstairs as a result of all of the traffic created by Bobo's girls going up and down the staircase at all hours of the day and night.

One day, Sally had the nerve to call me while I was in my kitchen, on the basement floor, and asked to speak to Bobo, who was on the top floor in the front room. I cannot recall my reaction at that time, except to say what a nerve she had, calling on my phone and asking to speak to Bobo, who was on the top floor, and she wanted me to go up and call Bobo and tell him that he was wanted on the phone . . . not his phone, but my phone.

I am a loyal person, but enough is enough. I went upstairs and called Bobo and told him that he was wanted on the phone . . . my phone. Sally was calling from the hospital. I then opened the door leading to my living room, pulled the phone out into the hall, and gave it to Bobo. I was lucky to have a long cord that enabled me to take the phone into the hall. Bobo had the decency to thank me for letting him speak to Sally on my phone.

Several days after Sally was discharged from the hospital, my phone rang. The caller wanted to speak to Sally. I answered the phone. I said in a loud and a disgruntled voice, "Miss Sally does not live here. I am the owner of the house, and this is my phone."

The caller said, "I am sorry," and hung up. In addition to free rent, I guess Bobo wanted me to give him free telephone service.

I was familiar with most of Bobo's girls, that is, the older girls that were coming by to see Bobo shortly after he moved upstairs. This was the fourth phase of Bobo's tenancy, and I can imagine that he could be in the process of getting a new set of girls.

A few days after I returned from my vacation, my bell rang, I answered the door. A girl about five feet, four inches tall and weighing about 145 pounds was standing at the door. I did not recognize her. Most of the girls that visited Bobo came by on a daily basis, and I learned their names as well as their features. I had not seen Bobo as yet and did not know whether he was upstairs or not. I said, "Yes," and was waiting for the girl to identify herself and to state her reason for coming here and ringing my bell. I did not recognize her as one of Bobo's girls.

Suddenly she simply displayed one key that she was holding in her hand, and she was saying, "This is one of the keys that Bobo gave me, but I lost the key for this door here, the entrance door," as she was pointing at the entrance door lock. She suddenly rushed past me and ran upstairs. She appeared to be very agile. When she reached the hallway upstairs, Bobo was there and he attacked her, and they were falling against the banister.

This was the same banister that I was given a violation for because the banister was not sturdy, as reported by the inspector who filed the violations against me for not meeting the requirements of the city of New York for an area where a tenant was living. This was probably why the banister was not sturdy when the inspector gave me a violation for the banister not being sturdy. If Bobo got into a fight with one of his old girls before, I must have been away, because I did not hear him fighting and falling against the banister before.

Later, when I saw Bobo, he told me that the girl's name was Jose. She was by to see him about three weeks ago, and he, Bobo, told her not to come back. Bobo told me that he heard her story that he had given her keys to the house and to his room upstairs. He said that she was lying, because he did not give her keys the house and to his room. Bobo further stated that he and Jose got into a fight before and Jose gave him a hard time, because Jose could rumble. Bobo was used to taking advantage of the other, smaller girls, but not Jose. Jose could take care of herself, and Bobo did not like that; he wanted to dominate the girls.

With emphasis, Bobo told Jose that she was not invited back to see him, because he did not want to see her anymore.

The girls that were usually dominated by Bobo were small or petite girls. With this domination, Bobo felt like a hero over the girls. But Jose, who was robust and could rumble, made Bobo feel inferior and a loss of prestige over the girls.

Bobo's experience with Jose made him more careful in selecting new girls to join his clan.

15

The Fifth Phase of Bobo's Tenancy

One day while I was sitting in my living room, I had just turned my stereo on, with the volume low. I heard Bobo coming downstairs. When he reached the lower hallway floor, it seemed that he hesitated awhile, then he started to go back upstairs. By this time, I was increasing the volume on my stereo. When Bobo heard the sound of music, he returned downstairs. I knew that he wanted to talk to me or see me for one of his optimistic reasons. He tapped on my door to the livingroom. I opened the door and I saw Bobo standing as he held a lot of papers in his hand.

Here a man, whom I had spent a lot of hours in court with a case against for not paying his rent for the room upstairs, having to listen to a judge who ignored what I had to say in court against my tenant Bobo, listening to a judge who always favored my tenant Bobo, who could forget about my experiences with a man who went through the Dr. Jekyll and Mr. Hyde changes, I accepted as a friend and let him come into my living room for me to give him my advice, which would eventually help him shape up his future. It seemed that I was always mindful of the fact that he grew up without the guidance of his father. Maybe I was trying to replace his father's image and give Bobo the help that he needed as a father in the home.

Anyway, I let him come into my living room without any remorse.

Bobo did not stay long. Reason: He had a brief in his hand regarding an accident that he was involved in while he was a truck driver. Bobo told me that he had gotten a new lawyer to handle his case and this was the brief that he wanted me to read to give him my opinion about the case. He needed my advice to proceed with the case. Bobo said, "Take your time," and he returned upstairs.

Bobo said, "Take your time to read those papers." That I did. It took me about two weeks to read the document about Bobo's accident.

When I finished reading and making notes that I figured Bobo should adhere to, I called him downstairs, and I gave him my advice about his case.

I did not see Bobo for several days and wondered what he was doing. He finally showed up . . . telling me that he had his new lawyer. Bobo informed me that he had won his case and he would be receiving an undisclosed amount of money. Bobo did not tell me the amount that he would be getting as a result of the accident case.

At this time, when Bobo won his case in court, he did not owe me a lot of money for unpaid rent, but he had his reason for not wanting to let me know how much he received.

Bobo did, however, discuss with me his plans on how to use this money to his greatest advantage. On one of his visits to my living room, he told me that there was a vacant store on the corner of MacDougal Street and Ralph Avenue and he was going to rent that store.

Bobo continued, saying that he was going to open a short-order restaurant in that store. Bobo was a good cook. This was one of the skills that his mother taught him when he was a young boy, since he did not have the opportunity to learn from his father, who was, most of the time, on the road driving his truck.

Bobo paid one month's rent on the store and had some minor repairs made to shape up the image of this short-order restaurant.

For several days I saw Bobo going back and forth to the corner. I thought that he was ready to operate the store. It seemed that Bobo was formulating his plans on how he was going to operate the short-order restaurant, until one day he stopped by and told me that he did not want to operate the restaurant himself and was looking for someone that he could trust to run the restaurant for him.

I could not offer any suggestions to him of a qualified person I knew that Bobo could rely on to operate the restaurant for him. I did tell him that he was doing the right thing investing his money in that manner and not spending money buying old cars like one of my previous tenants did, several years ago, ending up with nothing.

Bobo recalled that he had a very good friend and said that he was going to look him up and maybe he would be willing to take care of and run his business for him, like he would like him to do. Bobo said that his friend visited him when he first moved upstairs, but he had not seen him since then.

Bobo continued, saying that he and his friend worked together many years ago and they had a very good relationship at that time. He said at that time his friend was one whom you could rely on and one that you could depend on for dedication and reliability, his honesty in being as what you could say at that time a vice-president of the business. Certainly, he had the skills to do so at that time, as I remembered him when they worked together, many years ago.

Bobo set out to find his friend. He did not have any addresses, nor did he remember anybody else who knew his friend from years back to the time when they worked together.

Bobo depended on his own intuition to guide him to his friend's neighborhood. Bobo visited sections where he remembered his friend used to hang out. Bobo toured the neighborhood where he and his friend use to hang out and left messages with people that he came in contact with and asked them to rely his request to his friend named Bob. Bobo then returned back to his restaurant on MacDougal Street.

One day, while Bobo was sitting on the stoop, he saw his friend Bob coming up the street. Bob was coming to visit Bobo when he was notified by one of the people that Bobo had left a message that he wanted to see Bob.

I remembered that on one occasion Bobo introduced me to Bob. This was during the time when Bobo had a lot of young girls coming by to see him. On one of these nights, I clocked the number of girls coming by to visit Bobo. During this clocking period, I observed that one of the girls appeared to be very shy. This was why her name or nickname was given to be Timid, which fit her pattern of behavior.

I recalled one night that Bob was visiting Bobo, Timid came by and went upstairs. I was accustomed to hearing a lot of noise upstairs when these girls were visiting Bobo. Tonight was no exception. I did not hear any unusual noise; it appeared to be as usual. Some of the girls left after staying a few hours upstairs, but I did not see Timid leaving. I did not let my curiosity cause me to sit up late, to do any more clocking of the girls coming and going. I simply went to bed.

The next morning, about nine o'clock, I heard footsteps coming downstairs. This, too, was not unusual, to hear footsteps coming down or going up the stairs at this hour in the morning.

When I looked out at the girl that was leaving, I noticed that it was Timid. It had been about eight months since I had seen Timid. The last time that I saw her was when she stayed upstairs with Bobo's friend Bob. From this association of Bob and Timid it seemed that they had a good relationship with each other. Maybe Timid was not shy after all. At least, Bob was able to tame her, because she appeared to be stable now.

Now that Bobo had located Bob, I guessed he would open the short-order restaurant that he wanted to operate.

I saw Bobo and Bob going to check on the vacant store where Bobo was going to set up his business. I never asked questions. I simply waited for Bobo to tell me about his plans. It was my good neighbor who told me that Bobo had invested about three hundred dollars to do some repair work in the store, and as far as I knew, the place was all cleaned up and ready to put in the fixtures.

In about one month, Bobo returned to my living room. He gave me his final plans for the restaurant. Bobo told me that he had given Bob an undisclosed amount of cash to get the business started and that Bob would be the sole manager, running the place properly, and would be solely responsible for the operation of the business. Bobo simply waited for Bob to report to him regarding his progress in getting the business started.

One month passed, and Bob had not reported to Bobo on his progress in getting the business started. Bobo simply waited and waited, but Bob did not report to him.

Finally, Bobo had to pay a month's rent on the store, even though his business was not in operation. Bobo waited and waited. Meanwhile, Bobo and I had to reappear in court for another court hearing for my case against Bobo for nonpayment of his rent.

Our last court appearance was the twelfth time that we appeared in court in my case against my tenant Bobo. We were now approaching our thirteenth time in court in my never-ending case against my tenant Bobo. So far, Bobo had won all of the previous court hearings. At this point, I knew from the lack of consideration that I received from the judge concerning my case against my tenant Bobo that I would have to make some changes as a petitioner against a respondent in this case.

It was only now that I found out why my lawyer, Mr. Jasper, told me that I had a lot of problems to face in court with my tenant Bobo.

On one of Bobo's visits to my living room, he told me that Mr. Jasper was his lawyer on several occasions when he was a member of the street gang. Bobo continued, telling me that he used to get into a lot of trouble when he was a member of the street gang. Bobo said that his father had hired Mr. Jasper to represent him in court several times, several years ago.

After Bobo told me that Mr. Jasper was his lawyer on several occasions, hired by his father to represent him in court, when he used to get into a lot of trouble when he was a member of the street gang, I was able to figure out why Mr. Jasper told me that I was going to have a lot of problems with my case against Bobo in court. Mr. Jasper did not tell me that he knew Bobo and that he was, in fact, Bobo's lawyer at one time, several years ago.

At this point, I decided to write a letter to Mr. Jasper, revealing my concern about the ineffectiveness of my case against Bobo in court. So far it had been a waste of time for me and the court system, as I did not get any results after all of these court hearings.

Somehow, I felt that Mr. Jasper had a conflict of interest in my case, since he use to represent Bobo several years ago.

Mr. Jasper failed to show up at some of the court hearings, and one time that he did not show up I had to represent myself. In my letter to Mr. Jasper, I told him that I thought that I was in court as a result of a holdover proceeding that I had requested him to issue on my tenant. Instead, the hearing was in response to an order previously issued to collect ($852.50) in back rent payments. I only collected $750.00 of the money, as a result of that order.

I had pointed out many reasons why I wanted Bobo to move, but nothing seemed to materialize with my case against Bobo in court.

One of the reasons that I wanted him to move was because I could not sleep in my own bedroom at nights, and now I had to leave and return through the basement door, which led to the yard. Another reason was because I could not sit on my own stoop anymore. Still another reason was that Bobo had created a complaint to present to the judge in court so he would be given more time to remain in his room for another month or so.

I continued, saying that I was a senior citizen now and could not bear these burdens with Bobo any longer. My life span might be shortened as a result of what I was experiencing with my tenant Bobo. This ended the letter to Mr. Jasper.

In preparation for my thirteenth appearance in court, I knew that I would have to get a new lawyer to represent me.

I did not know another lawyer that I could get at this time, so I visited my friend Marvin on the corner of the street by my house.

Marvin owned at least three houses at this time, and I knew that he knew or did have his own lawyer to represent him on several occasions.

I told my friend Marvin that I was having a lot of problems with my tenant Bobo and it did not seem to do any good to take him to court, because after all of these appearances in court Bobo still seemed to have the upper hand. The judge seemed to be in favor of Bobo and not me, the landlord.

Marvin suggested that I use his lawyer, Mr. Harmond, to represent me in court. Marvin gave me his address and telephone number. I made an appointment with Mr. Harmond, which was about a week later.

I visited Mr. Harmond's office as scheduled and discussed my case with him. Mr. Harmond advised me that he did not represent anyone with cases like mine, but he recommended another lawyer, at the office of Mayo and Moss, Attorneys, about one and a half blocks away.

Meanwhile, Mr Harmond called Mr. Mayo and told him that he was sending me to his office. Mr. Harmond further stated that Mr. Mayo handled cases like mine.

When I entered the office of Messrs. Mayo and Moss, Mr. Mayo greeted me, saying, "Come in, please"; he checked my case carefully and said Mr. Harmond always assigned him hard cases. Mr. Mayo accepted my case, but he warned me, on the spot, that his fee would be more than my previous lawyer's. "More expensive," he said. The word *expensive* registered with me, but at this point I needed results, especially a lawyer who would be able to present my case to the judge. It seemed that the judge did not pay any attention to my first lawyer. This was why I felt sorry for my previous lawyer, when the judge ignored what he was trying to say in court. I think the reason was because my first lawyer was black, so my new lawyer was white. My sole reason was to get results with my case against my tenant Bobo.

Mr. Mayo did not hesitate; he reported to the courtroom and informed Judge Swan that he would be representing me in court from this day on. I could see, right away, that the judge recognized my new lawyer and accepted him with respect and greeted him spontaneously. Maybe it was because he was white. Anyway, my thirteenth appearance in court was postponed until a later date, possibly to let my new lawyer prepare his case on my behalf, which was to be heard in court in two months.

Now Bobo and I had two more months to wait for the next hearing. By this time, Bobo had paid the second month's rent on the vacant store, and still there was no sign of Bobo's good friend Bob. I felt optimistic that Bobo would be a successful businessman and would pay the back rent that he owed me. By this time, Bobo began to realize that his future plans to operate a short-order restaurant were beginning to look bleak.

When Bobo finally stopped by my living room to bring me up-to-date on his progress in becoming a successful businessman, he said that his friend had accepted his money with a promise that he would place all of the necessary fixtures in the store and start operations in about one month. Bobo was still waiting for this to happen. Meanwhile, Bobo did not pay the third month's rent on the store. He simply waited hoping that in the meantime his friend would show up.

Bobo told me that he heard that Timid was with Bob, wherever he was. I had my own idea about Bob. I said that Bob and Timid had eloped with Bobo's money. Bobo visited the old place where Bob used to hang out, but there was no sign of Bob being in the area since he left. Bobo was still waiting.

16

The Sixth Phase of Bobo's Tenancy

With my new lawyer I hoped that my case against my tenant Bobo would soon end. Remembering that the judge showed respect for my new lawyer made me feel very optimistic that I would collect my rent and would be able to force my tenant Bobo to move. My thirteenth appearance would take place in two more days.

On my way to court, my chest felt like it was sticking out with confidence that the judge would listen to my lawyer and my case and would give me a chance to prove that I indeed had removed all of those violations brought against me through my tenant Bobo and the inspector representing the city of New York.

These violations dated back one year or more since they were charged against me. As I sat in the courtroom waiting for my new lawyer to arrive, I saw a young man walking into the courtroom, and as soon as he positioned himself he called my name. I went over to him and identified myself to him. He told me that Mr. Mayo had sent him to court to represent me and my case to the judge. He identified himself as a student from the Brooklyn Law School. I had no choice but to accept him as my lawyer to represent me in court, since Mr. Mayo did not show up to represent me.

The student lawyer gave his name as Mr. Dupree, and he whispered to me, since we were sitting in the courtroom, that Mr. Mayo had another case he had forgotten about that he had to represent, which was the reason that he asked the student lawyer to represent me. The student lawyer told me that he was capable of representing me with a case such as mine and that I should not worry, because he could get the same results as Mr. Mayo could get with my case.

Mr. Dupree did not have time to review my case before appearing in court to represent me. He could only follow his own intuition in presenting cases such as mine and follow the general procedure usually followed in such cases as mine.

One thing that I noticed right away was that the judge handled Mr. Dupree with respect. More respect than he used to give Mr. Jasper. Maybe it was because Mr. Dupree was representing Mr. Mayo. Mr. Dupree appeared to be Hispanic. It does not matter what nationality you are; if you are a lawyer and if you have a case in court, the judge should recognize you as a lawyer and give you respect and allow you to present your case as it should be presented.

Nothing new was added to my case, and nothing was changed in my case. Mr. Dupree did say that if he represented my case again, he would prepare before appearing in court to have a hearing.

After the court hearing, Mr. Dupree said that he recognized my case as one in which I was trying to collect unpaid back rent. He continued, saying, "That's no big deal . . . you either pay your rent or you move. Just as simple as that." I told Mr. Dupree that maybe that's how it should be, but in my case there were a lot of violations brought against me by Bobo and the city of New York and it seemed to never end.

Mr Dupree said that he could not comment any more concerning my case because he might not be asked to represent me on my case anymore. But if he represented me in court again, he would prepare my case before the hearing, so he would know what to argue as strong points geared to winning my case against my tenant Bobo. He continued, saying that he would have to evaluate my case to see if it warranted a quick settlement or not.

Since Mr. Mayo did not represent me in court, at my earliest convenience I went by his office to speak to him about my case. I told him that I felt that he should review the testimony heard in my case for at least the last four hearings and he would see that what was discussed in my case was repetitious and should be revised.

I continued explaining to Mr. Mayo that there were a lot of violations, some created by Bobo himself and some that were there for a long period of time and had not changed accordingly to the Building Code. I showed Mr. Mayo some of my valid receipts removing some of those violations, but these violations remained as current violations against me involving my case. Mr. Mayo promised me that he would review my case before the next hearing and what needed to be changed would be changed.

When you report to the court building for a hearing, it is customary that you check the court calendar first, to see if your case is listed on the calendar. Then you go into Room One. This is the room where all cases are called by a judge or whoever is responsible for assigning the cases that are to be heard on that particular day.

If the person calling and assigning the cases that are to be heard sees that one party is disabled, he will call those cases first. As Bobo was pretending to be disabled, my case would be one of the first cases to be heard. Bobo would always carry his walking cane and would walk with a limp; this was an easy way to convince the judge that he was disabled.

This procedure allowed the disabled to be assigned a room where their case would be heard. The next step would be to go to that room and wait for the judge to come in and discuss your case. When it was over, you would go home.

One thing that was in my favor was that I did not have to sit around for long periods of time waiting for my case to be heard. The only thing that was not in my favor was that the judge would give my tenant Bobo a chance to speak and would not listen to me. Not one time did I have a chance to testify against my tenant Bobo. Even when my first lawyer was in charge of my case, the judge did not give Mr. Jasper a chance to speak on my behalf.

The reason that I got a new lawyer was because I thought that the judge would give the new lawyer a chance to plead my case and that would help me in collecting my rent and I would be able to force Bobo to move. Here I was almost preparing for the fourteenth hearing and my new lawyer had not shown up as yet to represent me in court.

Thus far, the judge always gave Bobo a chance to speak. Usually, I discussed my case with my good neighbors, especially the one that was a police sergeant at another precinct. He seemed to understand my case, and since he was one of the owners of the house next door to mine, he checked with me to see how my case was progressing. When I told him about how the judge gave him first preference in speaking in the testimony of the case, he, the sergeant asked, "Is your tenant related to the judge?" because there seemed to be a close relationship between the judge and my tenant Bobo. Even when the judge made his personal inspection at my house, he seemed to favor my tenant Bobo over me.

When Bobo gave his testimony in court, the judge put it down as genuine testimony and did not give the landlord a chance to prove his side of the case. Would you classify that as favoritism on behalf of Bobo?

If the answer is yes, then a complaint should be filed indicating that the court system is one-sided and unfair.

Our next hearing, which would be the fourteenth appearance in court involving my case, landlord against tenant, would be heard in three days. I already knew that the judge would give my tenant Bobo the first chance to speak and I would not be given a chance to prove my innocence by showing proof of those violations' removal receipts.

The other part that I had to worry about would be, if my new lawyer would represent me in court, today.

My fourteenth appearance in court was no exception, I simply reported to the courtroom as usual and waited for my name to be called. Today, the case before mine was late and they were still occupying the room where my case was to be heard. As I attempted to go into the room assigned for this date, I was stopped at the entrance door and was told to go into the adjoining room and wait for this case to end.

I went into the adjoining room, sat down, and was waiting for the other case to end when my name was called. I looked around and saw a young man calling my name. I checked him out and found him to be a Mr. Axley. Mr. Axley told me that Mr. Mayo had asked him to represent me in my case in court. Mr. Axley said that he was a student lawyer from the Brooklyn Law School and Mr. Dupree had brought him up-to-date on what my case was all about.

Remember, I was having problems with my case in court because the judge favored my tenant over me and I was not getting any consideration from the judge in ending my case and forcing my tenant to move. My solution was to get a new lawyer to represent me in court, especially before this judge. What had happened to this point? My new lawyer showed up at the end of a court session and informed the judge that he would be representing me from then on with my case. I had not seen him since in court to represent me at all. This was the second student lawyer to represent Mr. Mayo, my new lawyer, in presenting my case in court.

In view of my new lawyer's lack of interest in my case, my case against my tenant Bobo could go on forever. However, my new lawyer had prestige and he would be able to testify on my behalf in front of this judge without any remorse. The two student lawyers got the same consideration as Mr. Mayo, because of Mr. Mayo's prestige before the presiding judge, but they did not seem to be capable of defending my case with positive results. This discrepancy could be the lack of preparation of my case.

At this point, the lawyer or lawyers representing my case should be able to eliminate all of those violations that they were continuing to list as present violations or current violations. I informed my new lawyer that I had valid receipts removing those violations, but when I showed him my receipts he casually looked at them and it seemed that each lawyer was letting the judge dismiss the case, based on my valid receipts. I was beginning to be skeptical about my new lawyer. It seemed that he was passing the buck and I was losing the buck, with my case in court.

I had to ask myself a question: should I accept Mr. Axley, the second student lawyer from the Brooklyn Law School, or should I ask for an adjournment and my case being heard at a later date? At least, I had the power to ask for an adjournment, but would that be the right thing to do at this point? All of these questions and I did not seem to get the right answers; that's where I needed a lawyer to get the right answers to my case.

The only positive answer that came into my mind was that the judge recognized the student lawyers when they represented me in court, but was that enough . . .? The judge gave them a lot of respect, but was that enough?

My case was heard for the fourteenth time in court. Results; you guessed it; my case ended as before, the old status quo. Same as before.

Since I had not seen my new lawyer since he reported at the end of one of the hearings to let the judge know that he was going to be my lawyer for the rest of the duration of my case in court. Then I was obligated to go by his office to see what his intentions were concerning my case.

When I arrived at his office, what did I find? I found my new lawyer was sitting in a chair in his office, drinking a soda and talking on the phone. Yet he assured me that my case in court would end soon. What about my rent money? He did not mention that. What about Bobo moving out of my house? My new lawyer did not mention that, either.

At this point, my new lawyer felt that he had to appease me in one way or another, so he told me his lawyer's bedtime story. I was not sleepy, and all I wanted to know or hear was that he could and would win my case and I could get or collect my earned unpaid rent money, plus force the tenant to move.

My lawyer's bedtime story started off like this: "I once had a case in court when I represented someone like you and a case similar to yours. After several hearings, the tenant failed to show up at one of the hearings; it was then that the judge ordered the tenant to move out of the landlord's house." The tenant did move out of the landlord's house, but he did not pay any rent before he moved. This meant that the landlord sacrificed his unpaid rent in order to get the tenant to move out of his house.

This was not all in favor of the landlord; the landlord was able to fix up his apartment, and he rented it to another tenant, and he collected his rent on time for several months thereafter.

Then the lawyer said, "Wouldn't you like to be able to do the same thing like that landlord?"

When you hire a lawyer to represent your case in court, the lawyer tried to impress you that he is doing all that he can to represent you in your favor, as far as your case is concerned. Mr. Mayo is no exception; he tries to impress you that he is doing all that he can for your case. Yet I had not seen him in court for the last two hearings. This was the fourteenth hearing, and my case had remained the same since 1991.

He was not mindful of the fact that I was in court for a reason. Lawyers should know that when you go to court it is for a reason. When you went to court, you wanted to win your case. Otherwise, why would you pay a lawyer to represent you in court?

Did I have to assume that when I went to court next time, I would win my case? According to my index number 59172-1991, that means that I filed or had the lawyer file an order to collect my unpaid rent, and here it was in 1992 and I did not collect any rightful due rent since that time. How I was scheduled to appear in court for the fifteenth time, in about three weeks, and I had not collected any rent since March 5, 1991.

I should be able to blame someone for this discrepancy. Should I blame my lawyers?

Going to court repeatedly since 1991 and not getting any results meant that those hearings in court were beginning to be like "a broken record," which repeated the same thing over and over again and again, for the last fourteen appearances. Now we were appearing in court for the fifteenth time. Should I expect the same thing to happen at this fifteenth hearing?

There was a change in the general appearance of our case in court. Bobo was assigned a Legal Aid lawyer (female) to represent him for his side of the case in court. Would that make a difference in the general setup of the case in court? You can assure yourself that it would have a dynamic effect on this case in court.

A few days earlier, I saw this young lady visiting Bobo in his room, at my address. I was accustomed to seeing young girls visiting Bobo, but seeing this young lady, I could tell that she was different. She appeared to be businesslike in her gestures as she was interviewing Bobo. Bobo knew that I was suspicious about her visit to his one room. Therefore, the first chance Bobo was available, he came down to my living room and told me that she was a Legal Aid lawyer and that she was going to represent him in court for his side of the case. This was the fifteenth appearance in court with this same case.

I found out later that her approach to this case was as follows:

1. She asked the judge for notes based on this case dating back to 1990.
2. She picked out the most important parts of the judge's notes that she thought would be more effective against the landlord in this case.
3. Then she documented the reasons why the landlord brought this case against the tenant. She listed all violations that she thought would be most effective to present against the landlord in court.

This outline that I was able to get concerning what procedure that the Legal Aid lawyer was going to use in court against me left me uneasy, because so far my new lawyer had not represented me at the last two hearings.

I had not seen or heard from my new lawyer since the last hearing. Would he represent me this time in court? It was doubtful that he would represent me in court.

We followed the usual procedure, this time, in preparation for the fifteenth appearance in court. I usually got to the court building and the courtroom a few minutes before the court session started or began.

As I sat watching the people, as they came into the courtroom, this was when I was able to see my lawyer when he was coming into the courtroom before he saw me.

After sitting in the courtroom for about ten minutes, I saw Mr. Dupree coming into the courtroom. He stopped over in the section where the lawyers usually sat, and he sat down. Less than five minutes later, I saw Mr. Axley coming into the courtroom, and he went over to the same section where Mr. Dupree was sitting and sat down next to Mr. Dupree.

As I was looking at the two student lawyers, I noticed that they were reading from sheets of paper that they were holding in their hands. I could only assume that what they were reading was something pertaining to my case in court, which would be heard later.

I found out later that this document that the two student lawyers were reading was a document drawn up by the Legal Aid lawyer representing Bobo for his side of the case. I found out later that the Legal Aid lawyer drew up her document and presented it to Judge Swan, who, in turn, had it transferred to the legal form of the court system.

The Legal Aid lawyer had drawn up her document on her personal stationery. The judge felt that her own personal stationery was not sufficient to present a legal document in Court.

This legal form used by the court system indicated the petitioner and the respondent of the Civil Court of the City of New York as a "Stipulation of Settlement Document." I also noticed that the judge wrote: "2 Atty's" on the top of the right side of the document indicating that there were two students, who were lawyers from the Brooklyn Law School. They were sharing in representing my side of the case in court.

From this point of the case, I would like to quote part of the wording of this document drawn up by Bobo's Legal Aid lawyer, which pertained to my tenant Bobo. *"In consideration of Petitioner's agreement to waive any claim to rent through August 31, 1992, and to make all repairs listed in the Inspection Report, dated March 4, 1991, and the Judge's Order of February 14, 1992: To clean up the back yard as legally required and repair front door window."*

COMMENTS

Comment #1. This document disregarded the holdover (L&T, 59172, 1991, and 1992) for a rent payment.

How could my new lawyer sit back and let the Legal Aid lawyer enforce an order to disregard my right to collect my rent from a tenant who had been living at my expense for over one year . . . plus, in a way, helping or providing good conveniences to his girls on a daily and nightly basis, as they used my bathroom facilities, and providing other accommodations for these girls, as well, an expense to the landlord? These bills had to be paid for with cash, not promises. Who was going to pay these bills? The landlord, who else?

My new lawyer was letting the Legal Aid lawyer pull the wool over his and my eyes. And she was getting away with it. The two student lawyers could not rescue me from the Legal Aid lawyer, because she had the upperhand of this case in court.

Maybe I was not supposed to know any better; therefore, I should just sit back and let the "chips fall where they may."

Concerning the holdover proceeding, the judge said that the reason the holdover proceeding was issued was because my tenant Bobo complained about certain violations existing in his room, kitchen, and bathroom. The holdover proceeding was thrown out . . . disregarded, by the judge himself.

Comment #2: "To waive any claim to rent through August 31, 1992." This meant that I could not collect any rent from my tenant Bobo from March 5, 1991, when Bobo only paid part of his rent. Now his Legal Aid lawyer was saying that I could not collect any rent from my tenant Bobo through August 31, 1992. In summing all this up, you will find that my tenant Bobo had been living at my expense from about February 1991 through August 31, 1992, without paying any rent at all. How could the court system of the city of New York take advantage of a retired landlord, living on a fixed income? Yet they wanted the landlord to keep his property in good repair. This area was where my new lawyer should have placed his priorities in favor of his client.

Comment #3: After Judge Swan's personal inspection, he said, "Clean up the backyard as legally required." Here, when the judge was in Bobo's kitchen, Bobo pointed out some lumber that I had stored on a metal rack, at the extreme rear of my backyard, for future use. The judge commented to me, "The fire department could give you a violation for storing that lumber at the rear of your backyard. They could say that this is a 'fire hazard' and is dangerous to the surrounding area."

This was my house, this was my backyard, I was paying the real estate taxes on my property for my personal use and for my personal convenience, and I do not think that any judge or anybody else has anything to do with what I do or how I use my personal property as long as it is not detrimental to my health or anybody else's health, and it looked like the way that I had it stored was neat and it was not creating a "fire hazard" to anything around it.

The Legal Aid lawyer was looking for something to accuse the landlord of as a reason to waive the right for the landlord to collect his rent overdue at this time. The Legal Aid lawyer felt that these statements made by the judge's notes were genuine and they existed because the landlord neglected his duty to have them removed.

This was where I needed someone who could reach the Legal Aid lawyer and could point out that these statements were not true, because they did not exist anymore. They were corrected by the landlord several months ago.

Comment #4: "No rent to be paid through September 30, 1992." I could not see a reason for Comment #4, because Comment #3 explained that I was not entitled to collect any rent through August 31, 1992, except it seemed to be extended through September 30, 1992.

Comment #5: "Make all repairs listed in the Inspector's Report." Here was another part of the Legal Aid Lawyer's Report that my new lawyer could have challenged. He was not, even, here to represent me with my case. The two student lawyers from the Brooklyn Law School represented me, and one of them; Mr. Dupree was sharp enough to observe from my valid receipts, that I had, indeed, removed all of these violations on the Inspector's report, dating back to about one year ago.

After Mr. Dupree had noticed that I had corrected those violations, he asked me; "What does the judge want you to do? Does he want you to repair these violations, again? That means that you would be repairing these violations for the second time. . . . That does not make any sense, the judge should give you credit for removing those violations, by checking your valid receipts closely." It seems that the judge was not mindful of the fact that I had completed the necessary repair work to remove those violations. For one thing, the judge did not give me a chance to speak in court to explain my side of my case. He did not interpret the meaning of my valid receipts, and those violations continued to exist.

The only existing violations, at this time, were the ones that were created by Bobo himself and the ones that were created by his female friends.

Comment #6: "Entrance door glass window broken." Check out this violation carefully to see who was responsible for this violation.

Late in the afternoon, one of Bobo's girls—this one was once his girlfriend—came by to see him. Bobo did not want to see her. To spite him, supposedly, after he did not want to let her into his room, she broke the plate-glass window, because Bobo refused to let her into his room. Did she think that this was one way to punish Bobo for refusing to let her into his room?

In breaking the window, did she really think that she was hurting Bobo? Instead of hurting Bobo, she was destroying the landlord's property, and the landlord would be responsible for this violation, not Bobo. If you checked some of these violations, you would find out that the landlord was not responsible for several of the violations. They were created by a malicious act.

It was my duty to file a complaint against my tenant Bobo. The nearest precinct to my house was the Thirty-first Precinct. They gave me the complaint number 7270, dated September 7, 1990. Can you see how far back this was? But because of the mishandling of my case, it was still listed as a current violation.

Bobo knew that I had filed a complaint against him for this violation at the precinct because he saw the squad car and the cops that came to check this broken plate-glass door window in the entrance door. Bobo did realize that this episode by Sally destroyed part of the landlord's property, and he paid to have the plate-glass window replaced.

Now, how could Bobo's Legal Aid lawyer accuse the landlord of not replacing the plate-glass window in the entrance door? I, the landlord, was accused of being negligent by not replacing the plate-glass window in the entrance door. Bobo paid to have the plate-glass window glass replaced, but they were still listing this violation as a current violation.

If a lawyer was assigned to defend his or her client in a case such as this case, landlord against the tenant, the lawyer had to get some way that he or she could accuse them, in this case landlord, of not providing adequate service to his or her tenant and therefore charge him with negligence for not providing the service that he was legally responsible to provide and could be punished for not taking care of his responsibility.

In this case, the Legal Aid lawyer was assigned to represent the tenant. Now the Legal Aid lawyer's complaints had to be drawn up against the landlord. Then the Legal Aid lawyer (female) knew that she would have to check previous hearings notes from the court clerk's records to find out what the case was all about. She (the Legal Aid lawyer) was guided to the judge where she found the judge's notes on his personal inspection visit and the inspector's violations, and from the court clerk's notes she was able to draw up her complaints against the landlord. Since most of her information concerning this case came from the judge's notes, she thought that the judge's notes were true and accurate.

At this point, the Legal Aid lawyer did not know that the judge was negligent in recording his notes, and not giving the landlord credit for removing those violations at the time that they were removed was the basis of the Legal Aid lawyer's report, erroneously drawn up against the landlord.

For an instance, the plate-glass window in the entrance door was broken on September 7, 1990, and the Legal Aid lawyer's report was drawn up May 20, 1992. Even though the plate-glass window was removed in 1990. It was still listed as a current violation in May 20, 1992.

This was how the criminal justice system treated my case of landlord against tenant for fifteen hearings.

What happened to the landlord from this point on? The student lawyers from the Brooklyn Law School who were representing me in court for Mr. Mayo cornered me in one section of the courtroom. They presented me with a copy of the Legal Aid lawyer's report. After they gave me a chance to read this Legal Aid lawyer's report, they said, "All you have to do is sign this report and your case against your tenant will be over."

What did they do to accomplish their aim? Where we were standing was not good enough, so they simply called me to the back of the courtroom. In a low tone of voice, each of them tried to persuade me to sign this document, drawn up by the Legal Aid lawyer. I knew that this document was not true. Mr. Dupree knew that this document, containing a breakdown of the old violations against the landlord, was not true. So why did they want me to sign this report?

In a situation like this, you cannot visualize that getting still another new lawyer to represent you might not work, either. Getting a different lawyer at this point might be a waste of time and money, and you might end up closing this case in the same manner . . . in favor of the tenant.

I reluctantly signed the Legal Aid lawyer's report above the line where "landlord" was written.

Did Mr. Mayo close his books as a winner of this case? Indeed he was a winner; he did not put anything into the case, yet he was paid double to handle the case. Sure he was a winner; the landlord was a loser.

* * *

To begin this part of Bobo's tenancy, I was mindful of the fact that my case of landlord against tenant Bobo spread out to and included the fifteenth appearance in court. My tenant Bobo's Legal Aid lawyer won the case. Everything was in favor of her client Bobo. I did not have anyone to dispute her proposal. Exactly what she had on her report, that's what she got, without any opposition whatsoever.

My tenant Bobo was winning from the beginning. The judge always listened to my tenant; he did not give me a chance to speak out in court. He, the judge, only spoke of putting me in jail, and he constantly reminded me that he would put me in jail. Maybe it made him feel good to have the power to put me in jail, or maybe he would always say that to intimidate me.

Since my tenant won the case in court, where did I go from here? Realizing that Bobo did not want to move, I felt that I was stuck, again, with him. I could end up back in court with my tenant Bobo. If, however, I would qualify for a Legal Aid lawyer, I might have a chance to win my case against my tenant.

Going back to court would give my tenant Bobo another chance to create more violations against me. At this point, I felt that Bobo would do almost anything that he felt would help him to remain upstairs in his room. I think that he liked it upstairs. At least, it appeared to be convenient for his girls to come by to see him. Another thing that he would feel that would be in his favor would be not paying any rent and maybe that he would be able to cash a two-party check and nobody would investigate the disappearance of the two-party checks. I did report that I was not collecting my rent. I also reported to my tenant's supervisor. He made promises but did nothing about the disappearing checks. I returned two stale checks to him, and I did not get them back, either.

I have always heard that any type of forgery is a crime and this pattern of behavior by anyone who commits this type of crime would be punished. It seemed that my tenant Bobo was not even questioned about the disappearance of those two-party checks. It seemed that nobody cared, as long as only the landlord was losing; then the perpetrator went unpunished.

Based on the report drawn up by Bobo's Legal Aid lawyer, my tenant Bobo won the case May 20, 1992. In addition, speaking of the financial part of the case, I lost the following:

1. Bobo's rent money from February of 1992 to August 31, 1992 which amounted to: $4,267.
2. (a.) Replacing the entire roof: $1,700.
   (b.) Replacing the gas line from basement floor to the top floor: $1,500.
   (c.) Repairing a section of ceiling in Bobo's room: $130.
   (d.) Expense derived from traveling to and from the court hearings, estimated to be: $5,250 not counting time lost in court.
   (e.) Legal fees: $2,150.
   (f.) Miscellaneous expenses: $750.

The total expense for the landlord, with the case in court against the tenant, amounted to $15,747.

It appears that the criminal justice system was not mindful of these expenses created by my tenant Bobo. Instead, he was given credit for good testimony . . . anytime that he could charge the landlord with negligence in providing essential services to the tenant.

God forbid, Did I have to go through this again? With my tenant Bobo?

It was now June 2, 1992, and I did not see any signs of Bobo preparing to move. He knew that the case was settled in his favor, and he knew that I could not collect any rent from him until after August 31, 1992, and he liked to stay upstairs in his room, since it was convenient for him for his contacts with his girls. This neighborhood seemed to be ideal for his type of operation. The bus was only one half-block away; the subway was only one half-block away. The post office was just in front of my house. Could you ask for any more than that?

It was the wording of Bobo's Legal Aid lawyer's report of May 20, 1992, that included free rent through August 31, 1992. Of course, this was not different from before, because Bobo had been living at my expense since March 5, 1991. In spite of this, the lawyers from the

Brooklyn Law School, representing Mr. Mayo, persuaded me to sign the Legal Aid lawyer's report.

This type of consideration for a landlord, who had prepared himself for retirement several years before he retired, and now he saw his dream go down the drain without qualm or fiction. It's painful, to say the least.

I recall once Bobo told me that he could take my house and not pay me anything for it. I did not take what he was saying seriously, regarding that statement, and did not give what he had said a second thought.

An elderly senior citizen (ninety-four years old) who attended the senior citizens' center where I went for some of my meals, told me one day that she remembered when a senior citizen living near where she lived was having problems with one of his tenants, and the tenant ended up taking over the senior citizen's house.

From the senior citizen's statement and having confidence in her, based on her age and her past experience, I thought carefully about what she said. I recalled in the past that there were some landlords who had problems with some of their tenants, who stopped paying their rent and damaged their property to the extent that they just walked out and left their investment, after being tormented by the tenants over the years, they just gave up and walked out, and that was a final good-bye to their future dream. Then the city would take over these buildings for nonpayment of real estate taxes. Soon thereafter, the city was called a slumlord. The city would declare the buildings unsafe to live in, the tenants would move, and then the city would demolish the building. This travesty occurred in a lot of areas throughout the city. Areas where the tenants' destroyed property became vacant lots.

After reviewing these possibilities in my mind, I could see, from my experience with my tenant Bobo, that it could happen to me and I would not get any compensation for my investment, like the landlords who abandoned their houses.

It is true that if a landlord has good tenants, his property is usually kept in good repair. I had that experience in the past, when I had some tenants that you could live with like your own family members, tenants that you could trust. Many times I left my children with some of my tenants while I was going to be away for long periods of time. I could rest assured that my children would be taken care of by the tenants as they would be taken care of by a close relative. It doesn't seem to be like that now. Where are the good tenants? Are there any more good tenants left?

Checking back further in my past experience dealing with tenants, I found out that the tenants who disrespected their landlords were the ones that destroyed the landlord's property. I continue to find out that it is the slum-living-way of the tenants who create or cause this type of destruction of the landlord's property.

Going back to that statement that I made previously, I was mindful of the fact that my tenant Bobo was still living upstairs in my house, and it was June 2, 1992, and I did not see any signs of his preparing to move. What could I say? He did not want to move out of my house.

Here is a "supposition" that I am mindful of: just suppose that Bobo would be stubborn, disrespectful, uncompromising, concerning the landlord, and remain upstairs, in his one room, with use of kitchen and bath, because he knew that he won the case in court and he knew that I could not collect any rent from him until after August 31, 1992, based on the report drawn up by his Legal Aid lawyer as of May 20, 1992.

Where could I get help to correct this condition in my house? It seemed that I could not rely on the criminal justice system for the landlord to get help in my case of landlord against tenant. If, however, I ended up back in court, the case might end up the same as before, the tenant winning the case with a Legal Aid lawyer.

There are some statements that prevail, but are they true? Such as:

1. All are equal in the eyes of the law.
2. There is equal justice for all.
3. Justice will prevail.

It seems that you cannot believe in these statements unless you are a tenant.

Let's think of good things to happen . . . positively. It's painful to think of things that might happen negatively, and I could not continue to absorb any more abuse from my tenant Bobo. If he decided to remain upstairs, then I would be forced to move myself. This apparently was what he wanted and what he expected me to do. Then I would be losing my investment, my retirement plans, and my overall image.

Where could I reach out to get some help? Nobody seemed to have an answer for that question, so I had no other choice but to sit back and let time march on.

Here it is, June 22, 1992, and I was on my way home. To me, today was no exception. I was simply on my way from wherever I was. I was going home. It's a good feeling when you can say, "I am going home." A home to go to is an asset in one's life cycle; whether it's peaceful or not, you can always say, "I am going home."

But today it seemed to be different than before. As I reached about one half-block from my house, I saw a lot of people standing on the opposite side of the street, in front of my house. As I got closer, I saw a squad car near the left side of my house, parked. As I got even closer, I saw a police barricade across in front of the house, next door to the left side of my house, and the barricade extended across in front of my house as well.

By this time, I had gotten close enough to see Bobo, as he sat in a chair on the opposite side of the street, facing my house. Bobo called me over to where he was sitting. As he pointed at the house next door, he was saying that a fire started in the house next door and he had to leave from upstairs, as demanded by the firemen, and he went across the street and sat down. Meanwhile, the water hoses were focused on the house next door. The extra firemen went into my house with their axes, wrecking bars, and hammers. Bobo continued, saying that the firemen that went into my house had remained in the house for several hours before they came back out. The firemen had left by the time that I had arrived. Only the cops were stationed outside.

As I walked over to the barricade, in front of my house, the cops stopped me. After I identified myself to the cops as the owner of the house next door, they let me pass.

As I walked through the parlor floor entrance, I could see that the firemen had broken the lock on the front door leading into the front room of the parlor floor. It was obvious that something had happened. The hallway floor was covered with debris. From where I was standing I could see that the lock on the door leading to what used to be my bedroom was broken, and as I looked to my left I could see that there was a big hole cut through the side of the wall midway up the steps leading upstairs.

This side of the house was the wall that separated my house from the house next door. The stairway was covered with debris all the way up to the top floor hallway. As I made my way upstairs, I could see that the skylight above the stairway was broken. You could look up and see the sky.

As I continued my tour, I went into the kitchen upstairs and saw a hole cut through the ceiling and the roof in the back of Bobo's kitchen. I could also look through this hole and could see the sky. The window was not broken in this area, but there was also debris in the kitchen on the floor, on top of the cooking stove, the kitchen table, and the chairs that were in the kitchen.

Reversing myself, I walked back toward Bobo's room, stopping at the door leading to the bathroom from the hallway on the top floor. As I entered the bathroom, I could see the sky as I looked up through the broken skylight. Bobo's room was not damaged.

I returned to the parlor floor and entered at the bedroom section. In that area, on the side, was a half-bath, that is, a commode and a washbasin. The firemen went into this area, and they broke a large hole in the ceiling. Realizing that above this ceiling was the floor for the kitchen on the top floor, they did not break a hole through the floor.

Continuing my tour, I went down to the basement area. When I reached the hallway in the basement, I could see that the firemen broke the lock on the door leading to the front room of the basement. Why did they break this lock on this door? The fire was confined on the left side of the house, next door, on the top floor. This area, here in the basement front room, was not in danger of the fire spreading down here. Why did they break this door open? This looked to be a malicious act by the firemen. The firemen then continued to the back room of the basement. They broke a panel from the center of the back door, reached in, and opened the door. At this point, they were exposed to the door leading to the backyard.

A few days later, I picked up my change box, which was on the mantel in the basement front room. The change box was empty. I picked up a few nickels and dimes from on the floor where the perpetrator had dropped them. This change box was made out of an old cigar box and was divided into sections for nickels, dimes, quarters, and bills. I used to travel a lot on toll roads, and I needed a lot of ready change to pay these tolls; that is why I made this change box. Usually I would have as much as forty-three dollars in this change box. All of this money was gone.

Realizing that it was a few days since the fire, I could not blame the firemen for taking my change. It could have been Bobo who took my change. I had no proof of this theft. I have heard that policemen as well as firemen who have access to your property if they see anything of value will also see it ends up in their pockets.

The entrance door to my house was not broken, because Bobo was at home at the time of the fire and he let the firemen into the house.

First it was my tenant Bobo who gave me a lot of problems; now it was the results of the damage created by the firemen, breaking virtually all of the locks on the doors. It was customary for me to leave all of the doors locked when I went out for long periods of time. It was a sure thing that I could not trust my tenant Bobo.

Now I had this big problem of repairing and replacing all of the broken locks on the doors that I felt could protect me from the evils of the outside force of evil itself. I could count at least five broken locks that I had to replace.

When I returned upstairs, on the parlor floor I was met by someone from the Red Cross. This representative from the Red Cross had already checked the fire damage, and he inspected the house in general. I do not know what he told Bobo, but he offered me some type of shelter, somewhere in one of the city's buildings. I refused his offer, because if you leave your house after a fire, when you return you might only find the structure of the house standing on the lot. I had to protect my house during the time that my tenant Bobo was staying here, and I had to protect it now after the fire.

There were guys out there on the streets looking for houses in this condition, so they could come into the house and rip out all of the plumbing pipes, fixtures, and anything else that they could get in order to sell them for a few dollars.

When I saw Bobo, he told me that the representative from the Red Cross told him that the house was livable. I could see from Bobo's statement that he did not want to move. At this time, Bobo had cleaned a narrow path between the debris on the steps, enough so he and his girls could walk up and down the stairway.

A few more days passed. After a light rain, I saw Bobo again; he approached me saying, "Mr. B, did you notice the broken skylights and the hole that the firemen cut open in my kitchen?"

I said, "Yes."

Bobo said, "If it rains, the water could damage your house. Maybe you should have those areas repaired, and it would save you money in the long run." I said that I was aware of those possibilities.

Can you image Bobo telling me that if I repaired my skylights and the hole in his kitchen it could save me money in the future? What about my rent money, Mr. Bobo? I had already earned my rent money, and I did not get the rent money, Mr. Bobo.

The second time that it rained, it rained harder, and I found out later that to prevent oneself getting wet while sitting on the toilet in the bathroom you had to hold an umbrella over your head. Maybe Bobo had that unpleasant experience, and he was trying to persuade me to repair or replace those skylights and fix the hole in his kitchen for his convenience.

After Bobo revealed to me the unpleasantness, I figured that this would be a good tool to force Bobo to move.

I had no intention of replacing the skylights or repairing the hole in Bobo's kitchen after I had found out that this was an unpleasant experience for my tenant Bobo. Instead, I could think of the different options that I could use to cause it to rain harder. I could pray for it to rain, or I could try performing the Indian Rain Dance ritual. Maybe I could get more results that way and that might force Bobo to move.

I continued to ignore the unpleasant experience that Bobo was having, and it was now that I felt that I had something to force my tenant Bobo to move.

A few days before July 1, 1992, I saw Bobo's Legal Aid lawyer coming to visit Bobo. I gave Bobo's Legal Aid lawyer credit for winning the case, landlord against tenant. The tenant won the case as a result of the report of Bobo's Legal Aid lawyer. On her visit to Bobo's room, it seemed that she was able to persuade Bobo to move.

On July 1, 1992, Bobo moved out. Was that the end of Bobo's tenancy? Not yet. Give him a few more days. This date was around the time that Bobo was expecting his check. Bobo came by around July 3, 1992, and asked me if I received his check, because he said that his check was scheduled to be mailed to him around this time. I told him no! Bobo did not believe me. Since he was talking loudly, my neighbor heard him. My neighbor told Bobo that the postman left his check at his address and he had given it back to the postman.

Bob left and apparently went by the Welfare office to pick up his check.

A few days later, I looked out and saw Bobo standing on the stoop, and it appeared that he was writing something on a mailbox.

The mailboxes were attached against the wall outside the entrance door to the house. I had two mailboxes, one for upstairs, Bobo's mailbox, and the lower mailbox for the downstairs area. The first chance that I got, I went outside and on the stoop. Looking up to the top mailbox, I saw that Bobo had, clearly written his name and Sally's name on the mailbox.

I can imagine that Bobo thought that if the postman saw his and Sally's name written on the mailbox, he would leave their mail in the top mailbox.

When I found out what Bobo continued to do at my house, I sorta felt that his presence would last forever here at my house. *Not so,* I said to myself. *Enough is enough with my former tenant.* I secured my screwdriver from my toolbox, and I looked up to the mailboxes; I carefully unscrewed the screws from the top mailbox, took it down, and carried it into the house and put it away.

Since Sally was living nearer my house, I knew that Bobo had asked her to keep the mailbox under surveillance to see if the postman left any mail in the mailbox for them. But when Sally came by, she saw an empty space where their mailbox used to be. I can imagine Bobo's reaction when Sally told him that there was no mailbox on the wall where their mailbox used to be.

Realizing how insistent Bobo was, I could feel that he had some other schemes. However hidden, he would reveal them in the near future. At this point, I was hesitant to say a final good-bye to Bobo.

Sure enough, a few nights later I heard someone upstairs. I could only think that Bobo had forgotten to take something and came back to get it. That happens to people who move sometimes; they forget to take something. I could go along with that.

About eight the next morning, I heard a noise upstairs. It seemed that someone was slipping out of the house. Whoever it was, it seems that he did not want to disturb me as he left. But hearing the noise of someone leaving the upstairs area, especially after Bobo had moved, was enough for me to take some action; this was happening after I had replaced the skylights and had repaired the hole in the kitchen upstairs. I also had cleaned all of the debris from the hallway and the steps. Everything was clean. The hole that you could see inside the room next door was repaired and painted.

I went to the hardware store and purchased a new doorlock cylinder for the outside entrance door, where you entered the vestibule. I figured that it was only necessary to replace the first door cylinder, because you had to open this door before you could reach the inside door.

With someone like Bobo, you had to give him more time to react. In this case, it did not take long; the next night, I heard someone trying to open the outside door with her key. After she found out that her key would no longer fit the lock, she called me, "Mr. B." It was obvious that it was a female's voice.

I went to the door and said, "Yes." The young lady identified herself as Bobo's niece. She told me that her Uncle Bobo had asked her to go by my house and get his mirror that he had left upstairs. I did not object to her request to get her uncle's mirror. I let her in. She was followed by a male friend. I told her that I would remain on the parlor floor and give her time to get the mirror and leave.

I waited and I waited, but they did not show any signs of leaving. I called upstairs but did not get an answer. At this point, I remembered that one of my students had given me one of his father's whistles that he used when he was a policeman.

I blew this whistle as loud as I could, but that did not arouse them I thought that the fact that this whistle was once a whistle of a policeman would make them think that a policemen was waiting for them to leave and they would come downstairs and leave.

I went downstairs and called the precinct and told them the problem that I was having with a couple who had gone upstairs to get a mirror, and they were still upstairs, and they were not showing any signs of leaving.

Later, two female cops came, one small female cop and a large female cop. I explained to them the problem that I was having with the couple who said that they came to pick up a mirror that her uncle had left when he moved and they were still upstairs.

The two female cops went upstairs, the smaller cop in front of the heavier cop. I followed them and I backed myself inside the opening where a door to the kitchen was at one time. The heavier cop knocked on the door: *Bang! Bang! Bang!* and yelled, "The police! Open the door!" There was no answer, but I assured them that was the right door, so we just waited for a while. This heavier cop had a heavier voice than the smaller cop, and with her heavier voice and a demanding voice the place seemed to vibrate.

As we stood there waiting, out came the male companion, and he was headed down the stairway like he was frightened. At this point, the female, Bobo's niece, who was left behind, yelled to the male companion, "Wait for me!" As soon as Bobo's niece said that, the heavier cop told the male companion to wait for her. He stopped about halfway down the stairway. Soon Bobo's niece was able to dress and come out of the room. She did not look up. I was about three feet away from her as she passed.

After they left, I returned upstairs to check to see what they were sleeping on in that room. I found that in this room Bobo once occupied that he had left that old box spring mattress, which was supported at each end with a crate. Four crates, to be exact.

I knew that I had a solution for that old box spring mattress. The next day, before the garage truck came by, I put this old box spring mattress out on the sidewalk.

The garbage truck finally came, and when they left I noticed that they had indeed carried away the old box spring mattress.

Now could I finally say good-bye to my tenant Bobo?

17
Bobo's Stepmother

On this date, September 12, 1992, I sat on my customary seat on my stoop. This was where I used to sit to enjoy the sun and outside view of the location in front of my house, which was located across from the rear of the post office building. I lost this favorite seat when I rented a room to my tenant Bobo. According to the story of my tenant Bobo, I lost my privilege of sitting out on the stoop, as a result of Bobo and his many friends. I did not want to share space on my stoop with people that I was not familiar with. To avoid this confrontation with other unknown people, I simply moved inside of the house or simply would stand inside the yard behind the metal fence. Bobo was forced to move on July 1, 1992. This was about two and a half months ago.

When Bobo moved, I was able to regain the space on the stoop. As I sat there observing the area around me, I saw a lady who was carrying a shopping bag. I noticed that this lady was looking up at the window where Bobo customarily sat and looked out on the street. As this lady approached my stoop, she stopped and asked me if Bobo was still living upstairs in his room. I told the lady that Bobo moved on July 1, 1992. She wanted to know where he moved. I could only tell her that he moved into the Brownsville area, but I did not have the address.

At this point, she identified herself as Bobo's stepmother, and she said that he visited her a few months ago and promised to return at a later date to see her, but he did not show up. It was in June when he was there to see her, and he promised that he would be back to see her and to bring her up-to-date on his plans for the future.

It was at this point that I invited her to sit down in my chair on the stoop. This lady was about five and a half feet tall, she looked to weigh about 150 pounds, she was light-skinned, and she spoke with a soft voice. She appeared to be very persistent in what she was saying.

Bobo's stepmother continued, saying that Bobo told her when he visited her in June that he was going to move into a senior citizen building, but he did not give her the address. She said that Bobo had two strokes and he was a diabetic. After he did not return to see her, she thought that he could have died as a result of the two strokes. She also said that he did not smoke or drink. After this lady unknown to me was telling me so many things about Bobo, I started taking notes about what she was saying and telling me.

I put a question mark after the word *smoke.* Smoking was one of the complaints that I had against Bobo and his friends. One day, I smelled a peculiar kind of smoke, which annoyed me. I ran upstairs complaining about this odor of smoke that I was smelling. When I reached the upstairs area, I saw just about a roomful of Bobo's friends. It seemed that I recalled that all of them were smoking something. One day before, I was complaining about the odor of smoke that I was smelling and Bobo told me that it was Ben-Gay. Bobo did tell me that he suffered from different types of ailments and he used something to relieve the pain. I simply said "No comment," and returned downstairs.

After my complaint to my lawyer about the odor of the smoke coming from Bobo's room, he, the lawyer, said that it could have been the smoke of reefer or a marijuana cigarette. After my persistent complaints to Bobo, it seemed that they stopped using or producing that type of smoke in the downstairs area of the house.

Bobo's stepmother continued, telling me that Bobo's mother died when he was nine years old, "and his father raised him until he married me." She, Bobo's stepmother, said that she had a lot of problems trying to raise Bobo.

Bobo's stepmother told me that Bobo's mother's dying at an early age, her son only, nine years old at the time, created a big problem in the Ryan household. Mr. Ryan's mother-in-law was there to attend her daughter's funeral, and because of the amount of turmoil she hardly had time to return to her hometown to get her clothing. But Mr. Ryan's mother-in-law was able to come to his rescue.

Sally Ann, Bobo's grandmother, was unable to continue her daughter's way of raising Bobo; she could only do what she was capable of doing in continuing to raise Bobo. Mr. Ryan realized that his mother-in-law had a serious problem in raising Bobo. The question was would she ever be able to convince her grandson that she could raise him properly?

This was a decision that Bobo's father had to make for the best interests of his son and for his son's future.

One year passed, then another year passed, and finally four years had passed and Bobo was on the streets, as a member of the street gangs. Bobo's father realized that to put his son back on the right track of life he had to make a drastic change. Certainly, every father wants the best for his child. Otherwise, in this case, Bobo would grow up as a bum on the streets of Brooklyn.

A bum, no way! Mr. Ryan was thinking of doing something concrete, now. Mr. Ryan visualized his son growing up in a society where he could live and respect others as good neighbors and would be able to plan his own prosperous future.

Mr Ryan was thinking that mothers could be replaced, and he was thinking that maybe he could find a good replacement for Bobo's sake.

Mr. Ryan's decision to remarry was uppermost in his mind, but he had to find the right person to fulfill those obligations of a real mother and one that could change the direction of a despairing boy.

Mr. Ryan had met Miss Susie (Sue) Bets on previous occasions when he attended various functions given by the Methodist church. Miss Susie Bets displayed a beautiful personality herself, but she sorta kept herself in isolation. She helped different organizations raise money for the church, but she did not join these organizations.

Mr. Ryan probed deeper into Miss Susie's life, and he found out that Miss Susie Bets was engaged to get married after she became pregnant. She, like Mrs. Callie Ryan, was from a southern state, but a more populated area. From a small town, to be exact.

Miss Bets's fiancé met with an accident before they were able to get married. Her daughter was born out of wedlock as a result of this accident, and it was this misfortune that made Miss Bets feel that she should keep herself in isolation. This incident could have been the reason that she did not join the various organizations in the church.

Nevertheless, Mr. Ryan could see the good qualities in her, and he did not hesitate to make his proposal to her. He felt that she would make him a good wife. And then he had to prove to her that he would make her a good husband. After they were able to convince each other that they could live happily together, they started making plans for their wedding.

Miss Susie Bets did not want a big church wedding, because of her unfortunate experience when her fiancé was killed in an accident. Mr. Ryan wanted to satisfy Miss Bets; therefore, he did not plan a big wedding.

After the members of the Methodist Church found out that Mr. Ryan was going to get married to Miss Susie Bets and had planned a private wedding, the members of the church spoke up.

"Mr. Ryan, how can you do that when you and your family helped this church to survive from its inception several years ago?

"Your wife was very active in the choir . . . we still hear her voice in the choir." After the members approached Mr. Ryan with their objections to his not getting married in the church, they offered these proposals:

1. "Your former wife died at an early age."
2. "You are still young, and you did not get a full life with your first wife, which was unfortunate."
3. "You should live the life that will, without a doubt, make you, and only you, happy. Because the church is where you belong and we are with you all the way."
4. "If you feel that you have found someone who will accept your son and will raise him as her own son, then the members of the church should be given the opportunity to suggest how you should select the place where you should get married. We members feel that you should not separate yourself from the church, because the members of the church feel that they are part of your family and that you should get married right here, in the church."

Mr. Ryan, after realizing that the members of the church would back him and be considerate about what he did or did not do, changed his mind and arranged to get married in the church, but not a big wedding like his first marriage to Callie, his first wife.

Mr. Ryan had to contact his boss on his job to let him know that he was going to get married in the church and that he would need more time off from his job to fulfill these obligations.

A date was set for the wedding of Mr. Ryan and Miss Susie Bets. It seemed that all of the members of the Methodist church wanted to participate in this wedding. With all of these members helping with the wedding, Mr. Ryan did not have to do too much himself. Mr. Ryan estimated that the members helped about 100 percent. This wedding was classified as a Methodist church wedding.

The date of the wedding, Mr. Ryan and his son, Bobo, were getting dressed for the wedding. Mr. Ryan, at this point, after the church members were so eager to see that this wedding made history, felt that he would have to be on time for the wedding procession to begin. Mr. Ryan looked for his son but did not see him. He assumed that Bobo had already gone to the church.

When Mr. Ryan reached the church, he looked for his son, Bobo but did not see him. He asked some of the members who had reached the church early if they had seen his son, Bobo. No one reported having seen Bobo.

According to what Bobo's stepmother told me while I was sitting on my stoop listening to her story, Bobo did not attend the wedding at all. Instead, he visited some of the gang members who had gotten into some trouble a day before. Bobo did not know this, so when the policemen came to arrest them, they took Bobo along with them, in spite of Bobo telling them that he did not participate in that crime.

When Mr. Ryan heard what had happened to his son, he went to the precinct house and bailed him out. Later Bobo was not charged with the crime.

Bobo's stepmother told me that Bobo's father was a Filipino and moved to the United States for economic reasons. He followed the footsteps of other Filipinos who proceeded him. When Mr. Ryan arrived in the United States, he was told that he could get a job as a long-distance truck driver. Mr. Ryan followed their advice, and he had a job less than two weeks after his arrival here in the United States. He settled down in the borough of Brooklyn, where he was surrounded by other Filipinos who had been here several years.

Mr. Ryan married an American lady, Mrs. Callie Mae Ryan. From this union they had one son . . . Bobo.

During Bobo's visits to my living room, he never talked about his father too much, and he *NEVER* mentioned that his father got married again after his mother's death. It appeared that Bobo resented what his father was doing or not doing when his mother was alive.

Retracting part of my story of Bobo's life, when he got married and went into isolation for a large number of years, his stepmother filled me in on what actually happened to Bobo during that period of time in his life. She said that he moved to California and lived there until 1985. He then moved back to New York. He lived with his stepmother until he got married for the second time. His first wife died in California, and maybe this was why he moved back to New York.

Bobo lived in Brooklyn after he got married, and then he moved upstate, where he purchased a small house, and at one point of his life, he owned two cars . . . one for himself and one for his wife.

Bobo's stepmother told me that Bobo was constantly getting into trouble. Sometimes he would spend a lot of his time in jail.

After a few years living upstate, Bobo lost everything that he owned upstate. He and his wife moved back to Brooklyn. Moving back to Brooklyn did not solve Bobo's problems. He continued to get into trouble with the law . . . and he would end up in jail again. His stepmother did not explain to me what kind of trouble Bobo would get into. She never revealed to me why he was put into jail. She did, however, tell me that he used to tell a lot of lies . . . And you could not trust him.

This type of behavior continued for several years after and his wife moved back to Brooklyn. Bobo's second wife reached the point that she could not continue living with Bobo anymore, and she put him out of the apartment.

Bobo returned to his stepmother's house and asked if he could move back with her. His stepmother looked him over . . . seeing that he was dirty . . . his clothes that he was wearing were filthy. She said, "No!" Then she realized that he was, in fact, her stepson, recanted, and told him that he would have to clean himself up first.

Bobo's stepmother asked him what size clothing he wore. She went out and bought him a new outfit of clothing and sent him into the bathroom to wash himself up. Good. She then told him to clean up the bathroom and he had to take a bath every day that he was staying in her house. She further stated that she could not live with his "odor." From that day when his stepmother laid down her rules and regulations, as he wanted to live in her house Bobo kept that bathroom spotless, from then until he moved to another location.

At this point, I told Bobo's stepmother that I had observed that he kept his bathroom very clean while he was living upstairs. He did not, however, keep the kitchen clean and spotless, as he did the bathroom.

Why did Bobo clean the bathroom and not the kitchen? His stepmother told me that he would eat his food and leave the dirty dishes in the kitchen sink. She was unable to break this this habit of his. I noticed that when he was living upstairs the kitchen was always filthy, as well as the refrigerator. The kitchen should be the place that should be kept clean. Because this is where you cook your food and this is the place where you ate your food. Shouldn't that section of the apartment be kept cleaner than the bathroom?

At this point, she introduced herself as Mrs. Susie (Sue) Ryan, and I introduced myself as Mr. B., the landlord. But many people thought that Bobo was the landlord while he was living here. Mrs. Sue Ryan returned to her apartment, which she said was about two blocks away.

When Mrs. Sue Ryan, Bobo's stepmother, left, I remained on the stoop for a while. As I sat there, I saw a young lady, a very attractive young lady, approaching from my right. I noticed that she was looking up at the famous window that Bobo spent a lot of his time looking out, throwing out his house keys so someone could open the front door and come in, just looking out and talking to someone on the sidewalk or street.

Bobo had a lot of nice-looking girls coming and going when he occupied the room upstairs. This was not an uncommon practice, for them to look up to the window as they passed, because after a number of times that you looked up at this special window it became habit-forming.

If I were not sitting on the stoop as this young lady passed, she, no doubt, would have called, "Bobo!" which was a common practice, for the girls to call Bobo to let them in.

Bobo's stepmother's visit to my house to find out about the whereabouts of her stepson was a welcome visit, because I had the opportunity to learn that Bobo had a stepmother and I found out about Bobo's father. Bobo never talked about his father very much. During Bobo's visits to my living room, he talked a lot about his mother, his grandmother, and sometimes his Aunt Sarah . . . but never about having a stepmother, and he talked very little about his father.

From the information revealed to me by Bobo's stepmother, I found out that Bobo's father was a Filipino. He came to this country in or about 1930. He came from Luzon Island near the Pacific Ocean, in the Republic of the Philippines. As Mrs. Sue Ryan pointed out, the main crops there were coconuts, sugar cane, rice, maize, tobacco, and hemp. They also, as Mrs. Sue Ryan pointed out, produced minerals like gold, silver, copper, lead, etc.

Bobby Ryan was engaged in the cultivation of rice, sugar cane, and tobacco. His income from the cultivation of these products was very low. His decision to come to this country was enhanced by some of his uncles who had lived in this country in earlier years.

Bobby was told by his uncles that he could get a good job in this country as a long-distance truck driver. Bobby was told by his uncles that he could accumulate his wealth in a matter of a few years.

Bobby was a silent listener. He was young at that time, but he did not forget what his uncles told him. When he, Bobby, grew up, he saved his money, and when he had accumulated enough, he left Luzon Island, and when he arrived in the United States he had no intention of returning to Luzon Island.

Bobo's stepmother continued, saying that Bobby came from one of the islands in the Republic of the Philippines and it was like he was desperate to make a change in his way of living. He was met upon his arrival in the United States by one of his relatives, Jocko, and Bobby stayed in his apartment until he learned his way around the city of New York.

Bobby was lucky to have someone who knew his way around here in this country, someone who knew where Bobby could get a job. After Bobby got a job, it seemed that his future just unfolded before him . . . and for him it was a new life! A new place to live! Currency in his pockets so he could get the things that he wanted.

Bobby was so anxious to move away from his country, and he did not want to be constantly reminded of his life back in his country, so he got married to an American lady. They had a son called Bobo.

Bobo's stepmother continued telling me that Bobo's mother died at an early age. Bobo, she said, did not accept her as his stepmother. He did not attend their wedding, he did not like his father's decision in selecting her as his second wife, and Bobo held that grudge against his father until his death.

When Bobo's father died, Bobo still had a grudge against him and did not attend his father's funeral. Bobo's stepmother continued, saying that she tried to persuade Bobo to come to the church his father was being buried from, but Bobo refused. She said that she could only assume that he was out on the streets with some of his old gang members.

Mrs. Ryan got up and said, "It was nice meeting you, Mr. B., and I must be going now."

I replied by saying, "I am glad that you stopped by to check on Bobo, and to bring to me the additional information about my tenant Bobo."

18

Bobo's Hispanic Friends

Several days after Bobo's stepmother appeared at my address, on September 12, 1992, I heard someone from the sidewalk calling, "Bobo! . . . Bobo!" Bobo had moved since July 1, 1992, and you would not expect that someone from the outside would be calling him from the street. However, this was how his friends were able to reach him when he was living upstairs in his room.

I went to the front door. I saw a lady who looked to be Hispanic. I saw a male sitting at the steering wheel of the car. This lady asked for Bobo. I told her that Bobo had moved.

"Where?" she asked.

But I was unable to give her Bobo's address.

This lady continued, saying that her brother had asked her to bring Bobo his money, which was in the amount of $1,500. She said, "That's my father in the car. I asked him to bring me here to pay Bobo."

Meanwhile, her father got out of the car and was standing near the car, which was parked in front of my house. She said that her brother had gotten into trouble and was unable to bring the money himself.

At this point, I told the lady that Bobo had moved owing me back rent in the amount of $4017 dollars and I would appreciate it if she would give me the money and I could accept the money as part of the back rent that he owed me.

The lady told me that she could not give me the money without the consent of her brother. "He is locked up," she said.

Why did the Hispanic lady's brother owe Bobo that kind of money? Was it from a drug transaction? What else could Bobo have done to earn that kind of money? These questions will not be answered, since Bobo does not live in this area anymore.

19

Summary

In summarizing this case, you look back to the beginning and let your mind wander through the story to the end of this case . . . in the court, with your tenant.

During your life cycle, you want the best for yourself like: (1.) a place to live when you retire; (2.) provisions made for yourself; (3.) financial plans; (4.) health plans; (5.) pension plans; (6.) and the location where you want to live. With these plans, you approach them one by one with a long outlook toward your future.

When you buy a house, you think of the days when you will be living on a fixed income. Then you want a house with rentable space for that little nest egg, to help you with the maintenance of your house. Then the next step is to select or try to select a good rent-paying tenant. But if you are misled, like in my case, you may select one who depends on the Welfare system to pay his rent; then you are in trouble.

If, however, you select a Welfare recipient and when you start having problems with your tenant, they will issue two-party checks, which means that the landlord and the tenant will have to sign each check before you can cash it. Then you feel secure in collecting your rent and on time. Not so with my tenant Bobo.

I managed to get a stale check and I thought that I could take it to the center in person and get an updated check. Upon my arrival at the center, I called upstairs to let Bobo's supervisor know that I was there to see him on behalf of Bobo. After I waited about an hour, a female social worker came downstairs to see me. I did not get to first base with her. Then there was another long wait. It was about lunchtime, so I waited until I saw the social workers returning from lunch.

I called upstairs, again, to see and to speak to Bobo's supervisor. About an hour later, he sent another female social worker down to see me.

The second female social worker that Bobo's supervisor sent down to see me was like the first social worker that he sent down to see me. At this point, I gave her the stale check and she promised that I would get a replacement in the mail. I never received any check in return for that stale check.

I asked myself a question, "Where do I go from here?" I would like to quote an editorial delivered over CBS April 7, 1994, by one of the news reporters. I will not give his name: "Ask the mayor." Welfare recipient, receives money to pay the rent. The rent is not paid. The landlord is left with his bills to pay and he did not collect his rent.

"What happened to the money that the tenant received to pay his rent? The rent is not paid to the landlord. What happened to those checks? Nobody from the welfare system ever investigated this fault. As long as the landlord is losing, nobody cares."

In my case, I wrote a letter to the commissioner of social services. I was late receiving a reply, and by that time Bobo had moved. The commissioner let me know that nothing could be done about my case, because the tenant had moved. I have a copy of that letter in my files.

Again, I have to ask myself a question; "Where do I go from here?" In spite of my fixed income, I had to get legal help to represent me in court. My lawyer was black. The judge was also black. The judge virtually did not listen to my lawyer's side of the case . . . in court. Watching the judge as he completely ignored what my lawyer was saying at one of the hearings made me feel sorry for my lawyer.

It was on one of Bobo's visits to my living room that he told me that my lawyer was also his lawyer when he was active in one of the street gangs.

This was many years ago, when my lawyer represented Bobo in court when he got into trouble when he was active with the street gang.

When I found out, through Bobo, that my lawyer was also his lawyer many years ago, I felt that there was a conflict of interest among my lawyer and me. I was sorta forced to get another lawyer to represent me in court. This lawyer was white and the judge did listen to the white lawyer, but the white lawyer charged more and he only represented me in court one time, when he came into court to let the judge know that he would be representing me in court from that date until the court case was settled.

It was my new lawyer, however, who sent students from the law school downtown Brooklyn to represent me at the rest of the court hearings.

At this point, Bobo found out that if he had a complaint against the landlord, he was able to get more court hearings. He, Bobo, had the upper hand against the landlord if he had a complaint against the landlord. What did Bobo do to find complaints against the landlord? He went down and through the welfare system he was able to file complaints against the landlord of not providing certain services to the tenant in the house where the tenant occupied a certain amount of space.

An inspector was sent out to inspect my two-family house and through these few complaints filed by Bobo created a chain reaction of complaints against the landlord. About sixty years ago, gas lights were used to furnish lights in the house. These pipes that enabled the gas to flow through were never removed when electricity replaced gas. The pipes were closed, but according to the city inspector, that was dangerous to my tenant Bobo.

There were other violations that Bobo could render, recurring violations like: (1.) Doorbell not working (Bobo used to jam the bell because all of those girls ringing his bell at all hours of the night and in the daytime annoyed him and once, in jamming the doorbell, he blew my new transformer); (2.) A clogged water drain from the kitchen sink (if Bobo needed a complaint and if he did not have one, all he had to do was pour cornmeal from his surplus food supply down the drain; when it reached the trap, it would remain there, and when it swelled, thereby clogging the drain; during his tenure he has used rice grains to get the same results); (3.) A leaking roof over Bobo's room. (During one of Bobo's visits to my living room, he told me that he once worked for a roofer and knew how to repair roofs and how to make a roof leak.) This was one of the complaints.

It was these violations that stretched the court hearings to fifteen in number. Even my new lawyer, who happened to be white, did not investigate my case. It was, however, one of the student lawyers who, looking over my receipts, saw a receipt dated about one year ago. He then asked me, "What did the judge want?" Did he, the judge, want me to do these repairs over again?

It was one or both of the students from the law school representing me in court who observed that some of my valid receipts were dated over a year ago. The judge did not accept any of my valid receipts, and my new lawyer did not check to find out what was going on in the court system. Yet the court system wanted me to do the repairs, using money from my fixed income . . . while my tenant Bobo was living at my expense.

Several times I was asked, "Is the judge related to Bobo?" I did not know the answer. They could be relatives. Maybe that's why the judge was in my tenant's corner when we appeared in court.

The court system seems to work this way. For instance, I am going to quote two articles from one of the leading newspapers here in the New York area. One article was dated January 29, 1994. It said: "Woman arrested for evicting crack-addicted relative." According to the article in the newspaper, she sought help but received none. The other article, dated May 1, 1993, said: "Slain student's mom is frustrated by Court delay." This murder took place at one of the high schools here in Brooklyn. "She is frustrated and tired of the Court System which is treating her as if she committed the crime." She said, "The boy who shot my son has high-priced lawyers and because of that, he gets all *the postponements he wants,* plus he and the Judge laugh as if the whole thing is a joke."

The criminal justice system, how does it work? Does it work with

1. equal in the eyes of the law, and
2. justice prevailing, or
3. as a miscarriage of justice?

After I was put through hell by Judge Swan and the Legal Aid lawyer, Bobo's lawyer, won the case, I took a vacation. Usually when I take a vacation it's in the South. The reason that I went to court in the first place was to collect my rent from my tenant Bobo. I did not collect any rent. I could have handled the case myself; at least, I would have saved the lawyers' fees.

I have a good neighbor who happens to be a police sergeant at one of the precincts in Brooklyn. It has always been my practice to tell him when I am going on vacation. My good neighbor knew about the problems that I was having with my tenant Bobo.

While I was away, my good neighbor saw an article in the newspaper regarding the judge that was presiding over my case. He saved that article for me and gave it to me when I returned home in the early part of January 1995. The date of the newspaper article was December 14, 1994. The headline read: "Housing Judge Jailed on Bribery Charges."

From this article, I was able to get articles related to the same story from three different newspapers here in the New York City area. The first newspaper said: "Rotten to the Court," "Housing Judge nabbed in eviction scam," and "Tenants tell of hell to put them through." The second newspaper reported: "Housing Court Judge Is Charged with Bribery." The third newspaper: "Judge is charged with taking bribes. Investigation say he solicited money to fix cases in Housing Court."

From these accusations of the judge that presided over my case in court I can only think maybe he wanted me to pay him to resolve my case in court against my tenant Bobo. Now the question is, Was Bobo paying the judge to operate on his behalf in court?

Normally the court order read:

Mr. B. Petitioner—Landlord
—Against—
Bobo, Respondent—Tenant

But the way my case against my tenant Bobo went, it appeared to be reversed, like.

Bobo, Respondent—Tenant
—Against—
Mr. B. Petitioner—Landlord

Bobo was depending on the welfare system to pay his rent. They did pay his rent. What did Bobo do with the money?

I would like to quote part of one of the court orders, which read: "The tenant testified credibly at this hearing that petitioner neither further inspected nor attempted to make any repairs in his apartment (room) during the last six (6) months! The Court finds the petitioner, Mr. B——to be in civil contempt of the Court's Order dated May 28, 1991. The petitioner is fined $100.00," which was paid in open court to Bobo on or about February 17, 1992. Did that money go into Bobo's pocket or did it end up in the pocket of the judge?

Finally, my good neighbor saw Sally returning from somewhere all dressed up. My good neighbor asked her where she was coming from. Her answer was "From Bobo's funeral."

"He died?" my good neighbor asked.

"Yes," said Sally.

"Oh!" My good neighbor gestured "Was he sick?"

Sally answered saying that he was a diabetic.

My good neighbor relayed the news to me. A few days later, I saw one of the girls that had visited Bobo when he was living in my house. She asked me, "Did you hear about Bobo?"

I said, "Yes."

"He had sugar," she said.

I said, "Oh," shrugging my shoulders as I spoke. Thinking about the past, as I lived with my tenant Bobo, I just walked away.

One day as I was about to enter the post office, I met Deacon Jack, leaving the post office. He asked me whether I had heard about Bobo? I said, "Yes."

He continued, saying, "Did you hear what or why or how he died?"

I said, "No."

Deacon Jack said, "He was stabbed to death." But Deacon Jack did not know whether it was a man or woman that stabbed him to death.

Mrs. Callie Mae Watts Ryan (1907–43), the mother of my tenant Bobo, was a high school graduate, yet when she realized that she was totally responsible for raising her son, Bobo, she adopted a plan of her own, whereby she would be able to raise her son in a way so that he would be able to compete with any of his peers, scholastically and socially.

She did not know, however, that the way that she chose to raise her son, in shaping his future by training him to learn by doing, was, in fact, in a way similar to theories of the greatest educators based on the same concept many years earlier. They were as follows:

Friedrich Froebel (1782–1852), German founder of the kindergarten and an influential educator. It was in the USA that the Froebelian movement achieved its greatest success.

Johann Pestalozzi (1746–1827), Swiss educator. He established an orphanage where he attempted to teach neglected children, agriculture and simple trades . . . hoping that they might lead productive, self-reliant lives.

John Dewey (1859–1952), U.S. philosopher, psychologist, and educator. John Dewey's theories led to the Progressive Education Movement in the United States and abroad.

After Mrs. Ryan molded her son for a better future, no one after her death was able to change Bobo's way of life.

Glossary

(The following definitions provided by the author are based on his general knowledge with peripheral references to the general collegiate dictionaries of Random House and Webster.)

A

a-ban-don: v. to give up wholly and finally; to relinquish; to surrender.
a-bide: v. to stay; reside; to tolerate.
a-bil-ity: n. quality, state, or condition of being able.
a-ble: having skill, strength to perform a task; competent.
a-board: on board within a vessel; on a train.
a-breast: side by side; in a line with.
ab-rupt: broken off; steep; describing a sudden change of subject.
ab-sence: being absent; failure to appear when cited to a court of law. absent; not present.
ab-solute: unconditional; without restraint; absolutely: adv. positively; very; entirely.
ab-sorb: to swallow up; drink in; soak up. absorbing: soaking up.
a-buse: to make a wrong use of; to violate. abusive: practicing abuse; rude.
ac-cept: to take; to receive; to agree to.
ac-cess: a coming to the means or way of approach; admission; entrance.
ac-com-mo-date: to render fit or suitable; provide room for.
ac-com-mo-dation: a loan of money; room or space for.
ac-com-pa-ny: to go with. accompanied: went with.
ac-com-plish: to carry out; to finish; to complete; to perform.
ac-cord: agreement; to grant; settle; compose. according: in accordance; agreeing; suitable.
ac-count: a report; to record accounting: as a profession. accountant: one skilled in recording financial transactions.
ac-cum-u-late: to heap up; to collect; to grow into a mass.
ac-cu-rate: correct; correctly. accurately: with accuracy.
ac-cuse: to charge with a crime or fault; to blame.
ac-cus-tom: to make familiar by use. accustomed: often practiced; ordinary.
ache: continous dull, heavy pain. aching: to be in pain.
a-chieve: to bring to a successful end; to accomplish. achievement: performance; accomplishment.
ac-quire: to gain; to get. acquisition: the act of acquiring.
a-cross: from side to side.
act: to perform, upon a stage.
ac-tion: a thing done; physical movement; function; a battle.

ac-tive: having the power to act; agile; busy; alert.
ac-tivity: to do or perform an act.
ac-tu-al: existing now or as a fact; real. actually: actively; existing.
add: to join, unite to form one sum or whole.
ad-dict: to apply habitually. addicted: wholly given over to; devoted.
ad-e-quate: equal to. adequately: made equal to.
ad-here: to stick fast; to be devoted to; to hold to.
ad-ja-cent: lying close to; adjoining, bordering on.
ad-journ: to put off until another day; to postpone. adjournment: putting off until another day.
adjust: adapt to; to make fit or suitable; to put into working order.
ad-mire: to admire with wonder and approval; to praise highly. admiration: high regard for.
a-dopt: to receive a child of another and treat as one's own. adopted: selected and received as one's own.
ad-vance: to bring or push forward; to raise in stature.
ad-van-tage: any state or means favorable to some desired end; upper hand.
ad-ven-ture: risk; bold undertaking; chance.
advert: to turn the mind or attention to; to remark upon.
ad-vice: opinion offered as to what one should do; counsel. advise: to give advice to; to counsel. adviser: one with power to advise.
af-fect: to act upon; to produce a change in.
af-ford: to yield; to supply or produce; to be able to bear expense.
af-raid: filled with fear; frightened.
a-gent: a person or thing that exerts power to act and to trust with honesty.
ag-ile: having the power of quick motion.
a-gree: to be of one mind; to resemble. agreement: agreeing; bargain.
ag-gress-ive: an unprovoked attack.
ail: to trouble; disturb; to pain. ailment: illness; pain.
a-larm: sound giving notice of danger.
al-co-hol: pure spirit; a liquid of strong, pungent taste; distilled liquor.
a-lert: watchful; vigilant; brisk.
al-i-bi: a plea that the prisoner was elsewhere when the crime took place.
al-low: to acknowledge; to permit; to give.
al-read-y: before this; even now; previously to the time specified.
al-tar: a table or raised structure in a place of worship.

al-ter: to change; to become different.
al-ter-nate: occuring by turns, one following the other in succession.
a-maze: to fill with astonishment or wonder; to perplex.
am-bu-lance: a covered vehicle for the transport of the injured or sick.
a-muse: to entertain agreeably; to occupy pleasantly; to divert.
a-nem-ic: a disease characterized by a defficiency of blood or hemoglobin.
an-gle: a corner; a point at which two lines meet.
an-i-mos-i-ty: violent hatred; active enmity.
an-nounce: to give first public notice of; to proclaim. announced: gave public notice.
an-noy: to torment; to tease. annoyed: teased; disturbed.
an-other: not the same; different; one more.
an-swer: to speak or write in return; to reply. answered: spoke of; wrote to; replied to.
an-tic-i-pate: to be before another; to be beforehand in thought or action.
anx-ious: uneasy; eager.
any-way: in any way or manner; anyhow.
a-pol-o-gy: something spoken in defense. apologize: to make an apology.
ap-pear: to come in sight; to become visible. appeared: became visible.
ap-pease: to quiet; to calm; to pacify; to satisfy.
ap-ply: to place one thing upon another; to agree with.
ap-point: to set apart; to assign; to ordain; to designate, for an office. appointment: the act of appointing.
ap-proach: to come near; the act of drawing near. approaching: the act of drawing nearer.
ap-pro-pri-ate: to take as one's own; to set apart for a particular purpose; to claim.
ap-prove: to be pleased with; to commend; to accept. approval: acceptance.
ar-bi-trate: to hear and give an authoritative decision in a dispute. arbitrator: a referee; an umpire; a judge.
ar-gue: to prove by reasoning; to persuade by debate. arguing: the process of proving which is right. argument: a reason offered.
arm: a weapon. armed; equipped with or supported by arms.
a-round: in a circle; near; on all sides of.
a-rouse: to excite to action; to awaken.

ar-range: to put into order; to prepare; to adapt; to adjust. arrangement: the act of arranging; the way or manner in which things are placed.

ar-rear: the state of being behind. arrears: money still owed.

ar-rest: to stop; to check; to hinder; to seize by authority of the law. arrested: seized by an arresting officer.

ar-rive: to reach a point; to come to; to reach the end of the journey.

ar-ti-cle: a clause or term in contract; a paragraph or section.

as-pect: look; appearance; position or situation; view.

as-sas-sin: one who murders by secret or treacherous assault; a hired murderer. assassinate: to murder by sudden violence.

as-sets: funds or property available for payment of a debt; the entire property of a business, company, association, or society.

as-sign: to allot; to apportion; to give out; to fix; to transfer.

as-sist: to help; to aid; to give support to. assisting: giving of your support to someone.

as-so-ci-ate: to join with as a friend, colleage, confederate, or a partner; to class together. associated: joined as a partner. association: a group of colleagues or friends.

as-sume: to take upon oneself; to take for granted; assumed: supposed. assumption: the act of taking to or upon oneself by force or right; the act of taking for granted.

as-sure: to make sure or certain; to affirm; to ensdure. assured: made sure or certain of. assuring: making certain of the facts.

at-mos-phere: the mass of air, clouds, gases, vapor surrounding the Earth or other heavenly bodies.

at-tach: to bind, fasten; to bind by affection.

at-tack: to fall on with force; to begin to affect.

at-tempt: to try; to endeavor to do. attempted: made an attempt to do.

at-tend: to accompany; to be present with or at. attending: giving medical care to. attention: careful observation.

at-tire: to dress; to array in splendind garments, apparel; dress.

at-ti-tude: posture of a person; mental or moral disposition.

at-tract: to draw toward; to cause to approach; to lure.

au-dience: an assembly or hearers or spectators.

au-to-bi-og-raphy: the story of a person's life, written by himself.

a-vail: to profit by; to take advantage of; to benefit. available: capable of being used to an advantage.

av-er-age: containing a mean proportion; ordinary; normal.

a-void: to shun, to elude; to keep clear of; to abstain from; to escape.
a-ward: to adjudge; to determine; to decide authoritatively.
a-ware: watchful; mindful; conscious of; possessing knowledge of.
awk-ward: unskillful; ungainly; clumsy; difficult to manage.

B

back: the upper or hind part of the trunk of an animal; a football player whose position is behind the line of scrimmage.
back-fire: an internal combustion engine's premature ignition, of fuel.
back-ground: part behind foreground, of a picture or stage setting.
bad: ill or evil; wicked.
bade: past tense of a verb, bid.
bail: a scoop; a shallow vessel for clearing water from a boat.
bail: security taken by the court that a person charged will attend court at a future date to answer the charge.
band: a cord; an ornamental strip separating moldings on a building or dividing a wall space. band: players of musical instruments.
ban-is-ter: same as baluster: a stone or wooden shaft turned and molded, used to support a handrail.
bar-ri-cade: a makeshift fortification, build as an obstruction; an obstruction that hinders passage for the public.
base: bottom; starting place; fixed point.
ba-sic: relating to a base. basically: that which is primary.
basis: that upon which a thing rests; foundation.
beat: to strike or hit repeatedly; to crush; to defeat. beating: the act of giving blows; a thrashing.
be-came: past tense to become: to pass from one state to another: to suit or be suitable to.
be-gin: to enter on; to start; to commence; to take the first step. beginning: one who begins; the first part.
be-half: favor; advantage; benefit; support.
be-have: to conduct oneself.
be-hold: to look at; to fix the eyes on or upon; to observe carefuly.
be-ing: existence; that which exists.
be-lieve: to regard as true; to trust; to have faith.
bench: a long seat; a table on which work is done; the seat in court.
ben-e-fit: an act of kindness; a favor conferred; an advantage; profit.

be-reave: to make destitute; to deprive of; to be deprived of by death.
bev-er-age: a refreshing liquid suitable for drinking.
be-wil-der: to lead astray or into confusion. bewildered: confused.
bid: to ask; to invite; to offer a price. bidding: an offer of a price.
blade: the cutting part of a knife or tool.
blame: fault; to speak evil of.
blast: a gust or puff of art; a forced stream of air.
bleak: without color; pale; desolate and exposed.
bleed: to draw blood surgically; to extort m oney from someone.
bless: to consecrate; glorify; sanctify; to give thanks to. blessing: source of happiness or gratitude.
bliss: the acme (acme: the highest point; the top) of happiness.
blow: to produce a current of air; to breathe hard or quickly; to puff.
blue: the color of the clear sky; one of the seven primary colors.
blurt: a sudden outburst; to give information suddenly.
blush: to redden in the face from shame or confusion.
boast-ful-ly: expressive of pride.
bold: daring; ready to meet danger; brave. bold print: printed with heavy, thick strokes.
booze: alcoholic beverage (liquor).
bor-der: the outer part or edge of anything; the exterior of a place.
bored: fatigue from body exertion; tired out.
brace: a support; a fastener.
brass: a yellow alloy of two parts of copper to one part of zinc.
brave: courageous; fearless.
bra-zen: shameless; to face a situation in a bold, impudent manner.
break: to shatter by force. breaking: dividing into several parts.
bribe: to influence by gifts.
bud-get: a plan for systematic spending; to plan one's expenditures.
building code: building: form; construction; house, etc. code: an orderly collection of laws; the proper law for a construction.
bulge: anything rounded that juts out. bulging: the act of sticking out.
bull-head-ed: obstinate, headstrong and stubborn.
bur-den: anything difficult to bear, a care, sorrow.
busy: having plenty to do; active and earnest in work.

C

cabal: a small group of plotters.
cab-i-net: a council advising a sovereign or executive: a piece of furniture with shelves and/or drawers.

cal-i-brate: to determine, check, or rectify the gradation of measurement.
calm: without motion; still; not windy; free from excitement or passion.
ca-pa-ble: having much intelligence or ability; efficient; able.
cap: a covering for the head. capped: a special headdress; covered.
cap-tain: one who is at the head of or in authority over others; chief.
cap-ti-vate: to charm by beauty or excellence; to capture.
cap-tor: a person who captures to take by force; take as a prisoner.
car-eer: progress of a person through life; an occupation, profession.
care-ful: cautious in one's action. carefully: cautious in work.
care-tak-er: a person who takes care of a thing, place, or person.
car-go: a big load of goods being transferred from one place to another.
car-riage: a wheeled vehicle for conveying persons, usually drawn by horse.
cas-u-al: happening by chance; without any definite intention.
caught: to catch; to capture, after pursuit, to grasp.
cau-tious: having or showing caution; being careful of what you are doing.
cease: to put a stop to; to discontinue.
cel-e-brate: to make famous; to mark by ceremony, as an event or festival. celebration: the act of celebrating.
cen-tral: relating to or placed in the center; chief; important.
ce-re-mony: a sacred rite; formal observance; formality; a function.
cer-tain: sure; settled; undoubted; constant.
cer-ti-fi-cate: a written testimony to the truth of a fact.
chain: a series of metal links or rings connected and forming a cable.
chal-lenge: an invitation to a contest or duel; defiance; a sentry.
char-ac-ter: a mark, letter, figure, sign or stamp of moral excellence.
chari-ta-ble: liberal to the poor; generous.
charge: a load of burden; price or cost; care or trust.
check: a stop; a restraint; a mark placed against items in a list.
chime: the musical sound of bells; a set of bells tuned to musical notes.
choose: to pick out; to select; to take one thing in or over another.
cho-rus: a band of singers and dancers; a combination of voices.
circuit: the act of moving around in space enclosed in a small area.
cir-cum-stance: a particular fact, event, or case.
ci-ta-tion: an official notice of appearance; quoting.
ci-vil: to city, state, or citizen, polite.
clad: dressed, clothed.
claim: to demand as a right or as due; to call for.

clan: a tribe bearing the same surname; group of persons with common interest.
clasp: to shut or fasten to another with a catch or hook.
class: an order or division or group of people of a certain order.
client: one who employs another (a lawyer); a customer.
clique: a narrow circle of persons with common interest.
clogged: obstructed; hindered; choked off or up.
close: shut up; confined; tight; near at hand.
clum-sy: ill-made; awkward.
clus-ter: a bunch; a collection of things together.
code: an orderly collection of laws; a system of words, symbols.
cold-water flat: apartment without heat.
cold shoulder: spiritless and not accepting responsibility.
col-league: an associate or companion.
col-lect: to bring together; to gather; to assemble.
col-lege: an institution for higher learning (education).
come: to approach; to arrive; to occur.
com-fort-able: promoting or enjoying comfort; consoling.
com-mand: to praise; to speak favorably of; to present favorably.
com-mence: to begin; to start; to originate.
com-ment: to make remarks, notes, criticisms; an explanation on behalf.
com-mit: to entrust; to give in charge; to be guilty of.
com-mit-ted: appeared for trial.
com-mode: a small piece of furniture containing a chamber pot.
com-mo-tion: violent motion; agitation; public disorder.
com-mu-ni-cate: to impart information; to reveal; to convey.
com-pan-ion: one who is in another's company; an associate or partner.
com-pare: to notice or point out the likeness and differences of.
com-pari-son: the act of comparing.
com-pat-i-ble: consistent; agreeing with.
com-pel: to force, to overpower; to bring about by force.
com-pen-sate: to reward; to pay; to make amends.
com-pete: to strive against another; to win something.
com-plain: to express distress, grief; to grumble.
com-plaints: dissatisfaction; ailments.
com-plete: entire, finished; perfect, with no part lacking.
com-plex-ion: color of skin.
com-pli-ca-tion: folded or twisted together.

com-ply: to yield to; to agree; to conform; to adapt oneself to.
com-pose: to form by uniting parts; to arrange; to put into order. composition: the act of composing to form by uniting parts.
com-rade: a close friend or companion; a mate.
con-ceal: to hide or to keep secretly; to withhold from knowledge.
con-cen-trate: to bring to a common center; to condense.
con-cept: a mental impression of an object; the act of conceiving.
con-cern: to relate or belong to; to be of importance to.
con-clude: to bring to an end; to close; to finish; to complete.
con-crete: made of sand and water for cement.
con-di-tion: a thing on which a statement, happening, or existing demands.
con-dolc: to offer sympathy. condolence: an expression of sympathy.
con-duct: the act of guiding; guidance; management. conducted: led.
con-fess: to admit; to own. confession: admission of something.
con-fide: to hand over to the charge of. confidence: trust.
con-fine: to keep within bounds; to limit; to enclose; to imprison.
con-flict: to dash together; to clash; to be at odds with.
con-form: to make like; to bring into agreement; to comply.
con-front: to face boldly; to oppose.
con-fuse: to mix up; to jumble together.
con-sent: an agreement; permission.
con-sider-a-tion: reflecting upon carefully; being of opinion; the act of considering.
con-sist: to be composed of. consistent: compatible; constant in adhering to principles.
con-stant: fixed; steadfast; invariable; permanent.
con-stant-ly: steadfastly.
con-tact: touching; a meeting; to get in touch with. contacted: got in contact with.
con-tempt: scorn; disagreement; disregard.
con-ti-n-ue: to prolong or extend in direction; to go on with; to last.
con-tin-u-al-ly: remaining in existence.
con-tour: a bounding line; outline.
con-strict: to draw together; to reduce to a lesser volume.
con-tri-bute: to give or pay to a common fund.
con-trol: to have under command; to regulate; to check.
con-trol-ler: one who controls.

con-ven-ient: fit; suitable; handy or easy of access.
con-verse: to talk with.
con-ver-ted: applied to another; changed.
con-vince: to bring to a belief; to persuade by argument.
con-voy: to accompany or escort or protect by sea or in the air.
co-op-er-ate: to act jointly with others, to unite for a common effort.
cope: to contend on equal terms with success.
cor-ner: the point where two lines meet; the part of a room where two sides meet; an angle.
cor-rect: right; free from faults; accurate. correction: amendment; a change to remedy a fault.
cor-rode: to eat away by degrees; to rust.
cos-me-tic: product for beauty of the skin.
couch: to cause to lie down; to lie down.
coun-cil: an assembly summoned for consultation or advice.
coun-sel: advice; opinion, deliberation together; one who gives advice.
cov-er-age: protection against risks.
cre-ate: to bring into existence. creating: bringing into existence.
cre-at-ed: brought into existence.
crea-ture: any living being; anything created.
cre-den-tials: testimonials showing that a person is entitled to beliefs or credit.
cred-it: belief; trust; to believe.
cred-i-bly: believable; putting trust in.
cred-it-able: reliable; meriting credit.
crime: violation of the law; an offense.
cringe: to shrink; to cower.
crop: the cultivated produce of any plant or plants on a farm. cropper: one who cultivates produce on a farm.
crush: to press beween two hard bodies so as to break, bruise, or crumple.
cud-dle: to caress; to hug; to fondle; to lie close or snuggle.
cue: the last words of an author's speech as a signal to the next actor to speak; a hint.
cul-ture: tillage or cultivation; mental training and development.
cum-ber: to burden or hinder with a useless load. cumbersome: burdensome, clumsy and unmanageable.
cun-ning: wily; sly; artful; skillful.
cur-i-ous: eager to know; inquisitive. curiosity: eagerness to know.

cur-rent: belonging to the present time. currency: money in use or circulation.
cur-ric-u-lum: a specified course of study at a college or university.
cush-ion: any stuffed or padded surface used as a rest.
cus-to-dy: a keeping or guarding; care; guardianship.
cus-tom: fashion; usage; habit. customary: according to custom; usual. customer: one who enters a shop to buy.
cy-cle: a regularly recurring succession of events or phenomena.
cy-lin-der: a rollerlike body with straight sides.

D

dai-ly: happening each day; a newspaper published each day.
dan-ger: injury or evil; jeopardy. dangerous: exposing to danger.
dea-con: an assistant to a priest or minister; a laymen elected to perform certain duties in the church.
deal: to divide; to dole out: dealing: buying and selling.
de-bris: fragments taken collectively.
de-cade: a group of ten things; a period of ten years.
de-cant: to pour off liquid without disturbing the sediment.
de-cease: to die. deceased: dead.
de-ceit: fraud; duplicity; wile. deceitful: crafty.
de-cent: fitting or becoming; modest.
de-cide: to determine the results of; to make up one's mind about. decision: the act of settling; settlement.
de-clare: to proclaim; to make clear; to state publicly.
dec-o-rate: to beautify; to make beautiful; to embellish.
dec-o-rum: behavior in keeping with social customs.
de-crep-it: worn out or enfeebled by old age; infirm; broken down.
ded-i-cate: set apart and consecrate to a holy purpose.
de-duce: to draw from; to reach a conclusion by deductive reasoning.
deed: that which is done; an act; exploit; a legal document.
deep: below the surface.
de-fect-ive: imperfect; failing in duty; incomplete; imperfect.
de-fend: to protect; to ward off an attack.
de-fray: to bear the cost of; to provide the money for.
de-lay: to put off; to postpone; to stop temporarily.
del-i-cate: dainty; frail; nicely adjusted.

de-liv-er: to liberate from danger or captivity; to distribute or hand over.
delve: to carry on an intensive research.
de-mand: to act authoritatively; to question; to require.
de-mo-lish: to destroy; to pull down; to ruin.
dem-on-strate: to prove by pointing out; to exhibit.
de-ny: to declare to be untrue; to refuse a request; to disavow.
de-part: to go away; to leave; to die. departed: the dead.
de-pend: to rely on. depending: relying on.
de-press: to deject or cast gloom over.
de-rive: to obtain or draw from a source; to have as an origin.
de-scribe: to represent the features of; to portray in speech.
de-serve: to earn by service; to merit.
des-ig-nate: to mark out and make known; to nominate or appoint.
des-per-ate: reckless from despair or loss of hope.
des-ti-tute: in want; needy; deprived of means of sustenance.
de-stroy: to pull down; to turn to rubble; to put an end to.
de-tail: to relate minutely; to record every item.
de-ter-mine: to fix the limit to; to decide; to define.
det-ri-mental: injurious; harmful.
dev-as-tate: to lay waste.
de-vel-op: to cause to grow; to unfold gradually.
de-vote: to give oneself wholly to. devoted: giving oneself wholly to.
di-a-be-tes: a disease marked by excessive flow of sugar in urine due to failure of pancreas to produce insulin.
di-ag-no-sis: a scientific discrimination of any kind; identification of a disease.
di-ag-on-al: joining two opposite angles in a rectilineal figure; having an oblique direction.
di-am-e-ter: a line passing through the center of a circle.
dif-fer-ent: unlike; not the same.
dif-fi-cult: hard to do or understand; not easy.
di-plo-ma: a document or certificate conferring some honor, privilege, or degree.
di-rect: in a straight line; to aim at. directly: in a straight line.
dir-ty: filthy.
dis-a-ble: to make incapable or physically unfit.
dis-a-gree: differing in opinion.
dis-ap-pear: to vanish; to become invisible; to cease to exist.
dis-be-lieve: to maintain to be untrue; to refuse to believe.

dis-card: to put aside; to cast off.
dis-charge: to free from a load or weight; to unload a cargo.
dis-con-nect: to separate.
dis-cov-er: to find out; to bring to light.
dis-cuss: to examine critically; to exchange ideas on.
dis-guise: to change the outward appearance of; to misrepresent.
dis-man-tle: to strip of furnishings; to take apart.
dis-may: to become alarmed; to take apart.
dis-miss: to send away; to disperse; to allow to go.
dis-place: to put out of position. displaced: put out of position.
dis-pute: to consider for and against; to debate; to discuss.
dis-re-gard: to take no notice of; to ignore.
dis-re-spect: want of respect; difference; rudeness.
dis-tance: the space between two objects; the interval between two events.
dis-tress: extreme pain, mental or physical; misfortune.
dis-turb: to upset the normal condition of; to ruffle.
ditch: a trench dug for drainage or defense; a natural waterway.
div-i-dend: the sum to be divided by the divisor to obtain the quotient.
do-cu-ment: an official paper containing information giving instructions or establishing facts; to furnish with written facts.
domain: property.
dom-in-ate: to rule; to tower over.
doubt: to disbelieve; to hesitate; uncertainty.
doze: to sleep lightly; to be half asleep; to nap.
dras-tic: very powerful; harsh.
dread: overwhelming apprehension; awe; terror.
dress: to put on clothes; clothing.
drift: state or process of being driven.
du-al: consisting of two; twofold; denoting two.
du-pli-cates: doubles; each exactly resembling the other; exact copies.
du-ra-tion: continuance of time; the period anything lasts.
du-ty: that which is due; that which is demanded by law.
dwin-dle: to grow less and less; to shrink; to fade.
dy-nam-ic: to force in motion.

E

ea-ger: inflamed by desire; ardent; yearning; earnest.
earned: gained money by labor; got; received money through it.

echo: repetition of sound produced by sound waves reflected from an obstructing object; reverberation; repetition.
e-co-nom-ics: wise expenditure of money; careful use of materials.
ef-fec-tive: in a condition to produce desired results; efficient.
ei-ther: one or the other; one or two; each.
e-lab-o-rate: to put much work and skill on; to work out in detail.
el-der: older; senior; one who is older.
el-e-gant: graceful; tasteful; refined.
el-i-gi-ble: legally qualified; fit and worthy; desirable.
e-lim-i-nate: to remove; to get rid of; to set aside.
e-long-ate: to make longer; to lengthen; to extend; to draw out.
e-lope: to run away with a lover; to marry secretly.
el-o-quence: the art or power of expressing thought in fluent, impressive and graceful language; fluency.
else-where: to some other place.
em-bark-ing: being put on board a ship; going on board a ship.
em-i-nent: exalted in renk, office, or public estimation; prominent.
e-mo-tion-al: traumatic; with strong, generalized feeling; exciting.
em-pha-sis: stress on anything such as force or voice given to words or syllables.
em-ploy: to give occupation; to make use of; to hire.
en-a-ble: to make able; to qualify.
en-cir-cle: to enclose in a circle; to surround.
en-core: again; once more; the item repeated.
en-cour-age: to give courage to; to inspire with hope.
en-dure: to remain firm under; to bear with patience; to put up with.
en-force: to give strength to; to put in force; to impress on mind.
en-gage: to bind by contract, pledge, or promise; to hire.
en-gross: to occupy wholly; to absorb; to monopolize.
en-hance: to intensify; to increase in value or worth.
en-joy: to delight in; to take pleasure in. enjoyable: pleasurable.
en-thuse: to become enthusiastic; to show enthussiasm.
en-tire: complete in all parts; whole.
en-tit-le: to give a title to; to qualify for a title.
en-vir-on-ment: the surrounding area; the external conditions that determine modifications in the development of organic life.
ep-i-sode: an incident; a series of events.
e-qual: having the same magnitude of value; identical.
e-quip: to fit out; to furnish; to dress.

er-a: a fixed point in time from which a series of years is reckoned; time; age; a memorable date or age.
e-rect: to set upright; to raise as a building.
er-rand: a trip to carry a message; a short journey for a specific cause.
er-ror: to make a mistake; that which is incorrect, wrong.
es-cape: to gain freedom; to evade; to elude; to avoid capture.
es-cort: an armed guard for a traveler.
e-spe-cial: distinguished, preeminent; more than ordinary.
es-sence: the very being or power of a thing; essential part.
es-sen-tial: necessary to the existence of a thing.
es-tab-lish: to make stable or firm; to set up; to enact or decree by authority; to prove.
es-teem: to regard with respect or affection; to rate highly.
es-ti-mate: to judge and form an opinion of the value, size, weight.
eu-lo-gy: a speech or writing in praise, especially a speech praising a dead person.
e-val-u-ate: to appraise or determine the value of; to estimate worth.
ev-en-tu-al-li-ty: that which will happen.
ev-ery-thing: each of all; all possible; every place involved.
e-vict-ing: disposing by a judical process; expelling.
ev-i-dent: visible.
e-vil: having bad natural qualities; harmful; corrupt.
ex-act-ly: accurately; correctly; precisely.
ex-cel: to surpass, especially in good qualities; to be better than.
ex-cept: to leave out; to object. exception: the leaving out.
ex-cess: that which surpasses or goes beyond a definite limit.
ex-cite: to rouse; to call into action; to set in motion.
ex-ert: to put forth as strength, force, or ability; to exercise; to strive.
ex-haust: to draw or drain off completely; to empty; to weaken; to tire.
ex-ist: to be; to live; to subsist; to occur.
ex-pand: to spread out; to enlarge; to increase in volume; to extend.
ex-pect: to look forward to; to look on as likely to happen.
ex-pend: to consume by use; to spend; to use up.
ex-pe-ri-ence: practical knowledge gained by trial or practice or proof.
ex-pe-ri-ment: the action of trying anything; put to the proof of.
ex-pire: to breathe out; to emit; to exhale.
ex-plain: to make plain; to account for; to define.
ex-pose: to lay open; to leave unprotected; to exhibit.
ex-tend: to prolong in a single direction; to use as a line; to go beyond.

ex-tent: space to which a thing is extended.
ex-ten-sive: having wide extent; large; spacious.
ex-tra: additional. extracurricular: not included in a curriculum.
ex-treme: at the utmost point, edge, or border; outermost.

F

fa-cile: easy; fluent; easily done. facility: something built, designed or installed to serve a specific purpose function; something that permits an easier performance of action.
fail: to lack; to diminish; to miss; to be unsuccessful in.
fair: free from bias, dishonesty, or injustice in giving.
faith-ful: loyal, reliable, honorable.
false: untrue; inaccurate; dishonest.
far-ther: more far; to a greater distance.
fas-ci-nate: to enchant.
fa-mil-iar: intimate; informal; well-known; close acquaintance.
farm-land: a tract of land set aside for cultivation of crops.
fast: rapid; securely fixed; firm.
fa-ther: a male parent.
fault: a failing; blunder; mistake; defect.
fav-or: a gracious act; kind regard. fav-or-ite: a person or thing regarded with special favor; the likely winner.
fear: alarm; dread; anxiety; to anticipate as a disaster.
fea-ture: any part of the face; main attraction; to outline.
fee: payment for a debt.
feel: to perceive by the touch; to be sensitive to; to know by touch.
feel-ing: the sense of touch. felt: the sensation of touch.
fend: to ward off; to resist.
fes-tive: joyous event. fes-ti-val: a feast or celebration. fes-tiv-i-ties: merry making events.
fic-tion: literature dealing with imaginary characters or and situations. fic-ti-tious: imaginary; false.
fig-ure: outward form of anything; to reveal the diagram of a person.
Fil-i-pi-no: a native of the Philippine Islands.
filth-y: foul.
fin-al: the end; last; the last stage of anything.
fi-nance: the science of controlling public revenue and expenditures.

find: to come by searching; to meet with; to discover. find-ing: discovering.
fine: excellent; thin; slender.
fin-ish: to bring to an end; to terminate.
fist: the hand clenched with the fingers doubled into the palm.
fit: becoming; suitable; qualified.
fix: to make firm; to establish; to secure.
fix-ture: that which is fixed or attached.
flap-jacks: the nickname given to a form of pancakes, which are made of batter and other ingredients and fried in a pan, usually eaten with syrup poured over the contents on a plate.
flare: to burn with a glaring, unsteady, or fitful flame.
flat: level; flattened; even; uniform; spread out.
fledge: to supply with features for flight as an arrow; to acquire feathers.
flex-i-ble: bendable.
flight: the act or power to fly.
flirt: to move playfully to and fro, as a fan; to move about bristly.
flow: to run as a liquid; to rise as a tide.
fluf-fy: light, floating down; downy skin.
fly: a winged insect; a housefly.
fo-cus: the point at which rays of light meet after reflecting or refracting; any point of concentration; to adjust.
fol-low: to go after; to move behind; to succeed.
foot-steps: foot: the extreme end of the lower limbs; steps: to move and set down the foot . . . walking.
force: strength; energy; power.
for-eign: situated outside a place or country.
forg-er-y: making of imitation money and representing it as genuine; the act of falsifying a document.
fore-most: first in place or time; first in dignity or rank.
for-ev-er: always; eternity.
for-mer: preceding in time; long past; first mentioned.
form: in shape of; shape or appearance; a mold.
for-mu-late: to express in a definite form.
forth: forward, in place or time, into view.
for-tu-nate-ly: lucky.
found: discovered by searching.
fra-cas: noisy quarrel; a disturbance; a brawl.
frank: open; honest.

free-dom: liberty; immunity.
friend: one attached to another by esteem or affection.
fre-quent-ly: happening at short intervals.
fright-ened: caused sudden and violent fear, extreme terror.
frills: gathered cloth or paper edgings; a ruffle.
frus-trate: to bring to nothing; to balk.
ful-fill: to carry into effect; to execute; to discharge; to satisfy.
full: filled to capacity; complete.
func-tions: performances; the special work done by an organ; office ceremony.
fund-a-men-tal: basic; foundational; original.
fur-ther: more remote; additional.
fu-ture: about to happen; that to come hereafter.

G

gang: people banded together for some purpose, ususally bad, like street gangs.
gath-er: to bring together; to collect; to harvest.
gauge: to ascertain the capacity of; to measure the ability of; to estimate.
gav-el: a small wooden hammer used by a judge or chairman.
gear: equipment; a set of tools. geared: equipped to operate.
gen-er-os-ity: liberality in giving.
gen-tle: kind and amiable; mild and refined in manner.
gen-u-ine: real, true, pure, sincere.
ges-ture: a motion of the head or hands as mode of expression.
giv-en: to make a present of; to grant.
goal: an object of effort; an aim in a race; a winning post.
gos-sip: idle talk about others.
got-ten: received.
grabbed: grasped suddenly; snatched; clutched; seized.
grant-ed: allowed; yielded.
grat-i-tude: thankfulness.
great-er: larger in number; longer in time.
greet-ed: saluted; welcomed.
grieved: deep in sorrow; to be distressed.
grooves: channels or hollows; ruts.

ground: reason; motive; basis; surface of the Earth; dry land.
group: a selection or assemblage of persons.
grudge: to be reluctant to give or allow; to envy.
grum-ble: to complain.
guard: to protect from danger; to keep watch.
guide: one who shows the way; an adviser; to lead.
gus-to: keen enjoyment; zest; artistic style.
gym-na-si-um: a building or room equipped for physical training.

H

hab-it: custom; usage; tendency to repeat an action in the same way.
har-ass: to attack repeatedly.
har-bor: shelter for ships; a port.
har-mo-ny: agreement; friendliness; peace; musical notes sung in harmony.
har-vest: season for gathering produce; season for gathering crops.
has-ti-ly: speedily; quickly; hurried; accelerated.
hate: to dislike strongly; to bear malice.
haves and have-nots: those holding or possessing and those not having or possessing.
heal: to make whole; to restore to health.
health: soundness of the body.
hear: to receive with the ear; to perceive sound.
heed: to take notice of; to care for; to observe or notice; to use caution.
help-less: unable to take care of oneself.
hence: from this point; for this reason.
hes-i-tate: to feel or show indecision; to hold back; to pause.
high: elevated; tall; far up.
hire: to contract with for wages.
his-to-ry: the study of past events; a record of past events in life.
hob-ble: to walk lamely; to limp.
hold ov-er: to detain; to keep longer than the specified time.
hon-est: fair. hon-est-ly: with upright conduct or disposition.
hon-or: high respect; reputation.
hop-scotch: a child's game, played on an arrangement of squares.
horse: the male of the horse species; a frame for drying clothes.
huge: very large.

hu-man: having the moral qualities of a man.
hunk of plas-ter: a composition of lime and water and sand used for coating walls.
hus-tle: to push about; to hurry.

I

i-ci-cle: a hanging conical mass of ice slowly built up by freezing water.
i-dea: a product of intellectual action; way of thinking; thought.
i-deal: existing only in fancy; perfect.
i-den-ti-fy: to establish the identity of; to ascertain or prove; to recognize.
i-den-ti-ty: state of having the same nature of charactder with.
i-dle: doing nothing; inactive; lazy.
ig-nore: to refuse to take notice of.
im-age: mental picture.
i-ma-gine: to form in the mind an idea or image of a picture to be true.
im-i-tate: to follow as a pattern, model, or example; to copy.
im-me-di-ate: occurring at once; without delay.
im-mense: unlimited; very great.
im-part: to bestow or share a portion; to grant.
im-per-fec-tion: state of wanting some part or parts.
im-pli-cate: to involve; to include.
im-port: to bring in from abroad.
im-pose: to lay on; to force oneself.
im-pos-si-ble: incapable of existing in fact.
im-press: to press in or upon; to make a mark or figure upon.
im-prove: to make better; to make progress. improvement: act of improving.
im-pro-vise: to make the best of the materials at hand.
in-ad-e-quate: insufficient; incapable.
in-cep-tion: beginning; start; origin.
in-cest: sexual intercourse of kindred within the forbidden degree.
in-ci-dent: happening.
in-clude: to confine within.
in-co-her-ent: not connected or clear; confused.
in-con-ven-ient: awkward; unsuitable.
in-crease: to make greater; to extend; to lengthen.

in-de-pen-dent: not dependent upon; not subject to the control of others.
in-di-cate: to point out; to be a sign of; to denote; to show.
in-di-vid-u-al: not divided; single.
in-dulge: to give freedom; to allow one his own way.
in-ef-fi-cient: incapable of producing any effect; useless.
in-ept: not apt or fit; unsuitable.
in-ev-i-ta-ble: unavoidable; certain to take place or appear.
in-fe-ri-or: lower in rank, order, or place. in-fe-ri-or-i-ty com-plex: a lower state of condition; subconscious sense of inferiority.
in-fest: to inhibit. infested: covered with body parasites such as lice.
in-flu-ence: power over men or things; effect on the mind.
in-form: to tell; to accumulate knowledge; to give information.
in-her-it: to receive by descent or by will; to fall heir to.
i-ni-tial: occurring at the beginning, early. i-ni-ti-ate: to begin.
in-ner: farther in; interior; farthest in.
in-ner-ci-ty-boy-feel-ing: not sensitive to outside the city activities.
in-no-cent: free from guilt; blameless; harmless; simple.
in-se-cure: not securely fixed; unsafe.
in-sert: to put in; to place among.
in-sist: to dwell upon as a matter of special moment.
in-spect: to view narrowly and critically; to examine carefully.
in-spec-tor: one who inspects a completed job for accuracy.
in-spire: to breathe in; to infuse thought or feeling into.
in-stall: to place into position. in-stalled: placed in position.
in-stant: urgent; pressing; immediate.
in-stead: in the stead, place, or room; in one's stead.
in-struct: to teach; to inform; to order or command.
in-stru-ment: a tool; a person made use of. in-stru-men-tal: helpful.
in-su-late: to keep apart from other people; keep making contact.
in-sure: to make sure or certain; to make safe.
in-tel-lect-u-al: of high mental capacity; having the power of understanding.
in-tend: to propose; to mean; to have in mind.
in-tent: state of the mind bent on an object; eager in pursuit of.
in-ter-est: to engage and keep the attention of; the profit percent.
in-ter-pret: to explain the meaning of.
in-ter-rupt: to break in upon; to stop course of; to break continuity.
in-ter-val: time or distance between; a pause; a break.

in-ter-vene: to come between; to happen in the meantime.
in-tim-i-date: to force or deter by threats; to inspire with fear.
in-trigue: a plot to effect some purpose by secret artifices.
in-tro-duce: to lead or bring in; to bring forward.
in-trude: to thrust oneself in; to enter unwelcome.
in-tu-i-tion: immediate and instinctive perception of the truth.
in-vade: to attack; to enter with hostile intentions.
in-var-i-a-ble: not displaying change; always uniform; constant.
in-vert: to turn over; to put upside down.
in-vest: to lay out capital with a view to profit.
in-vite: to ask by invitation.
in-volve: to envelop; to wrap up; to include.
i-ron-ic: sarcastic; satirical.
ir-ri-tate: to excite anger; to annoy.
is-o-late: to place in a detached position; to place apart or alone.
is-sue: the act of passing or flowing out; the act of sending out.

J

jack-o'-lan-tern: a lantern made from a hollowed-out pumpkin with holes cut out to make a face.
jam: to squeeze tight; to wedge in; to block out.
jeal-ous: envious; suspicous.
join: to bring together; to fasten; to unite; to act in concert with.
jour-ney: to travel from one place to another; to travel.
joy-ful: glad; rejoicing.
judge: one who judges; to administer justice.
juice: sap; the liquid constituent of fruits or vegetables.
jun-ior: younger; a lower status.
just: true; founded on fact; proper; fair.

K

keep: to retain possession of; to detain.
knock: to strike or beat with something hard or heavy; to strike again.
knowl-edge: direct perception; understanding; practical skills.

L

lane: a narrow track between hedges or across fields; narrow street.

lan-gua-ges: speeches; expressions of ideas by words or written symbols.

lan-tern: something portable or fixed enclosing a light, protecting from the wind, rain, etc.

last-ing: continuing in time.

lat-tice: framework of wood or metal.

law: a rule established by authority.

lease: a contract for renting, land, houses, apartments.

lec-ture: a discourse on any subject; to instruct; a formal speech.

ledge: a projection, as from a wall or cliff; a shelf.

left out: omitted, unaccounted for.

le-gal: according to the law; defined by law; binding.

length: the measurement of anything from end to end.

les-bi-an: a woman who is sexually attracted to another woman; female homosexual.

lev-el: a state of equality; not having one part higher than the other.

lib-er-al: open-minded; generous; unbiased.

lib-er-at-ed: set free.

life-span: life; existence; the space between birth and death.

limit: boundary; edge; utmost extent. lim-it-ed: circumscribed; narrow.

limp: to walk lamely; lameness.

link: a single ring of a chain; a connection.

list: a register; a recorded group of words, names, etc., on a sheet.

lit-er-al-ly: according to the letter.

liv-ing quar-ters: a place to live; house, apartment, etc.

lo-cate: find a thing or person, place etc.

lone-li-ness: in a state of solitary confinement.

look: to turn one's eyes upon. lookout: from which a watchful visual is kept.

lose: to be deprived of.

lot: a separate part; a large number of articles sold as one set.

loy-al: a faithful follower of a cause.

lum-ber-jack: a man who prepares timber for a market to be sold.

lure: an artifical bait; to entice.

ly-ing: untruthful.

M

mag-ni-tude: greatness; size; importance.
main: in a middle position; average; meanwhile; in the intervening time.
main-te-nance: the act of maintaining. main-tain: to hold or keep in shape.
mal-ice: ill will; spite; desire to injure others.
mal-i-cious: spiteful.
ma-nip-u-late: to operate with the hands.
man-ner: way of doing anything; custom; style; social behavior.
man-tle: a loose outer garment; a cloak; a covering.
man-u-al: a handbook or small textbook.
ma-ri-jua-na: a type of hemp dried and used in a tobacco, having a narcotic effect.
ma-ter-i-al-ize: to give bodily form to.
ma-ter-nal: to a mother; motherly; related on the mother's side.
ma-tric-u-late: to enroll as a student in college.
mea-sure: an instrument for measuring.
mem-brane: a thin, flexible tissue forming or lining an organ of the body.
men-ace: to threaten; a potential body danger.
men-tion: a brief notice; to name.
merge: to cause to be swallowed up; to combine commercial or industrial firms.
mes-sage: a communication, verbal or written, sent by one person to another.
Mes-si-ah: an expected savior or liberator.
mess-rs.: plural of Mr. (mister).
meth-od: manner of proceeding; system; techniques.
mild-ly: gently; kindly.
mill-ing: without direction, as in milling around.
mind-ful: attentive; observant; aware.
min-gle: to join in. min-gling: blending.
min-or: lesser; inferior in bulk, degree, importance.
mis-chief: harm; damage; conduct intended to annoy.
mis-chie-vous: bad management; dishonest conduct.
mis-for-tune: ill luck.
mis-lead: to lead astray; to lead or guide wrongly.

mis-take: to misunderstand; to take one person for another.
mite: any small thing or person, very small.
mod-el: one who poses for an act or artist.
mod-er-ate: restrained; average; freedom from excess.
mod-ern: up-to-date. mod-ern-ize: to bring up-to-date.
mold-ed: to work into a required shape.
mon-i-tor: one who cautions; one appointed to help keep order.
mon-ster: a creature of unnatural shape.
mood: a disposition or frame of mind.
mor-tal-ly: subject to death.
mo-tion: the act of moving; movement. mo-tion-less: still; immobile.
mo-tor-cade: procession of automobiles.
mot-to: a maxim or principle of behavior.
move: to act in motion. move-ment: the act of moving.
muf-fled: deadened the sound of something.
mum-ble: to utter or speak indistinctly.
muse: to think over dreamily; to ponder.

N

nar-co-tic: substance that produces stupor or induces sleep.
na-tion-al: belonging by birth to a nation, a native.
na-tur-al: normal in state or nature; true to life.
na-ture: the world, the universe, known and unknown; the power underlying all phenomena in the material world.
nec-es-sa-ry: needful; that which must be done; a needful thing.
ne-glect: to disregard: to take care of; to fail to do.
neg-li-gee: a woman's loose dressing gown.
neg-li-gence: want of due care; carelessness; habitual neglect.
neigh-bor-hood: an adjoining district and its people. neighbor: one who lives or works near another.
nerves: one of the bundles of fibers that convey impulse from brain (motor nerve) to muscles.
nerv-ous: containing or affecting the nerves; uneasy.
nev-er: at no time; not ever. nev-er-the-less: in spite of that. none-the-less: notwithstanding.
night-mare: a terrifying feeling of oppression or suffocation.
nod-ded: inclined the head forward by a quick motion.

noise: sound; loud cry.
not-ice: to watch; to observe one's actions.
not-i-fied: to report or inform another of an occurrence.
not-with-stand-ing: nevertheless; however.
num-er-ous: very many; existing in a very great quantity, or large number of units.
nu-tri-ents: nourishing food.

O

oath: a solemn appeal to God or to some other revered person or thing.
o-bey: to be obedient; to comply with others.
ob-ject: to offer opposition; to put forward; a reason against.
ob-jec-tion: to bind by legal contract. obligation: the binding power of a promise or contract.
ob-li-gate: to bind by legal contract. obligation: the binding power of a promise or contract.
ob-serve: to watch; to take notice.
ob-vious: easily seen or understood; evident.
oc-ca-sion: to cause or bring about.
oc-cu-py: to take possession of; to inhibit; to employ.
oc-cur: to come to mind; to happen.
od-or: smell; fragrance; a strong smell.
of-fered: to present for acceptance of an act of offering.
off-set: away; away from.
op-en: not shut or blocked up; without any restrictions.
op-er-ate: to cause to function; to work; to produce an effect.
o-pin-ion: judgment or belief; estimate.
op-por-tun-ity: a fit or convenient time; a good chance.
op-po-si-tion: the state of being opposite.
op-ti-mis-tic: taking a hopeful view.
op-tion: the power or right of choosing.
or-di-na-ry: usual; regular; normal; plain.
or-di-na-tor: one who ordains; a person of the ministry.
or-chard: a garden or enclosure containing fruit trees or vegetables.
or-deal: a trying experience; a test of endurance.
or-ga-nize: to set up, arrange, and put into working order; to prepare for a transaction of business.

or-ig-i-nal: earliest; first; new, not copied.
or-phan-age: a home or institution for orphans.
out-let: a passage or way out; an exit; a vent; an opening.
out-line: the lines that bound a figure; a boundary; a stretch without details.
out-look: a looking out; a prospect; a person's point of view.
out-side: the outer surface; the exterior; the farthest limit.
over-come: to overpower; to get the better of.
own: to possess; to acknowledge; to admit.

P

pack: bundle for carrying on back; a set of playing cards.
pain-ful: full of pain; causing pain.
pale: faint in color.
pan-el: a rectangular piece of cloth or wood; a list of jurors; a jury.
par-all-el-o-gram: a four-sided plane figure with both pairs of opposite sides parallel.
par-cel: a small wrapped bundle; a package.
par-ents: mothers, fathers.
par-tic-i-pate: to have or take a part or share with others in some activity or enterprise.
par-tic-u-lar: pertaining to one and not to more than one; single; apart from
past-times: sports; amusements; that which serves to make time pass agreeably.
pa-tron-ize: to show favor or kindness to in a condescending manner.
pat-tern: a model, guide, or plan, used in making things.
pause: to make a short stop; to cease in speaking; to stop temporarily.
peace: freedom from disagreements, quarrels; restful minds.
pea-vey: a lumberman's cant hook, having a spike fixed on the end of it.
pe-cul-iar: belonging solely to; singular.
peer: an equal; one of the same rank or value.
peeved: bad-tempered.
pelt: to beat or stroke heavily and repeatedly.
pen-sion: a payment, not wages, paid to a person who had fulfilled certain obligations of servitude and reached a certain age.
per-cent-age: a given rate in every hundred; interest.

per-fect: complete in all respects; without defects.
per-form: to execute; to fulfill, as a promise or command.
pe-ri-od: to put an end to the interval between the events.
per-ma-nent: lasting or intended to last indefinitely without change.
per-mis-sion: the act of permitting or allowing; formal consent.
per-pe-trate: to do or perform something evil or criminal or offensive.
per-plex: to make a person uncertain, doubtful, or hesitant, confused.
per-se-vere: to maintain an effort thoroughly; not to give in.
per-sis-tent: refusing to relent; continuing, especially in the face of opposition; stubborn.
per-son-al-i-ties: the qualities of being a person; individualilties; a particular people with qualities.
per-suade: to cause something or someone to do something by reasoning, urging, or inducement.
per-tains: reference or relation to; relates; belongs properly.
petite: small and trim in figure.
pe-ti-tion: to make a request to; to ask from; to solicit. the act of soliciting.
phe-no-me-non: the appearance or observed features of something experienced or observed; features of something experienced as distinguished from reality or the thing in itself.
pick: to remove from fruit or fruit from a tree; to choose or select.
pic-nic: a pleasure outing at which a meal is eaten outdoors.
pid-dle: to trifle; anything of little value or importance.
piece: a part or fragment broken or separated from the whole.
pimp: to lure, to entice, to go between in an illicit sexual affair.
pitch: to fix or set up a tent for camping.
plan: an outline, a draft, a map, a scheme for making, doing, or arranging something.
plan-ner: a person or thing that plans.
plant-ed: put a tree or herb in soil for growth to maturity; implanted.
plate: a shallow dish, usually circular, from which food is eaten.
plead: to discuss or defend by argument; to declare oneself to be guilty or not guilty in answer to a charge.
plight: to pledge or engage; to bind by a promise.
poc-ket: a little bag sewn into clothing for carrying money and small articles.
point-ed: with a sharp end; aimed gun the direction of any object.

pol-i-cy: a written contract in which one party assures the other party that his investment is safe against a loss or misfortune, in consideration of periodic payments, called premiums.

pop-u-lar: well liked and accepted by most people, friends, and acquaintances.

pop-u-late: to be or become inhabitants of; to increase the number of people or inhabitants in one area.

po-si-tion: to put in a particular place.

posi-tive: direct; precise; specific; absolute; real; beyond all doubts.

pos-sess-ion: thing owned.

pos-si-ble: that can be; capable of existing; that can be done.

pos-si-bil-i-ty: quality or state of being possible.

post-pone: to put off; to delay.

post-script: a paragraph or note added to a letter after close.

po-ten-tial: that which can but has not yet come into being; that which is possible.

pound: a weight on a scale; to beat, to strike with a heavy object with repeated blows; to make an impression.

pov-er-ty: the condition of being poor; lack of means of substances; state of having inadequate means of support.

prac-tice: to do or perform frequently; repeated mental or physical action for the purpose of learning or to become more proficient.

prag-ma-tic: concerned with practical consequences; matter-of-fact.

pre-cinct: a subdivision of the city, ward, such as police precinct.

pre-cise: accurate; definite; distinct.

prem-is-es: pieces of real estate, houses, buildings and land.

pre-pare: to make ready; put together or make out of material.

pre-req-ui-site: requird as a prior condition of something.

pre-sence: the state of being present. present: being at a certain place.

pre-serve: to keep from evil or injury; to keep in a sound state.

pre-side: to be a chairman of a meeting; to direct; to control.

pressed: a condition of being distressed.

press-ure: the act of pressing; influence.

pres-tige: the power to command admiration or esteem; distinction, based on brilliance of achievement.

pre-tend: to make believe, as in she pretended she was a princess.

pre-vail: to overcome; to exist widely; to appear at that time of need.

pre-vent: to stop or keep from doing something, to keep from happening.

prev-i-ous: before in time or order; before something else.
pri-or: preceding in order, time, or importance.
priv-a-cy: a place of seclusion from public view.
priv-i-lege: a basic civil right; a right or immunity.
prob-a-bly: most likely.
probed: searched to the bottom; investigated with thoroughness.
prob-lem: a question proposed for a solution or consideration.
pro-ceed: to move past, advance, especially after stopping.
pro-ce-dure: a particular course of action or way of doing something.
pro-cess: the course of being done.
prod-i-gy: a person or thing causing wonder; a very gifted person.
pro-duce: to bring forward; to bring forth.
prod-uct: that which is produced, by nature or industry.
pro-fes-sion-al: engaged in a highly skilled occupation, a profession or calling.
pro-file: a side view of the face; an outline or contour.
prof-it: to gain in wages.
pro-gress: to move forward or onward; to push forward.
pro-ject: a plan of action. pro-ject: to protrude; to cause to stick out from a point.
pro-long: to lengthen in time; to extend the duration or time.
prom-ise: an oral or written agreement to do something; a vow.
pro-mote: to advance; to move up to a higher rank or poosition.
prompt: ready to act as quickly as possible.
pro-nounce: to articulate words correctly, such as persons' names.
pron-to: promptly; quickly; at once.
pro-pel: to drive forward; to press onward by force of wind or steam.
prop-er: conforming to an expected standard to good usage.
pro-pose: to form or announce an intention or design; to outline a plan. pro-po-sal: the act of proposing. prop-o-si-tion: something proposed.
pros-per: to cause to succeed; to thrive; to be successful.
pros-ti-tute: a woman who engages in sexual acts for a fee or an income.
pro-tect: to defend; to cover or shield a person from danger; to guard.
pro-test: to make an objection to; to express opposition to.
prove: to try by experiments to ascertain as a fact, by evidence.
pro-vis-ion: the act of providing.
pull: to exert force for dragging; to move away from by a dragging force.

pun-ish: to cause a person to undergo pain for a misdeed; to treat in a harsh manner.
pur-chase: anything obtained by buying.
pur-pose: that which a person sets before himself as an object to be reached.
pur-sue: to follow in order to kill, capture, or overtake; to follow after.

Q

qual-i-ty: that which belongs to something and makes or helps to make it what it is; any character that may make an object good or bad.
qualm: a fit of nausea; a sudden seizure of sickness.
ques-tion: inquiry; a problem; doubt; to seek an answer.
quick-ly: in a lively manner; with haste or speed; rapidly.

R

rack: a frame for holding hay; a frame with hooks for clothing to hang on.
ra-di-at-or: a series of pipes through which hot water passes or steam flows.
rad-i-us: a spoke of a wheel; the distance from the center of a circle to the circumference or outer circle.
rage: a furious uncontrolled anger; to show violent action or speech.
raise: to cause to rise to a higher level; to elevate in a special social position.
ram-page: to rush violently about; to act violently; an outbreak of violence.
rank: a social division; a class; a degree of dignity; eminence; a high social position.
ra-pid: swift; quick.
ra-ther: more readily or willingly; preferably. "I would rather go than stay."
rat-ing: a rank, class, or grade; an evaluation of the credit or financial standing.
reach: to extend; to stretch; to thrust out.

re-act: to act in opposition; to act in a reverse way to go back to a former condition.
re-ac-tion: return or opposing action.
read-i-ly: without hesitation; without delay.
re-al-ize: to make real; to bring into being; to understand fully.
re-a-li-ty: actuality; fact; truth.
re-ap-pear: to appear again.
rear: behind; at the back part.
rea-son: a cause or motive; to analyze; to think logically.
re-call: remembering; to call back; a calling back to mind.
re-cant: to withdraw or renounce; to abandon an opinion.
re-ceive: to take into one's possession; to take or get something.
re-ceipt: a written acknowledgment that something has been received, such as money, goods, etc.
re-cep-ta-cle: something to receive and hold something else; a container.
re-ci-pe: a prescription; a list of ingredients for preparing a dish or drink.
re-ci-pi-ent: a received.
re-ci-pro-cal: moving backward and foward; alternating.
re-cog-nize: to identify as shown before; to know by some detail; to accept as a fact.
re-com-mend: to present as deserving of acceptance.
re-col-lect: to recall to memory; to gather together again.
re-com-pose: compose again.
re-cord: to commit to writing; to make a note of; to register.
re-cur: to return; to happen again; to return periodically.
reef-er: marijuana.
re-fer: to direct to; to assign to; to send a person to someone for information.
re-frain: to hold back; to keep from action.
ref-uge: a shelter for protection from danger; a place of safety.
re-fuse: to deny or reject; to decline to accept, to not accept what is offered.
re-gain: to recover; to get back; to come to again.
re-gard: to observe; to consider; to take into account.
re-gis-ter: a written account; a record or list of events; a book where items for information are kept or recorded.
reg-u-lar: usual; customary; consistent.

re-ha-bil-i-tate: to make suitable; to restore to reputation or former position; to put back into good condition.
re-ject: to refuse to take; to discard a person or thing rejected as not up to standard.
re-lapse: a recurrence of illness; a falling back.
re-late: to tell the story of; to recite. re-lat-ed: recounted; told.
re-lax: to make less tense; to loosen; to rest from effort.
re-lay: a shift; to lay again.
re-lent: to soften in temper; to become less severe.
re-li-a-ble: trustworthy; honest; dependable; to be trusted.
re-lieve: to ease, lighten, to set free from burden.
re-lin-quish: to give up; to yield.
re-luct-ant: unwilling; opposed in mind. re-luct-ant-ly: in a reluctant manner.
re-ly: to place faith or confidence in; to depend on.
re-main: to be left behind; to be left over; to stay; to stay while others go.
re-mem-bered: called back to mind.
re-mind: to cause a person to remember.
re-mi-nisce: to call past events or experiences to mind.
re-model: to alter the structure of; to make over.
re-morse: a deep, torturing sense of guilt felt for someone's action.
ren-der: to give in return; to give up; to surrender.
ren-di-tion: the act of rendering.
re-neged: denied; deserted; broke the promise.
ren-o-vate: to make new; refresh; to renew.
re-or-ga-nize: to put back together; or organize again.
re-peat: to say or utter again; to say after someone else.
rep-e-ti-tion: act of repeating. re-pe-ti-tious: full of repetition.
re-place: to put in again or restore to a former place.
re-plied: to give an answer to in speech.
re-port: to make or present an account of; to relate; to give a formal statement; to present oneself.
re-pre-sent: to stand for; to act the part or role of.
re-pri-mand: to reprove severely.
re-proof: reprimand; rebuke; to charge with fault.
re-quest: to ask for; to ask a person to do something.
re-quire: to impose an obligation on someone; to compel; to command.
res-cue: to save as from danger; to take from legal custody by force.

re-sent: to feel or show displeasure and indignation.
re-sign: to give up a position; to give up one's job; to quit.
re-solve: to reach a decision; to describe or express by formal vote; to bring to a successful conclusion.
res-pect: the state of being regarded with honor or esteem.
res-pond: to make a reply; to act in return by an answer.
re-spon-si-ble: legally or ethically accountable.
re-store: to bring back into existence or use; to bring back to original.
re-sult: to end in a particular way.
re-tire-ment: the act of retiring.
re-trace: to trace again; to go back over.
re-tract: to take back; to draw back.
re-tri-bu-tion: just or suitable return; repayment.
re-turn: to go or come back from where you were.
re-veal: to divulge or disclose; to make known; to bring to view.
re-verse: turn backward in position or direction; to change to an opposite position or direction.
re-view: to look over, study, or examine. re-viewed: examined.
re-vise: to change or modify: to make corrections of the original copy.
re-vit-al-ize: to bring to life again; to restore.
rig-ors: harsh or trying circumstances; severe cruel acts.
risk: to expose to a chance of loss or damage.
riv-al: one who attempts to equal or surpass another.
roam: to move or travel without purpose or plan; to wander.
ro-bust: strong; full of health; powerfully built.
rock: to move back and forth or from side to side.
rod-ent: gnawing animal, like a rat, rabbit, or squirrel.
roof-er: one who lays or repairs roofs.
ros-ter: a list of personnel; an itemized list of persons.
ro-tate: to turn or spin on an axis.
rove: to wander about at random over a wide area; to roam.
rude: uncivilized; uncouth; without education or knowledge.
rule: mode of directing; an instrument to draw straight line.
rum-ble: to engage in a gang fight.
rush: to move or act swiftly; to hurry to perform with great haste.

S

sab-bat-i-cal: a leave, often with pay granted.
sa-cred: dedicated, consecrated, or belonging to a god or deity; holy.

sac-ri-fice: to sell or give away at a loss; a bunt that allows a runner to advance a base while the batter is retired.
safe: secure from danger, harm, or evil; unhurt.
sa-ga: novel describing the life of a family.
sanc-tion: authoritative approval that makes a course of action valid; to authorize.
sanc-tum: a holy place; a private place or room.
sar-ca-sm: veiled sneer. sarcastic: bitterly satirical and cutting.
sat-is-fy: to gratify fully; to pay. sat-is-fact-ion: settlement of a claim.
scene: a picture or a part of a play as seen by viewer; a place where an action or event occurs.
sched-ule: a list of items or details; to make a schedule.
scheme: a plan for doing something; to form a plot.
scold: to reprimand or criticize harshly. scold-ed: reprimanded or criticized.
score: record, as in keeping score of a game.
scream: to utter a long, loud, piercing sound.
seam-stress: a woman who sews by profession.
search: to look through in trying to find something; to examine thoroughly.
se-cret: hidden; concealed; kept from general knowledge.
sec-tion: a part separated from the rest; a portion of.
se-cure: free from danger; safe.
se-cur-i-ty: freedom from risk or danger.
seek: to try to locate or discover; to look for.
seg-re-gate: to separate or isolate from others. seg-re-ga-tion: the act of segregating from others.
sei-zure: the act of seizing; thing or property seized.
sel-dom: not often; infrequently.
se-lect: to choose from among several; to pick out.
self-em-ployed: working for oneself.
self-es-teem: pride in oneself.
se-mes-ter: a period of six months, half a year.
senior: above others in rank; father to a son; older.
sense-less: witout sense or meaning; lacking sense; foolish.
sen-tence: a combination of words that is complete expressing a thought; judgment passed on a criminal by court or judge.
se-par-ate: to set or keep apart; to space apart; to sort. sepa-rat-ed: sorted.

se-ri-ous: dangerous; harmful; earnest; important.
set-tle: to put in place, order, arrangement; to make secure or quiet.
sev-er-al: being of a number more than two or three but not many.
shade: partial darkness; a place sheltered from light.
shape: to mold or make into a particular form; to give shape to; pattern.
share: part allotted; portion; to give or allot a share.
sharp: having keen cutting edge or fine point.
shed: a small structure, either free standing or attached, used for storage.
shel-ter: place or structure giving protection.
shock: violent collision or impact; clash.
shook him up: caused him to become emotionally upset.
short cir-cuit: an accidentally established low resistance connection between two connections, or two points in an electrical circuit.
shred-ding: tearing into strips; the act of stripping or tearing into strips of paper.
shrug-ging: raising the shoulder as a gesture.
shy: bashful; timid; to draw back in fear or caution; bashful.
sil-ent: making no sound or noise.
si-mi-lar: having the appearance of something else.
sim-ply: in a simple manner.
si-mul-tan-e-ous: existing or occurring at the same time; operating at the time.
sit-u-ate: to place in a certain spot or position; to locate. si-tu-a-tion: the way in which something is situated.
skep-ti-cal: doubting; doubtful.
skill: the ability to use one's knowledge effectively in doing something.
slight-ly: to a small degree or extent.
slouch: a loose or dropping gait or posture; a lazy person; an awkward, lazy, or inept person.
slum: a heavily populated urban area marked by poverty and dirt.
smog: fog that has become mixed with polluted smoke.
snap: to break the sounds of voice abruptly.
so-ber: not intoxicated.
so-cial-ize: to fit with companionship of others; to make sociable.
soft: smooth or fine to touch; having a gentle disposition; tender.
sol-ace: comfort in grief; to console.
sole: being the only one; single.

so-lic-it: to seek by persuasion; to approach with a request or plea; to approach with an offer of sexual services for a fee.
so-lu-tion: the method of solving a problem; the action of breaking up.
som-ber: dark; gloomy; grave; melancholy.
some-where: in an unnamed place or unknown place.
so-phis-ti-cat-ed: having acquired worldly knowledge or refinement.
sort: to put in a certain place, to put in order of one kind or another.
sought: past tense of seek: to try to locate or discover.
source: a place or thing from which something comes or derives; point of origin.
space: an area; room; period of time.
speech: the power of speaking; vocal communication; a talk before an audience.
spend: to use up or put out; to pay; to pay up.
spite: ill will with a wish to annoy or hurt someone.
spon-sored: supported another.
spon-ta-ne-ous: happening or arising without apparent external cause; self-generated.
spot: a stain. spot-less: perfectly clean; free from blemish.
spree: lively frolic; drinking bout.
spur: anything that excites action.
spy: one who enters enemy territory secretly. spy-ing: watching others secretly.
sta-ble: a building for horses, divided into stalls; firm, fixed, steady.
stair-case: flight of steps.
stalk: stem on a main axis or a main structure that supports a plant.
stal-wart: sturdy; strong; brave; steadfast; muscular.
state: condition of the mind; social position. stat-ed: expressed in words. state-ment: the act of expressing in words; the summary of an account.
sta-ture: the height of a person.
steer-ing: guiding by means of a device such as a rudder, paddle, or wheel. steer-ing com-mit-tee: a committee that sets agendas and schedules of business.
stern: firm or unyielding; inflexible; sturdy.
stim-u-late: to make active or more active; to excite one's emotions.
straight: passing from one point to another by nearest course. straight-en: to make straight.
stout: strong; robust.

strange: previously unknown; unfamiliar.
strain-er: filter; sieve to separate the good from the bad.
strat-e-gy: a plan of action resulting from the practice or plan or method.
stray: wonder from the path.
stretch: to cause to extend from one place to another.
strict: stern; severe; allowing no evasion or escape; accurate.
strive: to struggle in opposition; to make an effort.
stroke: to pass hand gently over; an impact.
stroll: to walk leisurely from one place to another.
strug-gle: to exert muscular energy against another force.
stub-born: unduly determined to exert one's will; not easily persuaded.
stuck: past tense of stick.
stu-dio: an artist's room for work; a place for the study of an art.
stur-dy: substantiallay built; strong.
sub-let: to rent (property) to another tenant under a lease.
sub-side: to sink to a lower level; to sink to the bottom.
sub-stan-tial: existing as in substance; real; strong.
suc-ceed-ing: to come next in time or succession; to accomplish something.
suc-cess-ful: having a favorable outcome.
sud-den: without warning; unforeseen; swift.
sug-gest-ed: brought forward for consideration; reminded.
suit-a-ble: appropriate for a given purpose.
sum-ma-rized: made a summary of.
su-per-fi-cial-ly: not deep; on the surface; shallow.
su-per-vise: to oversee; to direct and control.
sup-ple-ment: something added to a thing to make up a deficiency.
sup-ply: to make available for use; to provide; to furnish or equip with.
sup-port: to keep from falling.
sup-pose: to assume as true. sup-posed: presumed to be true.
sur-prised: suddenly without warning.
sur-round: to shield from all sides; to encircle.
sur-veil-lance: close observation; close watch.
sur-vive: to live longer than; to outlive or outlast.
sus-pect: to imagine the existence of.
sus-pend: to bar for a period from an office or position; to make inactive.
sus-pi-cious: distrusted.

swell: to increase in size.
switch: a flexible twig or rod; to transfer a train from one track to another.
swi-vel: ring turning on pivot.
syn-the-sis: combination or putting together.

T

tac-tics: awareness of the right thing to do.
tame: domesticated; subdued; to discipline.
tan-gle: confused; to form into a confused mass.
taste: to perceive or test by tongue or palate; one of the five senses.
taught: past tense of teach.
tech-nique: skill acquired by thorough mastery of the subject or method of handling materials of an art.
tem-per: degree of heat or cold of the atmosphere or a human body.
ten-ant: one who occupies property for a fee for a period of time.
tend: to look after.
ten-ure: holding of an office for a period of time.
ten-sion: the act of stretching; strain; a state of being nerviously excited.
ter-min-al: extremely large; railway station, with yards.
ter-mi-na-tion: the act of terminating or finishing.
ter-ri-tory: large track of land; limit to a certain district.
tes-ti-fy: to bear witness; to give evidence.
the-o-ry: supposition put forth to explain something.
threat: to menace; to declare intention to do harm to; to pretend.
threw: past tense of throw; to fling, cast, or hurl; the act of throwing.
thrill-ing: emotional.
through: from end to end of; going in one side and out the other.
tide: periodical rise and fall of the ocean due to the attraction of the moon and sun.
till: to cultivate the soil; to plow the soil; to prepare the soil for cultivation.
tim-id: lacking courage or self-confidence; shy.
tol-e-rate: to permit to be done; to put up with.
tor-ment: extreme pain of the body; to inflict pain upon; to torture.
tor-ture: to inflict agony.
tough: not easily broken; firm; difficult to chew.

toured: journeyed from place to place in a country.
toward: in direction of; with respect to the future.
traf-fic: movement of people and cars in a given area; coming and going.
tra-ge-dy: sad or calamitous event.
train: to instruct or educate.
trait: distinguishing feature in character.
trans-ac-tion: the act of transacting.
trans-form: to change forms. trans-form-er: a device that changes the volume or circuit to a lower or higher rating.
trans-mit: to send from one person or place to another.
tran-spire: to emit through pores of skin; exhale.
trans-verse: in crosswise direction.
trap: a plot to catch a person unaware.
trau-ma: bodily injury caused by violence; emotional shock.
treat: to entertain with food or drink.
trek: to migrate; to journey by wagon.
trig-ger: catch of firearm, which when pulled releases hammer of lock.
tri-ple: consisting of three united; three times repeated; three times.
troop: large assembly of people; an army.
trou-ble: to stir up; to bother.
trust: to have confidence in; to have faith in.
tur-moil: commotion, as of a crowd.
turn-out: an outside gathering.
type: class or group; style or form of printing.

U

ul-ti-mate: farthest; final; primary.
un-able: not having strength to perform a task.
un-an-i-mous: all of one mind; agreed to by all parties.
un-bear-able: not bearable.
un-born: not yet born.
un-capped: not covered.
un-comm-on: not belonging to all or several.
un-com-fort-a-ble: not consoling.
un-com-pro-mis-ing: making no concession.
un-con-troll-a-ble: not being capable of being controlled; unmanaged.

un-couth: awkward in manner; strange.
un-der-stand-ing: to comprehend; to grasp.
un-dis-closed: not revealed; not brought to light.
un-dress: informal dress; off-duty military uniform.
un-fold-ed: spread out; disclosed.
un-fore-seen: unexpected.
un-for-tu-nate: not lucky.
un-i-den-ti-fied: not established to be the same person.
un-load: to remove load from.
un-known: not known.
un-pleas-ing: not fitted to please.
un-re-lat-ed: not related; no kinship.
un-ruly: lawless, disobedient.
un-safe: not free from harm.
un-us-u-al: not usual; uncommon.
up-dat-ed: brought up-to-date.
up-hol-stered: stuffed and covered furniture.
up-roar: violent; noisy.
up-set: to turn upside down; to knock over.
up-per hand: superiority; advantage over another.
up-per-most: to the highest degree; most that can be.

V

va-cant: empty; void; not occupied.
val-id: sound or well grounded; being justified.
val-ue: worth; importance.
van-dal-ism: damage of property.
var-i-ous: different; separate.
ven-ture: understanding of chance or danger.
ver-ba-tim: in exactly the same words; word for word.
ver-i-fy: to prove to be true; to confirm the truth of.
ver-sion: translation; account from a particular point of view.
ves-ti-bule: small room or hall between outer and inner doors at entrance.
vice: immoral conduct. vi-cious: grossly immoral; disposed to evil.
vi-cin-i-ty: neighborhood.
vic-tim: person or thing destroyed or sacrificed; person that suffers.

view: sight; inspection by eye or mind.
vi-o-late: to break a promise. vi-o-la-tion: the act of breaking promises.
vi-o-lence: force; improper force.
vir-gin: girl or woman who has not had sexual intercourse; maiden.
vir-tu-al-ly: being in essence or effect potential.
vis-i-ble: in view.
vi-su-al: relating to sight; used in seeing; visible.
vis-it: to go, to come, to see.
vo-cab-u-la-ry: a list of words in alphabetical order and explained.
void: empty; without; an empty space.
vol-ume: part of a work that is bound; power of voice or musical tone.
vol-un-teer: one who enters service of his own free will.
vul-ner-a-ble: capable of being wounded; offering open criticism.

W

waive: to give up claim to; to forego; to relinquish right.
ward: to repel; to turn aside; room for patients in a hospital.
ware: articles of merchandise; goods for sale.
warn: to notify by authority; to caution; to put on guard.
war-rant: to give justification for; to authorize or sanction with assurance.
waste: to expend uselessly; to use extravagantly; to squander; to wear away by degrees.
watch: the state of being on the lookout; close observation.
wealth: riches; affluence; abundance.
wean: to discontinue breast-feeding; to detach or alienate.
wea-pon: instrument to fight with.
weigh-ing: the art of finding out what an article weighs.
wel-come: receive gladly; free to enjoy or to use.
whis-per: to utter in a low tone of voice.
wild liv-ing: in a state of nature, not domesticated or cultivated.
win: to gain by success in competition or contract.
wings: organs of flight; extensions of a building.
with-out: on or at the outside of; not within.
wit-ness: one who furnishes evidence or proof.
won-der: surprise; to marvel.
word: spoken or written sign of idea. word-ing: precise words used.

work: exertion of strength; to operate; perform; effort to an end.
worth: quality of a thing that renders it valuable.
worth-y of re-spect: having great or adequate merit, character, or value.
wound-ing: injuring a man by cutting or stabbing him, damaging his body.
wrench: a tool with fixed or adjustable jaws for holding or adjusting nuts, bolts.

Y

yell: to cry out in a loud, shrill tone; to scream.
young: not yet old, not advanced in growth, life, or existence.